Is Peaceful Co-existence Possible?

LORD LINDSAY OF BIRKER

(Michael Lindsay)

Is Peaceful Co-existence Possible?

Michigan State University Press
1960

Contents

* (Before sections (7) and (8) had been completed it had become clear that a reply could not be expected from Peking or Moscow, so they were not sent. They are included here to make the case complete.)

Part III. CONCLUSION.

Preface

This book is the record of an experiment. It has not been possible to complete the experiment, but even the limited evidence it has yielded in its incomplete form is worth reporting because it is relevant to some of the most important international issues of today, in particular to the problems involved in a top-level meeting between Communist and non-Communist leaders.

The logical place for reviewing the evidence and drawing conclusions would be after a description of the experiment, but it may be more interesting for the reader to present a summary of the conclusions here at the very beginning. The experiment seems to show that Communists are not prepared to discuss questions which would provide test cases of whether or not the Communist claims to want peaceful co-existence are made in good faith. They are not willing to comment on a statement of the evidence which has led many non-Communists to suspect the claims of the Communist powers to want peace or to answer the specific questions about Communist policy which are suggested by this evidence. They are also unwilling to make a reasoned statement of the basis for Communist suspicions of the good faith of the non-Communist powers in wanting peace, suspicions which are continually stated in Communist publicity, and to allow this case to be critically examined from the non-Communist side.

It is a reasonable deduction from this that the Communist eagerness to secure a top-level meeting depends on the assumption that the non-Communist representatives at such a meeting would not insist on asking the questions which could provide test cases of Communist good faith, an assumption which was justified at the last top-level meeting at Geneva in 1955.

It follows from this that the ability of the Communists to derive a propaganda advantage from a top-level meeting, or from proposals for such a meeting, depends on the ineptitude with which the non-Communist powers present their case. If people in positions of responsibility on the non-Communist side were less reluctant to engage in fundamental and theoretical analysis of the problems involved in peaceful co-existence it is very likely that this propaganda advantage could be reversed. If the non-Communist leaders made clear that they would use a top-level meeting to ask the questions which have to be answered if such a meeting is to produce any progress towards peaceful co-existence or the lessening of world tension, it is very likely that the opposition to such a meeting would come from the Communist side. The non-Communist leaders would be in a position to show quite clearly to world opinion that they are fully prepared to work for peaceful co-existence and the lessening of world tension while the Communist leaders are not.

Another conclusion which is suggested by the experiment, though less clearly, is that even people in Communist-ruled countries working on international problems are not really aware of the strength of the case which can be stated against Communist policy. This suggests that the stability with which the Communist powers are committed to a continuation of the lines of policy incompatible with peaceful co-existence may be less than many non-Communists suppose.

The Background

Peaceful co-existence is a term which appears very frequently in both Communist and neutralist statements. Communist statements on the subject are often confused and contradictory, as I show later. Neutralist statements are usually sincere and well meaning but fail to face the important and difficult problems involved in attempts to realize peaceful co-existence. Outside pro-Communist and pro-neutralist circles the term is somewhat suspect. It is often criticized as a Communist propaganda slogan and statements by Communist leaders often justify such criticism by suggesting that peaceful co-existence, from the Communist side, is simply a stratagem for postponing hostilities until the Communists judge the time to be ripe for a final attack on Capitalism. But such criticisms lose a good deal of their effect because they do not admit that peaceful co-existence is an effective propaganda slogan precisely because the *prima facie* case for peaceful co-existence is so strong.

Why should the peoples of different countries fight one another because they are trying different systems of economic and social organization? Indeed, why should they fight one another at all under present conditions? At one time it may have been true that some countries could advance their national interests by war. Now that any major war is likely to be fought with atomic weapons it is very doubtful whether even the victor could gain by it. In this situation have not the people of all countries a common interest in peaceful co-existence, in agreeing to settle their differences by negotiation and in not trying to force their social system on other countries however much they are convinced of its superiority? Formulated in this way the case for peaceful co-existence seems to be obvious common sense. And this is the sort of formulation one finds in neutralist statements and in Communist statements intended for a non-Communist public and which does have simple and natural appeal to public opinion.

Of course, this formulation introduces the very dubious implicit assumption that decisions on war or peace are taken by "the people" of various countries. In fact they are taken by ruling groups some of which take very little account of popular opinion. But even allowing for this one can still ask: Why should the ruling groups in different countries want to fight because they are trying different social and economic systems?

A great many people have answered this question by arguments to show that one of the main systems of social organization in the present world is inherently aggressive; that is, a system which puts the control of policy into the hands of people who are determined to extend their power over other areas of the world and are prepared if necessary to use military force to do so. Such aggressiveness may come from fanaticism, a determination to impose some system regardless of the consequences; it may come from megalomania, a desire for conquest and power for their own sakes; or it may come from a situation in which a ruling group can only maintain its power internally by following policies likely to lead to war.

Obviously, peaceful co-existence is not possible with an inherently aggressive system. If one major country is controlled by people who are determined to extend their power and prepared to use military force to do so, the rest of the world has to choose between submission and resistance. If people are not prepared to submit, their only hope of avoiding an actual war is by making preparations for defense which will make clear to the leaders of the aggressive power that, if they do start a war, they will most probably be defeated. Such a balance of power situation is unpleasant and not very stable but, so long as some major power is inherently aggressive, it is the best that can be attained.

The weakness of the neutralist position is that those who hold it never face the problem of inherently aggressive systems. Such systems have certainly existed in the past. The evidence now available shows quite clearly that Nazism was inherently aggressive and that the people who thought that they could secure peaceful co-existence by negotiations with Hitler were simply deluded by their own confused and wishful thinking. And there have been many other historical examples of systems which were inherently aggressive.

It is, of course, possible for a system to be inherently aggressive at one period and not at another. Some defenders of the Indian neutralist position have argued that systems which fought for a long time did finally accept peaceful co-existence, citing as illustrations such cases as the peaceful co-existence between Protestantism and Roman Catholicism which followed the period of religious wars in Europe. The conclusion drawn from this is that the supporters of Communism and Capitalism should learn from historical experience and accept peaceful co-existence now without going through a period of wars in which it is unlikely that either side could win a complete victory. The weakness of this argument is its implicit assumption that systems remain constant. The Protestantism and Roman Catholicism which accepted peaceful co-existence in the 18th century were appreciably different from the systems which had fought in the 17th century. Peaceful co-existence was not possible so long as policy was controlled by people who said, like the Emperor Ferdinand II, "Better a desert than a country full of heretics." When peaceful co-existence became possible the more fanatical individuals who held this type of belief were no longer in positions of dominant power on either side. It is quite possible that some system which is now inherently aggressive may, in time, cease to be so; but this does not make peaceful co-existence possible now.

The crucial question in any study of the possibilities of peaceful co-existence is, therefore, whether or how far there is a valid case for holding that one of the major social systems in the world today is inherently aggressive. If there is a valid case a second question arises: How far would the system have to change for its inherent aggressiveness to disappear and what is the likelihood of such a change?

The arguments stated by non-Communists for holding that Communism is an inherently aggressive system are fairly strong but not entirely conclusive. The main point which they leave uncertain is how far Communist aggressiveness is determined by fear resulting from the Communist belief that Capitalism is aggressive. How far can the Communist actions and statements indicating a determination to destroy Capitalism be explained by a fear that the only alternative would be the destruction of Communism by Capitalism? How far would Communist aggressiveness remain if this fear were removed? Also, many of the people who state a strong case for believing that Communism is inherently aggressive seem too ready to assume that inherent aggressiveness is an essential element of Communism which could only disappear when Communism collapses or is overthrown.

The case stated in Communist publications for holding that Capitalism is an inherently aggressive system would often be fairly reasonable if one granted its initial assumptions about the nature of the social system in non-Communist countries. But the Capitalism whose inherent aggressiveness is deduced has very little relation to the actual social system of any major non-Communist power. In so far as the actual social system has some relation to the theoretical model of Capitalism assumed by Communist theory some tendencies to aggressiveness may exist; but the Communist view that these tendencies are dominant depends on completely distorted beliefs about the functioning of political systems and the distribution of power in non-Communist countries. A great deal of the evidence cited to show non-Communist aggressiveness can be much more simply explained as preparations for defense against possible Communist aggression. There is, however, a lot of evidence to suggest that many Communists quite sincerely believe that the United States and other non-Communist powers are controlled by inherently aggressive systems. What one would like to know is how far this belief is the result of a considered judgment and how far merely the uncritical acceptance of ideas which remained uncriticized in a Communist controlled environment. Would Communists still believe that major non-Communist powers are inherently aggressive if they took the trouble to study the evidence of what their actual social systems are like?

So long as one can only judge Communism from Communist publications and official statements it is very hard to get satisfactory evidencce on many of the most important questions related to peaceful co-existence. On many of the most important issues it is hard to make out what the Communist position really is because Communist statements never answer the questions which a non-Communist would like to ask. The most controversial points in the Communist case are not argued or justified by the citing of evidence but simply introduced as implicit assumptions or unsupported assertions. To make a better judgment about the possibility of peaceful co-existence one would need to know the Communist answer to questions which are always evaded in Communist statements. And so long as Communists cut themselves off from contacts or discussions with the non-Communist world it is not possible to ask these questions.

The Experiment.

In 1956 it seemed that the isolation of the Communist world might be breaking down. Colleagues from the Australian National University who visited China and Russia reported that there seemed to be a new readiness to have contacts with the non-Communist world and to engage in discussion with non-Communists.

These reports led me, in August 1956, to write the paper which follows in the next chapter suggesting that a serious discussion at the academic level of the mutual suspicions between the Communist and non-Communist powers could be very important in providing a theoretical foundation for peaceful co-existence.

I sent a copy to a friend in the Foreign Office in Peking with a covering letter suggesting a definite project. I suggested that I should write out a statement of the non-Communist case for suspicion of the Communist powers to which someone on the Communist side would write a critical examination and reply; and that someone on the Communist side should write a similar statement of the Communist case for suspicion of the non-Communist powers to which I would write a critical examination and reply. I argued that a correspondence on these lines might do a lot to clarify the disagreements between the Communist and non-Communist sections of the world and to disentangle the suspicions for which there was some real basis from the suspicions based on misunderstandings, such as the interpretation of preparations for defense as preparations for aggression. If this first stage of the project showed that there were some suspicions with a real basis, a second stage could go on to discuss what changes on either side would provide adequate evidence that the basis for suspicion had been removed.

I received a fairly prompt reply to this letter saying that the suggested project seemed interesting and possibly of real value to the cause of world peace and that Dr. Chen Han-seng, a Vice-President of the Chinese People's Institute of International

Affairs, would be interested in co-operating with me on the project.

I wrote to Dr. Chen Han-seng explaining the project and sent him, as I completed them, the sections of my statement of the non-Communist case for suspicion of the Communist powers. However, several months went by during which I had no reply to my letters. Finally I wrote rather strongly both to Dr. Chen and to my original contact asking for a definite answer on whether or not I could expect Dr. Chen's co-operation and complaining that a refusal to answer letters was the most discourteous form of reply. This produced a letter from Dr. Chen explaining that he would shortly be leaving on a trip to Europe and would not be able to do anything on my project for at least six months.

It seemed likely that this was an indirect way of saying that Dr. Chen would prefer not to co-operate, so I decided to see whether it would be possible to obtain co-operation in the Soviet Union. I had first tried to obtain co-operation in China because I had some personal contacts there, but the questions raised in my statement related more to Soviet policy than to Chinese policy and it seemed that this might explain Dr. Chen's reluctance to discuss them.

A colleague at the Australian National University who had met the President of the Soviet Academy of Sciences at scientific conferences offered to provide a letter of introduction to him. I wrote on 21st. December, 1956 enclosing this introduction and a copy of my original paper and explaining the project for which I hoped to get co-operation. This letter was sent by air mail so it presumably reached Moscow at the beginning of January, 1957. In the early part of March I received a reply (in Russian) dated 26th. February, 1957 from the Head of the Foreign Section of the Soviet Academy of Sciences. This said that the Academy had recently set up an Institute of World Economics and International Relations to study fundamental questions of contemporary international relations and continued, "Your letter has been sent to this Institute and I assume that you will be able to establish useful contacts with the scholars of this institute. You may be absolutely sure of the heartfelt readiness of the

Soviet scholars to collaborate with scholars of other lands in the high moral aims of maintaining and strengthening peace."

I wrote to the Director of this Institute mentioning the letter from the Foreign Section of the Academy of Sciences, explaining my project, and enclosing the completed sections of my statement of the non-Communist case. Up to the time of writing, more than a year later, I have not been able to get any reply.

I had hoped that it might still be possible to obtain co-operation on the project when I visited Peking during my study leave in 1958 and, in making my visa application, I mentioned the discussion of foreign policy issues as one of the objects of my visit. However, the entry permit issued at Peking on the 20th. December, 1957 was cancelled when I arrived at the Chinese border on 8th. February, 1958. I wrote to Chou En-lai on 19th. February saying that, though my wife and I were annoyed by the discourteous way in which our entry permits had been cancelled, I would still be interested in going to Peking if I could obtain the co-operation which would make the visit of some value for my work and mentioned this project as the most important. This letter has produced no reply.

It seems fairly clear from all this that there is almost no hope of obtaining the Communist co-operation needed for completing the project. But even the incomplete project has provided some interesting evidence about the Communist position.

Both in China and the Soviet Union the initial reaction to the project was favorable. (And the delay of nearly two months in answering my letter to the Soviet Academy of Sciences suggested that the reply may have followed some discussion or reference to higher authorities.) In both countries people in official or semi-official organizations seemed to agree that a serious discussion at the academic level of the basis for mutual suspicions between the Communist and non-Communist sections of the world could be important in providing a theoretical foundation for peaceful co-existence. And this favorable reaction came after reading my original paper in which I argued that the Communist position on peaceful co-existence had been confused and contradictory. In both countries the initially favorable response turned into a refusal to co-operate in the project as soon as people had read some sections of the non-Communist case for suspicion of the Communist powers, on which they were invited to comment.

It is a reasonable deduction that the statement of the non-Communist case raised questions which the Communists found so embarrassing that they were not prepared to attempt to answer them. And the initially favorable response suggests that this may have been unexpected. It is hard to see why the Communists should have expressed an interest in the project unless they expected that the statement of the non-Communist case would be a statement to which they could make an effective reply.

This case which the Communists refused to answer was not an expression of my personal opinions. It was, on the contrary, an attempt to state a case likely to command general agreement from most non-Communists seriously interested in international affairs. The personal element came only in the selection of test cases and in the arrangement of the material to present the issues in as clear and unambiguous a way as possible with the minimum of possibly controversial assumptions.

In publishing this statement of the non-Communist case which the Communists have refused to answer I have added comments to some of the sections to bring the material up to date and have included two sections on "Negotiation" and "The Nature of the Communist System" which are needed to make the statement complete though they had not been written when the earlier sections were sent to China and the Soviet Union.

PART I

The Case for Discussion

[This is the paper written in August 1956 and sent first to Peking where it produced a reply indicating that a Vice-Chairman of the Chinese People's Institute of International Affairs would be willing to co-operate in the project suggested. It was later sent to Moscow and produced a reply from the Head of the Foreign Section of the Academy of Sciences saying that members of the Institute of World Economics and International Relations would be willing to co-operate in the project.]

The increased opportunities for contacts between the Communist and the non-Communist sections of the world seem to offer a chance of reaching some genuine and permanent relaxation of international tension. This result is most likely to be attained if the new contacts are used for frank discussion, especially of the controversial problems of international relations.

It is obvious that there have been very deep-seated mutual suspicions between the Communist and the non-Communist systems. Some of these suspicions can be explained as the results of mere ignorance and prejudice and may be expected to disappear as contacts increase. But a great deal of suspicion has been based on reasoned arguments and is not likely to disappear unless these arguments are carefully discussed and examined.

In serious publications, both Communist and non-Communist, one can find attempts to deduce the motives and objectives behind the policies of the other system. There are differences in method. Communist studies tend to emphasize deductions from the nature of the Capitalistic system; non-Communist studies to emphasize empirical generalizations from Communist policies.

In many respects the conclusions reached are, of course, very different. However, on one issue of fundamental importance each side has reached very similar conclusions about the other. It has been argued that the Communist, (or Capitalist) system under Soviet, (or American) leadership is controlled by a ruling group with ambitions of expansion and world domination which it is prepared to pursue even by methods likely to cause war; and that this type of leadership with these objectives is a natural, or even an inevitable product of the Communist system (or monopoly capitalism). It is suggested that professions of desire for peace from the Communist (or Capitalist) leaders are not sincere and may be only propaganda maneuvers to give intended victims a false sense of security, and that little trust can be placed on the observances of agreements by Communist (or Capitalist) governments.

There is a wide variation in the presentation of these conclusions. As compared with a few years ago, recent Communist statements are usually more moderate in their language and less sweeping in the range of those whom they denounce as representatives of "imperialist monopoly capitalism"; but there are no clear indications of any basic revision of the thesis that the capitalist system is inherently aggressive.[1] On the non-Communist side, the view that the Communist system is inherently aggressive is sometimes presented in a propagandist form as an established matter of fact; but it is also presented as a reasoned deduction based on circumstantial evidence in serious works by reputable scholars.[2]

1. A good illustration of the Communist thesis against the United States was provided by Chou En-lai's report to the Second National Committee of the CPPCC. (Published as a supplement to *People's China*, No. 4, 1956.)

2. To give one illustration, W. W. Rostow in *The Dynamics of Soviet Society* (W. W. Norton, New York, 1953) argues in his conclusion that, "Given its persistent objectives, the regime would almost certainly initiate a major war if it felt with a substantial margin of assurance that war could be decisively won without endangering its hold on Soviet society." (pp. 249-50.) and, "It follows, therefore, that a true liquidation of the Cold War—as opposed to a mitigation convenient, perhaps, for both sides—hinges on the possibility of change in the nature of the Soviet regime, . . ." (p. 252.)

There is a complete disagreement between supporters of the Communist and of the non-Communist views. Those who maintain that the Soviet Union or China has objectives of expansion and conquest would nearly always deny that any good case could be made for supposing the United States or Britain to be aggressive, and vice versa. Neutralist opinion has been inclined to avoid any serious consideration of these problems. (If either thesis were true it would have very awkward implications for the neutralist position.)

Though the whole subject is so controversial, it is of very great practical importance. The thinking of many people in responsible positions in the non-Communist countries has certainly been greatly influenced by the arguments which seem to show that the Communist powers are potential aggressors, and it seems likely that similar arguments about the Capitalist powers have had at least as great an influence in Communist countries. The weight of evidence is strongly against the view that one or both sets of arguments are nothing but propagandist assertions made by people who do not really believe them.

It is not possible to make a realistic appraisal of the international situation without considering whether either version of these conclusions is valid, and if so, to what extent. The results of such consideration will determine what developments in international affairs are possible and what policies are most likely to prevent war.

There is an important practical choice between the objective of security based on a balance of power and security based on mutual confidence. If there is one system whose leaders have objectives of conquest and domination which they are not prepared to give up, then security for the rest of the world can only be based on a balance of power. The best that can be done in order to maintain peace is to produce a situation in which potential aggressors will hesitate to start a war because it is highly probable that they would be defeated. Any real relaxation of international tension must depend on the hope that, eventually, the aggressive system will change.

This was, roughly speaking, the situation in the 1930's. Looking back on the period in the light of the evidence now available, it is clear that it was not possible to reach peaceful agreement with either the Nazi leaders or the more extreme Japanese militarists and that the best hope of avoiding the last war would have been for the peace-loving powers to present a firm and united front ready to resist any acts of aggression. (And some people on both sides have discussed the post-war situation in terms of an analogy with the 1930's.)

Though in some circumstances a balance of power may be the best that is attainable, it is not a satisfactory situation. It involves a continuation of international tension and of large scale armament expenditure and a continuing risk that a miscalculation by either side may unintentionally start a general conflict. And there are influences which tend to make a balance of power situation unstable. For example, if one side sees that the balance of power is moving against it, it will have strong motives for starting a fight while the power situation is still comparatively favorable. There are also reasons for supposing that the present situation with only two really great powers is likely to be more unstable than earlier situations when there was a number of great powers.

A much more satisfactory situation can be reached if a certain degree of mutual confidence can be established. Two systems can exist together and can even compete peacefully provided that competition is conducted within the limits of rules which exclude policies likely to cause war. Each side must be able to have reasonable confidence that the other will not use military force, or the threat of military force, as a means to extend its power. There must be mutual confidence that any agreements will be observed and are not likely to be repudiated when either side considers that it can gain an advantage by doing so. Under such conditions there can be a real relaxation in international tension, a mutual reduction in armaments would become comparatively easy to arrange, and the risk of war would become very small. Both sides would obviously gain by a system of rules which made this possible. But the rules can only exist if each side feels confident that the other will accept them and will not try to gain the increase in its power which it might obtain by breaking them.

Even now one can point to cases in which this degree of

mutual confidence has been attained, where a country does not think it necessary to take any military precautions against attack by some of its neighbors because the risk of such attack is considered negligible.

Confidence is, of course, a matter of degree. It is not reasonable to expect a sudden transition from a situation of mutual suspicion and balance of power to a situation of complete mutual confidence. There is, however, a very wide difference between policies aimed at building up a balance of power against a system which is considered to be irreconcilably aggressive and policies aimed at increasing mutual confidence with a system with which genuine peaceful co-existence is possible. And the two types of policy are, to a considerable extent, incompatible.

If the objective of policy is to attain a balance of power, every issue will tend to be judged in terms of how it may influence this balance rather than on its merits. Every proposal for co-operation will be regarded with suspicion because of its possible effects on security or because it may produce dependence on the other side. It will be hard to reach agreements when neither side has confidence that the other will observe them; and even when agreements are reached under such conditions they will have comparatively little value. Furthermore, policies based on a balance of power are likely to increase mutual suspicions. To a very large extent preparations for defense are similar to preparations for attack. If one side increases its military strength to a point which makes it secure against possible attack, the other side will feel insecure because it has no confidence that this military strength will not be used for aggression. A chain reaction can easily develop of mounting mutual suspicion and competitive military preparations.

If, on the other hand, the objective of policy is to promote mutual confidence, there will be a readiness to deal with issues on their merits and to make mutual concessions. Proposals for co-operation will be welcomed. Each side will be willing to take some risks in trusting the other in order to induce reciprocal confidence in its good faith. Under such conditions there is likely to be a chain reaction towards increasing mutual confidence.

On both the Communist and the non-Communist side a great deal of confusion has been caused by attempts to evade the issue of whether the other system is one with which mutual confidence can be established, or one with which nothing better than a balance of power is possible.

Many Communist statements on peaceful co-existence have claimed, on the one hand, that peaceful co-existence between the Communist and Capitalist sections of the world is both desirable and possible and have asserted, on the other hand, that "imperialist monopoly capitalism" is an incurably aggressive system so that peaceful co-existence will only become possible when its representatives have been removed from power. An exceptionally clear formulation of this contradictory position was given by Togliatti in an article in the Cominform Journal of 21st. December, 1951. He argued that peaceful co-existence between different economic and social systems was "the sole correct path for mankind" but he also maintained that the peace-loving forces in the United States could only prevail when "a genuinely democratic system is realized by reorganizing the economic foundations of society along socialist lines;"—in other words, peaceful co-operation was only possible between different forms of socialism and not between communism and capitalism. Many other Communist statements have expressed the same confused position in a slightly less explicit form. They have, for example, claimed that peaceful co-existence is possible while denouncing as warmongers, or puppets of warmongers, every political group likely, in the foreseeable future, to attain power in America or countries allied with America. Some recent statements seem to identify peaceful co-existence with a balance of power situation. For example, an editorial in *International Affairs* on the 20th. Congress of the C.P.S.U. says, "So long as imperialism exists, the reactionary forces representing the interests of the capitalist monopolies will continue to strive for military adventures and aggression and may try to unleash war. In such circumstances war can only be prevented by the greatest exertions of the peace-loving forces. However, wars are not fatally inevitable now."[1] And the rest of the article shows that, in the editor's views, wars are not now inevitable only because the ruling groups of the capitalist countries face a balance of power made up of the Soviet bloc and the "peace-loving forces" in their own countries and are likely, in the long run, to be replaced by socialist systems.

This Communist position provides a very confused theoretical basis for any attempts by the Communist powers to lessen international tension. The view that peaceful co-existence between Capitalism and Communism is both desirable and possible implies a policy of negotiation and rapprochement with the Capitalist powers. The view that the representatives of "monopoly capitalism" are incurably aggressive and irreconcilably hostile implies that such a policy is bound to fail when directed towards the existing governments of the United States and most of its allies, and that the only purpose of negotiations can be to provide propaganda likely to strengthen the "peace-loving forces" opposing these governments. If the Communist leaders take their own theories seriously they must approach any negotiations with Capitalist powers with contradictory beliefs about what can be accomplished. If they do not take their own theories seriously they will approach negotiations without any considered basic policy. In either case the chances of successful negotiation will be small.

Also, in so far as the governments of the Capitalist countries take note of such Communist statements about peaceful co-existence, it is likely to strengthen their suspicions that the object of Communist offers to negotiate is to score propaganda points rather than to reach any settlement. They will also have some reason to deduce that the Communist powers are very unlikely to respond to any efforts to improve relations if these come from a government which has been classified as representing "imperialist monopoly capitalism", and some Communist statements have put both major parties in both the United States and the United Kingdom within this category.

On the non-Communist side the confusion takes a rather different form. One does not so often find incompatible views

1. *International Affairs*, 1956, No. 3, p. 14. (*International Affairs* has been used throughout as a convenient sample of statements of the Communist position.)

asserted in the same statement, but one does find a very wide
range of different views asserted by different people. At one extreme are people who describe "international communism" in
terms very similar to those which Communist writers use about
"imperialist monopoly capitalism",—as an incurably aggressive
system which could not accept peaceful co-existence without producing its own collapse. On this view it follows that nothing
better than a balance of power is possible until there has been
some sort of revolution in the Communist countries. Others
maintain that, while Communism was an aggressive system
in the later Stalinist period, the system might change in a way
which would make peaceful co-existence and mutual confidence
possible without ceasing to be communist.[1] A variant of this
second view has been held by some left-wing groups in the British
Labour Party who argued, on Marxian principles, that the highly
centralized and authoritarian political organization of the Communist powers is certain to change because it conflicts with the
requirements of the structure of productive relations necessary
for a highly industrialized system. Others again have argued
that the Communist policies which appear to be aggressive have
been the result of a Communist fear of Capitalist aggression and
might be expected to change if the non-Communist powers
changed their policies. Finally, at the other extreme, some writers
have argued for positions very close to the Communist view. This
list is by no means exhaustive. One can find all sorts of variation such as the view that any aggressive policies of the U.S.S.R.
have little to do with Communism and represent merely the
continuation of Russian power politics' objectives pursued by the
Tsarist regime.

The policies of the non-Communist powers have reflected this
wide variety of views about the nature of the Communist system.
The American authorities have, on the whole, accepted the view
that Communism is an incurably aggressive system. The policy
of building up military alliances and the slogans of "contain-

1. Recent issues of *The Twentieth Century* (December, 1955 to
March, 1956) have published an interesting controversy between G. F.
Hudson representing the first view and Edward Crankshaw represent-
ing the second.

ment", "liberation", "position of strength" and "massive retaliation" are logical implications of the view that nothing better than a balance of power is possible in the relations of the rest of the world with the Communist system. But even here policy has not been entirely consistent. One can point to statements and actions which seem to be based on a view that some development of mutual confidence with the Communist powers is possible.

In British policy one can detect a tendency to minimize the importance of ideological factors and to conduct relations with the Communist powers on the assumption that the fundamental issues are those of traditional power politics. In general, however, British policy and the policies of other non-Communist powers have been less consistent than American and show the influence of widely differing views about the Communist system.

This is only a brief summary of a very complex situation but it may have been enough to suggest that efforts to reduce international tension have been hampered by a confused and inadequate theoretical basis. On both Communist and non-Communist sides policy makers seem to have operated in a state of confusion or indecision on the fundamental question of whether the other system, at least in its present form, is one with which peaceful co-existence and mutual confidence is possible or one with which nothing better than a balance of power is possible.

If this thesis is accepted as being at least worth considering it follows that those concerned with promoting peace should try to work out a more adequate theoretical basis for policy. And this could be done most effectively if people from Communist and non-Communist systems were to co-operate in discussion.

It is fairly easy to suggest a list of the main questions which need to be examined. Firstly, what exactly is the evidence and reasoning which have led people on either side to believe, with varying degrees of confidence, that the other system is one with aggressive aims and with which, at least in its present form, nothing better than a balance of power is possible? Secondly, how far is this evidence correct and this reasoning valid; or how far can the supporters of either system show that the case for supposing their system to be aggressive has been based on incorrect evidence, on misinterpretation of the evidence, or on misunderstanding? It is possible that a frank discussion of these questions between people from the Communist and non-Communist systems would show that a good deal of the mutual suspicion has been based simply on misunderstanding, for example, on interpreting preparations for defense as preparations for aggression. If, after such critical examination, the representatives of either side still considered that they had some reasoned grounds for suspecting the other system, a third question would arise, namely, what new evidence would be required to remove these suspicions? Discussion of this third question would have very important implications for practical policy. It would show what changes either system would have to make in its actions or policies to convince the other side that it did not have aggressive intentions and that it was safe to change the objective of policy from building or maintaining a balance of power to working for mutual confidence. (The developments of the last few years suggest, as a possibility, that there may have been some attempts to switch policy in this way which have failed because neither side has known, even approximately, how far it would have to go before the other would respond.)

There are, of course, many other questions which would need to be discussed, for example, how far are the claims for unrestricted national sovereignty compatible with the degree of international organization necessary to maintain peace in the modern world? But the three set out above would seem to be the most urgent.

It is unlikely that such a process of discussion would rapidly produce complete agreement, but it might very much lessen the range of disagreement. There would be some hope of arriving at a situation in which representatives of both sides would be ready to say, "We think your suspicions of our system are unjustified but we realize that they represent a possible interpretation of the evidence available to you. We believe that the new evidence which will become available with the passage of time, or which the governments of our system may produce, will eventually convince you that our interpretation is correct and yours incorrect." This is the sort of disagreement which exists between the supporters of rival hypotheses in many scientific fields and, in the case of international relations, it is not the sort of disagreement which would involve the risk of war.

These questions have, of course, been discussed in the past, but nearly all the discussion has been highly propagandist and polemical and, to a large extent, the disputants have argued at cross purposes. The impression a non-Communist gets from most Communist arguments is that they simply ignore the questions he would like to ask or are based on assumptions which he would like to challenge. It is possible that non-Communist arguments have given a similar impression to Communists. As was stated in the first paragraph, the new opportunities for contacts between the Communist and non-Communist sections of the world seem to offer, for the first time since 1945 or even earlier, an opportunity for discussing the basic issues of international relations in a scientific spirit with people from the other system.[1]

There is a strong case for holding that such discussions, at least in their early stages, can be better conducted by intellectuals from both sides at the unofficial level rather than between governments. People in official positions cannot engage in dis-

---

1. People on the Communist side might disagree with the contentions of this paragraph and argue that there had been opportunities for discussion at the various "Peace Congresses" held under the auspices of the World Council of Peace and other organizations, for example at Helsinki in 1955 or at Peking in 1952. However, the published proceedings of such congresses and reports of those who attended them provide fairly clear evidence against this argument and show that the non-Communist case was not clearly stated and certainly not discussed. Responsibility for this rests with both sides. On the one side, delegates to earlier conferences who wished to state the non-Communist case have reported that all sorts of manoeuvres were used to prevent them from doing so. On the other side, the governments of the non-Communist powers have tried to discourage attendance at such meetings; (a policy which the writer of this paper has strongly criticized). As a result the delegations from non-Communist countries to later conferences have been completely unrepresentative and have consisted, with only a few exceptions, of Communists and Fellow Travellers who did not wish to state the non-Communist case or of non-Communists of general good will who were too badly informed and too woolly minded to be capable of stating it.

cussions without to some extent committing their governments,
even when the discussions are private and informal. So long as
mutual suspicions remain serious each side will be intent on
maintaining the balance of power and will be reluctant to engage in discussions which might weaken its security system. To
give concrete illustrations, the governments of the NATO
powers would feel that their security system had been weakened
if it became known that their representatives had been discussing the conditions under which the NATO might be dis-
solved; similarly the Communist powers would feel that their
security system had been weakened if it became known that
their representatives had been discussing the conditions under
which the East German or North Korean regimes might be
allowed to disappear through free elections in Germany or
Korea. On the other hand, people with no official positions
can conduct discussions in a scientific spirit of readiness to examine any hypothesis suggested by the evidence and to follow
any line of reasoning to its logical conclusions. And neither
set of governments would have valid reasons for fearing that
this would endanger its security system.

Also, in the non-Communist section of the world, people in
academic positions are better qualified for conducting such
discussions than people in official positions. The theories which
need to be examined have, in their more serious forms, been
produced by people in academic life or on the borderline between academic and official life. People in official positions
have certainly studied these theories and been influenced by
them but they have seldom had either the time or the inclination for serious theoretical work and in conducting a discussion
they would be subject to all sorts of limitations which, in the
non-Communist world, do not apply to people in academic
life.

The first steps in such discussion should be for people on each
side to set out as clearly as possible a summary of the case which
has produced a belief that the other system may be one with
which nothing better than a balance of power is possible. The
necessary material already exists but not in a suitable form. It

is scattered over a large number of books, articles and published statements. In most of these the authors have been writing for people who were already in general agreement with them and have, therefore, taken for granted many points which need to be made explicitly in a case intended for people who share the general outlook of the other system.

There is also a wide variation between serious arguments by responsible scholars or politicians on the one hand, and purely propagandist arguments or expressions of extremist, doctrinaire and irresponsible views on the other. Only the former really need to be discussed. It would be a waste of time to give careful consideration to arguments which responsible people on the other side of the discussion would dismiss as complete exaggerations or distortions of their position, but it is often hard for someone from the other system to make the classification. To give an illustration, an article in *International Affairs* quotes with approval a pamphlet alleging that the American economy is controlled by 127 men and continues, "This handful of big plutocrats are the uncrowned kings of America, from whom the presidents, secretaries of state, senators and generals of the United States obediently take their orders. These capitalist magnates determine at their own discretion the entire policy of Washington, both internal and external."[1] This seems to show a grotesque misunderstanding of the American political system but it appears in what would almost certainly claim to be a serious periodical. Should this argument be taken seriously or not? The largely uncontrolled press of the main non-Communist powers must present people in Communist countries with even more difficult problems of deciding what should be taken seriously and what can be dismissed as the expression of extremist and irresponsible opinion.

Finally, it would be a great advantage to start any discussion by considering cases which are both important and comparatively simple. Many of the disputed issues between the Communist

---

1. "Lenin's Theory of Imperialism Today." By A. Leontyev. *International Affairs,* 1955, No. 4, p. 25.

and non-Communist powers have been extremely complex and depend on controversial matters of fact about which it is hard to produce really satisfactory evidence. Discussion which started by considering this type of issue would be tedious and almost certainly inconclusive. It should be possible, however, to select a sample of issues where the facts are comparatively simple, where the evidence is fairly definite, and which seem to provide fairly clear test cases of the generalizations to be discussed. This is analogous to the method of natural science which begins by trying to select possible experiments or observations which can give definite results whose implications will be decisive in choosing between alternative hypotheses.

The material which follows tries to do this for the non-Communist side, to give a summary of the evidence and reasoning which has produced non-Communist suspicions of the Communist system. It does not try to state the complete case but only to give a sample of the issues that raise questions of principle which need to be answered if people on the Communist side wish to refute the non-Communist case.

It is to be hoped that this will call forth from the Communist side both a critical examination of this case with answers to the questions which it asks and also a statement of the corresponding case for Communist suspicions of the non-Communist powers.

PART II

A Statement of the Non-Communist Case for Suspicion of the Communist Powers

[This is the first stage of the project suggested in Part I. The first six sections were sent to the people in Peking and Moscow who had been indicated as willing to co-operate in the project. In neither case were they actually willing to co-operate in the project by making a critical commentary on this statement or by producing a corresponding "Statement of the Communist case for suspicion of the non-Communist powers."

The last two sections had not been finished when it became clear that the chances of co-operation from Peking or Moscow were negligible. They have, however, been finished and included to make the statement complete.]

Introduction

It is hoped that readers, especially Communist readers, will note the exact title of this part. What follows is explicitly a brief statement of the case for one side. It needs to be balanced by a corresponding statement of the Communist case for suspicion of the non-Communist powers. And this statement of the Communist case should really be written by a Communist. Any statement prepared by a non-Communist would inevitably be based on very imperfect knowledge and rather speculative deductions. One can suggest a number of issues which are likely to have produced Communist suspicions of the non-Communist powers and one can study the arguments used in Communist publications, but it is hard to know which issues people in Communist countries consider most important and, as was pointed out in the preceding section, it is hard to distinguish serious arguments from propaganda statements which need not be taken seriously.

A reasonably objective picture of the international situation could only emerge in the later stages of the discussion when each side has made a statement of its case and has made a critical examination of the case stated by the other side. What follows is not an attempt to give a complete and impartial picture but to state a case which needs to be presented as part of a process which might end by producing one.

A great deal has been left out for the sake of shortness but no issues have been avoided for the sake of not giving offence to Communist readers. It was argued in the preceding section that discussion at the academic level might be very important in providing an adequate theoretical foundation for policies on both sides aimed at securing peaceful co-existence. For this it is essential that each side should state its full case. If issues which have been important in producing mutual suspicions are not touched on in discussion at the academic level, they will remain to confuse policies at the official level. And at the official level they would be much harder to discuss. There is nothing in the case stated below which cannot be found in serious non-Communist publications and, what is perhaps even more important, in private statements by people in responsible official positions in non-Communist countries. To have suppressed part of this case for fear of offending Communist feelings would have been to destroy a lot of the possible value of frank discussion.

Anything like a complete statement of the non-Communist case would have run to a large book, perhaps to several volumes. The following summary is only a sample which has been chosen according to two principles. An attempt has been made to select a sample of issues which are both important and also provide clear test cases. Many important issues have been left out simply because they are complicated. For example, the German problem has been a very important source of disputes between the Soviet Union and the Western powers, but only the issue of East German rearmament has been discussed. In some respects the Berlin blockade was a more important issue which might easily have led to war, but it could not be adequately discussed without going into very complicated questions such as the dispute over German currency.

The selection of the sample has obviously been influenced by the particular interests of the writer and the most that is claimed for it is that it is reasonably representative and raises most of the basic issues of principle which have produced non-Communist suspicions of the Communist powers. Other writers might well have preferred to select a rather different sample of particular issues, but it is fairly certain that these would have illustrated the same basic general case against the Communist powers.

To non-Communists some of the following sections may seem to be labored, going into great detail to substantiate points that seem to be obvious. But much that seems obvious to non-Communists is unlikely to seem obvious to Communists. A statement of the non-Communist case must challenge many points that are taken for granted by most people in Communist countries, and what could be taken for granted in a statement intended for non-Communist readers needs to be clearly argued and substantiated in a statement intended for Communist readers.

In most sections some questions have been emphasized. These are questions which defenders of the Communist position would need to answer if they wished to refute the case for suspicion of the Communist powers. And they are questions which have almost always been evaded in Communist statements up to the present.

1

An examination of some Communist arguments

Communist statements often assert that any suspicions of the Communist powers are utterly ridiculous and cannot really be held in good faith. To give a typical quotation, "The reactionary imperialist circles try to screen their designs against peace and international security with talk about 'Soviet aggression,' 'international communism,' etc. But it is doubtful if anyone other than utterly naive people or people befuddled by the imperialist propaganda seriously believe the inventions about a mythical 'Soviet threat,' or the allegation that the Soviet Union, the Chinese People's Republic and the People's Democracies, busy with their peaceful labor, threaten the security of other countries. The enemies of peace and international co-operation need these falsehoods to maintain the 'cold war,' to justify the swollen war budgets, the arms drive, and, in this way, assure fabulous profits for the imperialist monopolies."[1]

It is easy for anyone in touch with public opinion in non-Communist countries to find out from direct observation that statements of this kind are simply untrue. Large numbers of people are obviously quite sincere in regarding the Communist powers with very deep suspicion. It is, therefore, necessary to examine the arguments by which the Communist case is supported and to consider why they have proved unconvincing.

Firstly, it is argued that a socialist society is inherently non-aggressive. To give again one typical quotation, "In socialist society there are no elements interested in war. There are no classes or groups that might take advantage of war to enrich themselves. On the other hand, the Soviet Union and all the countries of the socialist camp have sufficient land and sources of materials to ensure the prosperity of their economies. And

---

1. *International Affairs*, 1955, No. 12, pp. 22-3.

finally, a socialist society is not faced with the problem of finding markets, which is a cause of such bitter rivalry among the capitalist countries."[1]

Secondly it is argued that attempts to impose Communism by interference from outside or by conspiratorial tactics would be contrary to the doctrines of Marx and Lenin.

"The Communists do not go in for plots or 'exporting revolution.'

"Furthermore, they reject conspiratorial tactics, which they label Blanquism and condemn as barren, as incapable of furthering the communist movement. . . . Lenin taught us that for a revolution to break out there must be a revolutionary situation in the country, a situation produced by a series of factors, in which the 'lower' classes refuse to go on living in the old way and the 'upper' classes can no longer govern in the old way. In that case, given the existence of a revolutionary party, a certain level of class consciousness and organization among the dissatisfied classes, and a split in the 'upper' classes, a revolution may break out. Replacing these conditions by 'export of revolution' would be reckless gambling doomed to failure. The Communists build their strategy and tactics on a profound scientific analysis of the laws of social development and they reject, in principle, any kind of 'export of revolution.'

"The Communists are opposed to any country interfering in the affairs of another. . . ."[2]

Thirdly, it is argued that the Soviet Union, or other Communist countries, have never attacked other countries, have never interfered in the internal affairs of other countries, and have always strictly observed any international agreements into which they have entered.

"From the first days of Soviet rule, our socialist state has stood for peace with all countries. Violation of the peaceful co-existence of the two systems has always come from capitalist countries. . . . The U.S.S.R. has never violated peaceful co-existence with capitalist countries."[3]

---

1. *International Affairs*, 1956, No. 3, p. 9.
2. *International Affairs*, 1955, No. 4, p. 19.
3. *International Affairs*, 1956, No. 3, p. 8.

"Our confidence in the universal triumph of communism in
no way derives from an idiotic hope of transplanting communism from Moscow to other countries by interfering in their
internal affairs. We do not indulge in such activity."[1]

"Fidelity to international agreements is one of the basic
principles of international law. The Soviet Union has always
honestly and scrupulously fulfilled the obligations which it has
undertaken under international treaties."[2]

The same general arguments expressed in various ways can
be found again and again in Communist statements and publications. To a non-Communist who has made some study of international affairs they are quite unconvincing because they
seem to be contradicted by numerous instances from the actual
record of Soviet policy. And this raises a serious fundamental
question. Most non-Communists accept the basic assumption of
scientific method, that the truth or falsity of a generalization
about matters of fact is best tested by comparing its implications
with the available evidence. When Communists repeatedly make
assertions that are, *prima facie,* flatly contrary to the evidence
and make no attempts to explain these contraditions, does this
mean that they reject this principle? Do they believe that their
statements about Soviet policy cannot be disproved by empirical evidence? If this were so, no useful discussion would be
possible between Communists and non-Communists until they
had settled a basic philosophical disagreement about what they
mean when they say that a statement is true or false.

It is, therefore, best to begin the discussion of Soviet policy
by considering a sample which seems to provide clear test cases
on this point. This can be found in the acquisitions of territory
by the Soviet Union between 1938 and 1946. Most of the evidence
is quite definite and not really controversial — changes in frontier
lines, the published texts of treaties and official documents,
and Soviet actions about which Communist and non-Communist
sources agree.

A comparison between maps showing the boundaries of the

---

1. *International Affairs,* 1956, No. 3, pp. 10-11.
2. *International Affairs,* 1955, No. 2, p. 63.

Soviet Union before 1938 and after 1946 will show that every European country bordering on the Soviet Union in 1938, and even some which did not, had, by 1946 lost territory to the U.S.S.R. or been totally incorporated in the U.S.S.R. In the Far East it can be seen that the Soviet Union has taken over areas which in 1938 were Japanese.

There are distinctions between the various Soviet annexations of this period and they will be considered in turn, proceeding anti-clockwise round the boundaries of the U.S.S.R.

The Soviet annexation of Southern Sakhalin could be defended as the recovery of Russian territory which had been seized after the Russian defeat in the Russo-Japanese war. But in the treaty of 1875 Russia had voluntarily recognized Japanese sovereignty over the Kuriles. In particular, the southern Kuriles together with Shikotan Island and the Habomai group were territory which, until 1945, had always been Japanese and where no previous Russian claims existed. The Soviet annexations put the U.S.S.R. in a strong position to exercise economic and strategic pressure on Japan but they do not seem to be essential for the defense of any important areas of the U.S.S.R.[1]

The next case is that of Finland. According to statements made by Molotov, the object of the territorial demands made in October, 1939 and enforced in the treaty of March, 1940 was

---

1. In the early part of last century both the Kuriles and Sakhalin Island were areas where neither Russia nor Japan had established effective occupation and into which both were expanding. An agreement of 1855 divided the Kuriles north of Uruppu Island but left the status of Sakhalin undecided and in the Russo-Japanese Treaty of 1875 Russia recognized the Japanese claim to the whole of the Kurile chain while Japan recognized the Russian claim to the whole of Sakhalin. Under the Treaty of Portsmouth in 1905 Japan took from Russia the southern half of Sakhalin.

The 11th. edition of the *Encyclopædia Britannica* argued that Japan had good claims to both Sakhalin and the Kuriles and said of the 1875 Treaty, "It was a singular transaction. Russia purchased a Japanese property and paid for it with a part of Japan's belongings." Translated into modern terms it maintained that the 1875 Treaty was a piece of imperialist sharp practice by a European Great Power at the expense of a still weak Asian country. (As this was published in 1911 it cannot be accused of anti-communist bias.)

to obtain a better strategic frontier for the defense of Leningrad and of the Murmansk railway.[1] In order to obtain these demands the Soviet government denounced its non-aggression pact with Finland, made a military attack against Finnish territory, and recognized as the government of Finland an organization established in Soviet territory by Finnish Communists. By the Peace Treaty of 1947 the Soviet Union also acquired from Finland a considerable area in the north including the important nickel mines at Petsamo.

Next come the Baltic states. In the secret protocol to the Nazi-Soviet pact of 23rd. August, 1939 it was agreed that, "the northern boundary of Lithuania shall represent the boundary of the spheres of influence of Germany and the U.S.S.R."[2] while in the Nazi-Soviet agreement of 28th. September, 1939 Lithuania was assigned to the Soviet sphere of influence in exchange for parts of Poland. During the end of September and the beginning of October mutual assistance pacts were signed between the U.S.S.R. and the Baltic states under which Soviet armed forces were to have bases in these states. Statements by people connected with the governments of the three countries have claimed that Molotov threatened that the U.S.S.R. would use military force if these treaties were not accepted.

In May and June 1940 the Soviet government sent ultimata to the three governments alleging that the mutual assistance treaties were being violated and demanding that new governments satisfactory to the Soviet Union should be established and that Soviet troops should be stationed in all important centers. All three governments complied with these ultimata which they had no means of resisting.[3]

---

1. *Soviet Peace Policy,* By V. Molotov, Lawrence & Wishart, London, 1941, p. 62.

2. *Nazi-Soviet Relations, 1939-41. Documents from the Archives of the German Foreign Office,* Department of State, Washington, 1948, p. 78.

3. The main alleged violations of the mutual security treaties consisted of a failure to denounce the military alliances which existed between the Baltic states, secret conferences in December 1939 and March 1940, and the publication in Tallin of the *Revue Baltique.* On the other side it is claimed that the military alliances were long standing treaties

Subsequent developments in the Baltic states are considered in a later section.

Next comes the territory that was formerly part of East Prussia. This had had a predominantly German population for centuries and even in the southern part of East Prussia, now incorporated in Poland, the areas with a partly non-German population had voted for Germany in the plebiscite held after 1919. The motives for this annexation would appear to be revenge against Germany and a desire to modify the frontiers of this area to secure strategic and economic advantages for the U.S.S.R. (At the Teheran Conference in 1943 Stalin claimed Koenigsberg as a price for agreeing to the Curzon Line as the post-war Polish frontier.)

The Soviet annexations at the expense of Poland figure at length in negotiations during the war. The memoirs of the non-Communist statesmen concerned and other non-Communist discussions of the problem mostly agree that there was a case for revision of the frontier. The Curzon Line had originally been drawn in 1920 as an attempt to make the frontier coincide with racial boundaries and the frontier fixed by the Treaty of Riga in 1921 gave Poland large areas with non-Polish population. There are disagreements on points of detail, such as the area between Line A and Line B including the city of Lwow, but this is a complicated subject not worth discussing here.

The Soviet annexations prior to 1941 form a rather different case. The secret protocol to the Nazi-Soviet Pact of August 1939 said, "In the event of a territorial and political rearrangement of the areas belonging to the Polish state the spheres of influence of Germany and the U.S.S.R. shall be bounded approximately by the line of the rivers Narew, Vistula and San.

"The question of whether the interests of both parties make

---

which had been registered with the League of Nations and to which the U.S.S.R. had made no previous objections, (as late as March 29th. 1940 Molotov had stated at a meeting of the Supreme Soviet that the execution of the mutual assistance pacts was proceeding satisfactorily) ; that the alleged secret conferences were only the continuation of a practice of regular meetings between the foreign ministers of the three states; and that the *Revue Baltique* was only a publication of the Societies of Friendship of the Baltic Peoples devoted exclusively to economic, social and cultural matters.

desirable the maintenance of an independent Polish state and
how such a state should be bounded can only be definitely determined in the course of further political developments."[1]

The German documents record discussions between Moscow
and Berlin on the date at which the Soviet armies were to occupy
the part of Poland assigned to the U.S.S.R. They show that the
Soviet government was determined on this occupation but
wished to start it on a date after the Polish defeat by Germany
had become certain and before any German-Polish armistice
had been signed.[2]

On the 19th. September, 1939 Molotov informed the German
ambassador that, "The original inclination entertained by the
Soviet Government and by Stalin personally to permit the existence of a residual Poland had given way to the inclination to
partition residual Poland along the Pissa-Narew, Vistula-San
line."[3] On 25th. of September Stalin told the German ambassador that, "he considered it wrong to leave an independent
Polish rump state," and that he proposed that, "all the province
of Lublin and that part of the province of Warsaw, which
extends to the Bug should be added to Germany's share. In return, Germany should waive her claims to Lithuania."[4] This
proposal was accepted in the Nazi-Soviet agreement of 28th.
September.

The frontier changes at the expense of Czechoslovakia and
Roumania, like the final frontier settlement with Poland, can be
defended on racial grounds. The areas incorporated in the
Soviet Union had populations with majorities racially and
linguistically akin to those of adjoining areas of the U.S.S.R.
and these populations had been racial minorities in pre-war
Czechoslovakia and Roumania. For the Roumanian case there
is the additional argument that the Soviet Government had never
accepted the Roumanian annexation of Bessarabia. In the case of
Ruthenia there would seem to be the additional strategic motive
of giving the U.S.S.R. a common frontier with Hungary. Dis-
putable points remain which are not considered here.

---

1. *Nazi-Soviet Relations*, p. 78.
2. *Nazi-Soviet Relations*, pp. 86-100.
3. *Nazi-Soviet Relations*, p. 101.
4. *Nazi-Soviet Relations*, pp. 102-3.

Finally, it is worth noting a case of Soviet claims which were not actually realized. On 25th. November, 1940 Molotov gave the German ambassador the Soviet Government's reply to German proposals. This stated that the Soviet Government was willing to accept the German proposals for Soviet adherance to the Three Power Pact provided, among other things, that the U.S.S.R. obtained a military and naval base in Bulgaria and, "Provided that the area south of Batum and Baku in the general direction of the Persian Gulf is recognized as the center of the aspirations of the Soviet Union."[1]

This summary of the Soviet record in expanding the frontiers of the U.S.S.R. has avoided, as far as possible, cases where the facts are controversial. Even so it seems to be clearly incompatible with the Communist claims that the Soviet Union has always followed a completely non-aggressive policy entirely different from and superior to the policies of non-Communist states.

Can defenders of the Communist position give explanations of Soviet policy which would reconcile every case cited above with claims such as, "The U.S.S.R. has never violated peaceful co-existence with capitalist countries." or "The striving to seize foreign territory and subjugate other nations is alien to the socialist state."?[2] If they can not, are they ready to admit that this type of extreme claim about Soviet policy is false?

Unless such explanations can be given, which seems very unlikely, it is reasonable to consider what hypotheses could explain these Soviet actions. One obvious hypothesis is that the policy of the U.S.S.R. was not essentially different from that of any other Great Power pursuing its "national interest" as defined in terms of a system of unscrupulous power politics. The Soviet annexations could be explained by the motives of expanding frontiers to include populations racially akin to the peoples of the U.S.S.R. and of acquiring bits of territory which strengthened the strategic and economic position of the U.S.S.R. Similar motives could be traced in the policies followed by other Great Powers, including Tsarist Russia. A case could be

---

1. *Nazi-Soviet Relations*, pp. 255-8.
2. *International Affairs*, 1955, No. 1, p. 46.

made out for holding that, as compared with the standards
observed by most European Great Powers since the 18th. century
other than Nazi Germany, Soviet policy was rather more unscrupulous and rather more brutal in its treatment of the population in newly annexed areas, but this is a question of degree.[1]

If this type of Soviet policy is extrapolated into the future it
provides reasonable grounds for some fears of the Soviet Union
in other countries. The motive of expansion to racial frontiers
may have exhausted itself but the motive of acquiring territory
likely to strengthen the economic or strategic position of the
U.S.S.R. could still be operative. The strategic motive in particular, with the increasing range of modern weapons, might form
a basis for very wide extensions of Soviet territory.

It should also be noted that the Soviet annexations up to the
present do not disprove (though equally they do not prove),
the hypothesis that the Soviet Government has long term ambitions of world conquest. Up to 1939 Hitler's actions did not go
beyond the strengthening of Germany's strategic position and acquiring territories with populations racially akin to that of
Germany, but these were only the preliminary to large scale
attempts at new conquests.

The extreme claims made by the defenders of Soviet policy
must strengthen any suspicions of the Soviet Union. If people
in the Communist system admitted that, in a world where other
powers were acting in terms of unscrupulous power politics,
the Soviet Union had done the same, it would then be possible
to discuss the changes which all powers would have to make
in order to secure a world of peaceful co-existence. So long,
however, as they continue to claim that Soviet policy has always
been entirely peaceful and non-aggressive there is no reason to
suppose that Soviet policy in the future will be different from

---

1. There is, for example, clear evidence of large scale deportations
from the Baltic states and from Poland. Another case is the disappearance of Polish officer prisoners linked to the controversial question of
the Katyn massacres. (For a summary of this case see *Survey of International Affairs, 1939-46. The Realignment of Europe,* Oxford University Press, 1955, pp. 138-148.)

Soviet policy in the past. On precedents provided by Soviet actions in the past a policy which Communists would consider to be entirely peace-loving and non-aggressive would not rule out the possibility that the Soviet Government might demand, and use military force to obtain, territory which it considers of strategic importance, (as in the case of Finland) ; or that it might conclude an agreement with an aggressive imperialist power to partition the territory of another state, (as in the case of Poland), and so on.

In non-Communist countries similar claims are not generally made. There would, for example, be strong reasons for distrusting British policy if people in Britian generally maintained that there had been nothing wrong with the foreign policies of British governments in the 1930's. Actually, most British opinion would admit that the appeasement policies culminating at Munich formed a discreditable episode in British history. *Would Communists be willing to admit that the period of the Nazi-Soviet Pact formed a discreditable episode in Soviet history?*

A similar issue is raised by the Communist claims that the Soviet Union has always strictly and honestly observed its international agreements. Except in the cases of Roumania and Germany, every Soviet annexation was made from countries which, at the time of Soviet action, had treaties of non-aggression, mutual assistance, or neutrality with the U.S.S.R. If "the Soviet Union has always honestly and scrupulously fulfilled the obligations which it has undertaken under international treaties" it follows that, on the Communist interpretation, the strict observance by the Soviet Government of a non-aggression pact with another country does not rule out the Soviet use of military force to take territory from this country, (precedents of Poland and Finland)[1]; that strict observance of a mutual assistance pact stipulating "non-intervention by either Contracting Party in the internal affairs of the other Contracting Party" does not rule out a Soviet ultimatum demanding that an existing government should be replaced by one acceptable to the Soviet Government

---

1. Soviet-Polish Non-aggression Pact of 25th. July, 1932. Soviet-Finnish Non-aggression Pact of 21st. January, 1932. (renewed until 31st. December, 1945 on 7th. April, 1934.)

(precedent of the Baltic States);[1] and that strict observance of a neutrality pact stipulating the inviolability of certain territory does not rule out a declaration of war and the invasion of this territory, (precedent of Japan).[2]

Would defenders of the Communist position maintain that in every case cited above the U.S.S.R. had "honestly and scrupulously fulfilled the obligations which it has undertaken under international treaties"? If they do maintain this, can they explain whether non-aggression pacts offered by the Soviet Union since 1945 differ from these earlier pacts, and if so how?

There are, of course, many cases in which non-Communist powers have not fulfilled treaties but their representatives are willing, in most cases, to admit this and only try to excuse their breach of treaties by over-riding reasons of state. Such a position implies that some reliance can be placed on their future observance of treaties in a situation where similar reasons of state are not likely to arise. If Communists were willing to admit that the Soviet Union had in the past broken treaties, often from understandable motives of national security, there would be similar reasons for putting some trust in the future Soviet observance of treaties in less critical situations. It is the Communist claim that the Soviet Union has always fulfilled its treaties that makes the value of any future obligations especially doubtful.

This section has discussed at considerable length a comparatively small sample of Soviet policy because it seemed to provide clear test cases on an important issue of principle, whether or not Communists will accept the normal scientific standards of verification or disproof. If Communists are determined to

---

1. Mutual Assistance Pacts of 29th. September, 1939 (Estonia), 5th. October, 1939 (Latvia) and 10th. October, 1939 (Lithuania). It should be noted that Article 4 of the Estonian Pact said, "For the implementation of the present Pact and the solution of problems arising therefrom a Mixed Commission on the principle of parity is to be established, which will evolve its own rules of procedure." Even if the Soviet Government considered that the other party had violated the pact it should, presumably, have acted through this Commission before sending an ultimatum.

2. Soviet-Japanese Neutrality Pact of 13th. April, 1941.

maintain the extreme claims which have been criticized above it would seem to imply that Communists and non-Communists cannot join in any rational discussion of international affairs until they have settled fundamental philosophical disagreements. It would also seem to follow that, judged by non-Communist standards, no reliance can be placed on obligations undertaken by Communist powers.

2

The "Satellite States"

At the Geneva meeting in July 1955 the Western leaders proposed that the agenda should include a discussion of the countries of Eastern Europe but they did not press this proposal when Marshal Bulganin objected that this would be interference in the affairs of independent countries. As a result the conference failed to discuss one of the most serious issues dividing the Communist and non-Communist systems.

The term "satellite state" is used to describe a country which is nominally independent but whose government is in fact controlled by the government of some other country of which it is a satellite. The issue between the Communist and non-Communist systems turns on questions of fact, whether or not certain countries stand in this relationship to the Soviet Union.

Extreme anti-Communists have caused some confusion by applying the term "satellite state" to every Communist ruled country outside the U.S.S.R., but some of them should clearly be excluded. Stalin's policy towards Jugoslavia in 1948 could be explained by his belief that Jugoslavia was a satellite, that the Soviet Government was in a position to eliminate any Jugoslav leaders who acted in ways of which he disapproved, and this belief proved quite clearly to be false. In China, as in Jugoslavia, the Communist Party attained power without decisive Soviet assistance and there is strong evidence for holding that the Soviet Government is not in a position to control the Chinese Government. The countries for which non-Communist opinion would consider that there is evidence of satellite status are:— Bulgaria, Czechoslovakia, East Germany, Hungary, Mongolia,[1] North Korea, Poland and Roumania.[2]

1. The Mongolian People's Republic is in a special class. Attempts to increase Russian influence in Mongolia date back to last century and after the 1911 revolution in China the Tsarist Government supplied arms to the Mongols who wished to assert their independence

Before considering these countries it may be worth considering an earlier case which raises similar issues, namely the incorporation of the Baltic states in the U.S.S.R.

A recent publication by a British Communist summarizes the Communist version of the story.[3] He says, "Another charge of 'imperialism' is made against the Soviet Union in connection with the alleged forcible incorporation of the Baltic States against the will of their people. But this charge, too, is based on total ignorance of the facts." He goes on to argue that the pre-1940 governments were reactionary regimes imposed by foreign intervention after the 1914-18 war and concludes, "The popular upheavals, led by the local Communists which took place in 1940 because the mass of the workers were no longer afraid of their rulers, thus represented the righting of a wrong done to them mainly by foreign invasion twenty-one years before. . . . In all three Baltic Soviet Republics today the people have a far higher standard of material life, of educational opportunities and cultural amenities than before 1940. It is based, moreover, on a more balanced and flourishing economy." Similarly, when the question of the Baltic States was raised at various war time conferences Stalin claimed that the people had voluntarily chosen to join the U.S.S.R.

---

against China and worked to produce a situation in which Mongolia would be largely autonomous as regards the Chinese Government but subject to a considerable degree of Russian economic and political control. The Russian defeat in 1917 enabled the Chinese Government to reassert its influence but after the revolution Mongolia was entered first by White Russian and then by Soviet troups. In 1921 the Soviet Government established diplomatic relations with a People's Government of Mongolia and in 1924 the Mongolia People's Republic adopted a constitution modelled on the Soviet constitution and since then seems to have been under effective Soviet control. (For details see, *Outer Mongolia and its International Position*. By G. M. Friters, Allen & Unwin, London, 1951.)

Thus, while the satellite status of other countries was only established after 1945, Mongolia became a Russian satellite before 1917 and its status as a Soviet satellite goes back to the early 1920's.

2. Albania is probably another Soviet satellite and Vietminh may be a Chinese satellite but evidence about them is very limited.

3. *Peaceful Co-existence*. By Andrew Rothstein, Penguin Books, London, 1955, pp. 113-116.

The non-Communist version of the story is completely different. By the standards of Eastern Europe, Estonia and Latvia were quite progressive countries before 1940. A radical land reform in the first years of independence had produced an agricultural system based on family farms of reasonable size. Figures for the 1930's give the production per person dependent on agriculture as 99% of the European average in Estonia and 111% in Latvia as against 49% in Poland, 48% in Roumania, and 39% in the U.S.S.R.[1] Though parliamentary democracy had broken down in the 1930's the regimes were still more liberal than those of most other East European countries. Lithuania was less successful both economically and politically but still better off than some other East European states.

The governments set up to comply with the Soviet ultimata of 1940 were headed by left-wing intellectuals who were not actually Communists but the Soviet military occupation ensured effective Soviet control. To each country was sent a high ranking member of the C.P.S.U., Zhdanov to Estonia, Vyshinski to Latvia and Dekanozov to Lithuania. In July the new regimes held general elections at very short notice which were marked by terrorism and fraudulent practices against any opposition to the Communists.[2] The assemblies thus elected voted for incorporation into the Soviet Union. Large scale arrests and deportations aimed at eliminating the intelligentsia and middle classes as leaders of possible opposition but included a high proportion of workers and peasants.[3] The peasant farming economy

---

1. *Economic Demography of Eastern and Southern Europe.* By Wilbert E. Moore, League of Nations, Geneva, 1945.

2. "Investigations of Communist archives which survived the first Russian occupation showed that the Central Electoral Committee alone had forged 35,119 votes. Unfortunately, no evidence has remained of votes forged by the District Electoral Committees." (*A history of the Estonian People,* by Evald Uustalu, Boreas, London, 1952, pp. 242-3.) For a more detailed account see, *Baltic Eclipse,* by Ants Oras, London, Gollancz, 1948.

3. According to Uustalu (*Op. cit.,* p. 248) the deportation lists abandoned by the Soviet authorities in 1941 showed 42.7% manual and office workers, 26.3% owner farmers and 16.9% civil servants and technical personnel.

was replaced by a program of collectivization which appears to have reduced agricultural productivity.[1] Soviet rule was interrupted by a period of German occupation. When the German armies retreated about a quarter of a million refugees fled to Germany and about 30,000 to Sweden. The new period of Soviet rule was marked by more large scale deportations and the replacement of this population by settlements of people from other parts of the Soviet Union.[2]

Considerable numbers of Baltic refugees are now settled in Australia and their reports in most cases indicate that the period of Nazi occupation was rather less unpleasant for the mass of the people than Soviet occupation.

Though the Baltic states were only satellite states for a few weeks in 1940 they show in a crude and extreme form some features of later developments in other countries and illustrate the complete disagreement between the Communist and non-Communist versions of what actually happened.[3]

The non-Communist accounts of developments in Poland, Roumania, Bulgaria and Hungary show a similar pattern of development in each country. In all cases developments took place in the presence of Soviet occupation forces. In each case the new regime was at first a broad coalition in which non-Communists had leading positions but in which control of the police and some other key ministries was effectively in Communist hands.

Agreements between the U.S.S.R. and the Western Powers stipulated that free elections should be held,[4] but these agree-

1. See, "Estonian Agriculture under Soviet Rule." The World Today, May 1951.

2. See Survey of International Affairs, 1939-46. The Realignment of Europe, Oxford University Press, 1955, pp. 7 and 260.

3. A publication which I had not seen when this was written is the Third Interim Report of the House of Representatives Select Committee on Communist Aggression. 83rd. Congress, 2nd. Session. This report, prepared by the Legislative Reference Section of the Library of Congress gives a very full account of Soviet policy in the Baltic states largely documented from Soviet sources.

4. For example, the declaration of the Potsdam Conference stated, "The three Powers note that the Polish Provisional Government, in

ments were not observed by the Soviet occupation forces or the local Communists. Non-Communist official observers and non-Soviet members of the allied control commissions agree with non-Communist journalists and non-Communist local leaders in reporting that the elections in Bulgaria, Poland and Roumania were marked by wide spread terrorism and fraud. The first Hungarian elections were comparatively free and the Smallholders Party gained 57.5% of the votes but the Soviet occupation authorities prevented the party from exercising effective power and finally helped the local Communists to destroy it.

In all countries the new regimes at first stood for a general program of reforms but this gradually changed to a program of "Gleichschaltung" with the Soviet Union and all non-Communists not entirely subservient to the Communists were eliminated. This liquidation of non-Communist organizations was applied not only to right-wing parties but also to all socialist organizations which wished to preserve some measure of genuine independence.

This is only a very brief summary of developments about which a great deal has been published. Fuller summaries are given in *The East European Revolution* by Hugh Seton-Watson[1] and in the *Survey of International Affairs* prepared by the Royal Institute of International Affairs. This literature provides strong evidence for holding that, in all these countries, governments which had only the support of a minority of the people were imposed by terrorism and fraud in which the Soviet authorities played a decisive part. (North Korea and East Germany are in a rather different category as the Soviet authorities had direct responsibilities for administration which they gradually handed over to local governments. In East Germany there

---

accordance with the decisions of the Crimea Conference, has agreed to the holding of free and unfettered elections as soon as possible on the basis of universal suffrage and secret ballot in which all democratic and anti-Nazi parties shall have the right to take part and to put forward candidates and that representatives of the allied press shall enjoy full freedom to report to the world on developments in Poland before and during the elections."

1. Methuen, London, 1950.

was the same development from a fairly wide coalition to an almost entirely Communist regime. In Korea the local Communists started with more of an organization than any rival groups but the series of negotiations for Korean unification showed that the Soviet authorities were not prepared to allow any Korean elections in which the Communists would have to compete for popular support with rival parties.)

Communists would deny the conclusion that the regimes in Poland, Roumania, Bulgaria and Hungary were not based on popular support but were imposed by terrorism and fraud, but it is very doubtful if they could substantiate these denials. It is hard to show this in a short summary. The non-Communist case depends on the cumulative evidence of large numbers of independent reports about large numbers of incidents. All these can be explained by the hypothesis that the Soviet Government was determined to secure Communist regimes in these countries and to use whatever methods might prove to be necessary to attain this aim. On any particular incident a defender of the Communist position might argue with some plausibility that the facts were not clearly established or that the Communist interpretation of the incident might be correct, for example, that some particular non-Communist left-wing leader was not liquidated because he opposed the Communists but because he was really implicated in some Fascist plot. But this kind of argument becomes progressively less plausible with an increase in the number of cases in which it has to be used. On the one hand, the non-Communist version of events explains all the evidence in terms of one simple hypothesis. On the other hand, the Communist version can only be defended by explaining away a great deal of evidence. By the normal standards of scientific method it is reasonable to believe the non-Communist version and to disbelieve the Communist version.

One can pick out a few fairly clear test cases. Vyshinski's ultimatum to the King of Roumania at the end of February 1945 demanding the appointment of a new government and the arrest of Bela Kovacs by the Soviet authorities in Hungary in 1947 both seem to provide very clear instances against the Communist claim that developments took place without Soviet interference. In the case of Poland there is a lot of evidence to suggest that, by 1944, the Soviet government was prepared to subordinate the fight against Hitler to the weakening of non-Communist Polish resistance groups. Instances of this were provided by Soviet action at the time of the Warsaw rising in 1944;[1] and by the arrest of Polish resistance leaders invited under safe-conduct to Moscow.[2]

The small number of really clear test cases can easily be explained. While, on the non-Communist view, the Soviet authorities were determined to impose Communist governments they also had obvious motives for trying to keep up appearances. Actions which could have been cited as absolutely clear breaches of inter-allied agreements or absolutely clear cases of Soviet interference in other countries would have weakened the Soviet position.

It is worth considering one general argument which has been used against the conclusion that the Communists in the "satellite states" did not have popular support. At least in the early stages of the regimes, the Communists advocated programs which were likely to gain popular support, proposing reforms of which very large sections of progressive non-Communist opinion would be likely to approve. It has been argued from this that the masses must have been ready to support a party which promised to follow policies which were obviously in their interest. There is no reason to doubt that such considerations did have some influence and produced some genuine popular support for Communism, but they were largely offset by another consideration, the association of the local Communists with the Soviet occupation forces. There is very clear evidence that the Soviet armies in all countries outside the Soviet Union showed a very low standard of discipline towards the civilian population at least

---

1. Even if defenders of the Communist position could show that the Soviet advance was halted on the outskirts of Warsaw for military rather than for political reasons, they would still have to explain why the Soviet Government refused to give the facilities which would have enabled the British and American air forces to assist the insurgents.

2. For an account of this and of the methods to secure confessions at the subsequent trial see *Invitation to Moscow*. By Z. Stypulkowski. London, Thames and Hudson, 1951.

for a considerable period. Reports of widespread looting, rape and brutality came not only from ex-enemy countries but also from countries where the Soviet forces were ostensibly liberating an allied population. This naturally produced popular feeling against any local party closely associated with the Soviet forces. In the first Austrian elections one of the most effective slogans of the anti-Communist parties was, "If you love the Red Army, vote Communist."

The Soviet leaders have shown themselves very sensitive on this point. One of the first disputes to arise between the Soviet and Jugoslav governments came from a report that some of the Jugoslav leaders had made unfavorable comparisons between the behavior of Soviet officers and that of the British officers in war time missions. Much more recently[1] Mr. Khrushchev indignantly repudiated Dr. Adenauer's statement that the Soviet army had behaved badly in Germany. However, this kind of indignation at some accusation is not evidence of innocence, if anything the contrary. It is certainly not enough to refute the highly circumstantial evidence reported by a wide variety of observers.[2]

The reaction of Western opinion to these Soviet policies in the "satellite states" was rather slow. There was an inclination to make excuses for Soviet actions. It was argued that, after the experience of the German invasion, the Soviet Government had

---

1. During Dr. Adenauer's visit to Moscow.

2. It is probably worth citing one source which Communists might now accept as reliable, *Tito Speaks,* by Vladimir Dedijer, London, Weidenfeld & Nicholson, 1953, pp. 271-2. Dedijer describes how, wherever the Soviet Army passed, there were complaints of rape, robbery and murder. The Jugoslav Communists first tried to explain these to the people as isolated incidents but the number of crimes steadily increased and became a serious political problem. He gives figures for cases reported to the Jugoslav authorities and particulars of some cases. The Jugoslav Politburo tried to make a complaint to General Korneyev, head of the Soviet Military Mission, but Korneyev refused to listen and said, "In the name of the Red Army Command I protest against these things because they are untrue!" There is an obvious similarity between Korneyev's reaction to Jugoslav complaints and Khrushchev's reaction to Adenauer's complaints about Soviet Army behavior.

good reasons for wanting governments it could trust in the bordering states and that the non-Communist parties were often strongly anti-Russian. It was admitted that parliamentary democracy had failed to work in Eastern Europe in the inter-war period and that the Communists were only following precedents set by previous right-wing regimes in conducting fraudulent elections and in using terrorism against political opponents. It was realized that drastic social and economic reforms were needed in Eastern Europe and it appeared for some time that the policies of the various Communist parties did not go beyond such reforms which, perhaps, could only be put through by a fairly authoritarian regime. Arguments of this sort can still be found in some recent non-Communist publications and they had much more influence before 1948.

The Communist coup d'etat in Czechoslavakia produced a change in non-Communist opinion because none of these considerations could be applied to it. President Benes and other non-Communist leaders were not anti-Russian but rather the reverse. Czechoslavakia was the only country of Eastern or Central Europe in which parliamentary democracy had worked fairly well until overthrown by the German occupation and it seemed to have been revived after the war. Because pre-war Czechoslovakia had been a fairly progressive country the case for any drastic social or economic changes was not so obvious as in other countries and, at any rate, the government was committed to a fairly left-wing program.

Czechoslovakia provided a clear test case showing that the Communists were not willing to base their power on popular support. In May 1946 the Communists had won 38% of the vote in elections which were generally agreed to have been free and honestly conducted. With Communists holding the positions of Prime Minister, Minister of the Interior and Minister of Information they had no reasonable grounds for fearing that the elections due in 1948 would be biased against them or that they would not be allowed to take over complete control of the government if they won a clear majority. The coup d'etat of February 1948 and the developments leading up to it seemed to show that the Communists were not prepared to accept the results of free elections because it seemed likely that they were losing popular support. A public opinion test conducted by the Ministry of Information in January 1948 indicated a drop in the Communist vote from 38% to 28%, (a similar test before the 1946 elections had proved accurate to within ½%) and there were other signs of increasing opposition to the Communists. For example, the Social Democratic Party Congress in November, 1947 had dismissed the fellow travelling Fierlinger from his position as chairman of the party.

The immediate occasion of the coup d'etat was the resignation of non-Communist cabinet ministers but this was a reaction to the refusal of the Communist Minister of the Interior to obey a majority cabinet decision against actions designed to put the police completely under Communist control. Most non-Communist accounts agree that the tactics of the non-Communist parties were stupid and gave the Communists a pretext for the coup. But they also agree that the policy of bringing the police completely under Communist control was only part of the evidence indicating that the Communists were determined to find some pretext for preventing free elections in 1948.

The elections actually held in May were certainly not free. The electors only had the choice between accepting or rejecting a single list of candidates in whose selection the Communists had had a decisive influence. Even so non-Communist observers report that there was no secrecy of the ballot and widespread falsification of results.

The part played by the Soviet Government is controversial. It is not clear whether Valerian Zorin ever explicitly threatened that resistance to the Communist coup d'etat would produce intervention by the Soviet army but there is clear evidence that many non-Communists were deterred from resistance by fear of possible Soviet intervention. It is also clear that non-Communist opinion in the Western countries took developments in Czechoslovakia as evidence that the Soviet Government was not prepared to allow any country where it could exert influence to follow a policy of non-alignment but was determined to extend Soviet control as far as possible. By giving this impression, the Communist seizure of power in Czechoslovakia played a large part in securing popular support for the Brussels Pact and its development in the N.A.T.O.

The split between Jugoslavia and the Soviet Union provided very clear evidence that the other Communist regimes in Europe were in fact satellites. One of the Soviet charges against the Jugoslav government was that the Jugoslav leaders had insisted that Soviet missions should obtain information through official channels and should not have the right to recruit intelligence agents within Jugoslav organizations. The same issue appeared in the trial of Kostov in Bulgaria who was accused, among other things, of having applied the Bulgarian law about state secrets against Soviet agents. The Soviet demands revealed in these cases are fairly clear evidence of satellite status for the countries which accepted them. It is extremely unlikely that a genuinely independent country would grant another power the right to recruit intelligence agents within its government organizations, especially when this right was not reciprocal.

Even before the Jugoslav-Soviet split there was some evidence to show that the satellite states were being subjected to economic exploitation by the Soviet Union. The material revealed by the Jugoslav authorities provided very clear confirmation of this. The exploitation took a number of forms. Trade agreements forced the satellite countries to trade with the Soviet Union on terms less favorable than could have been obtained in world markets. Joint organizations were established in which the assets contributed by the Soviet Union were over-valued and the assets contributed by the satellite country were under-valued and which claimed special privileges amounting almost to extra-territorial rights. Soviet advisers had to be paid at extremely high rates, and so on.[1] The effect of such measures was to decrease the national income of the satellite country and increase that of the Soviet Union and it is again very unlikely that genuinely independent countries would have agreed to be so exploited.

The Jugoslav-Soviet split was followed by purges in the Com-

---

1. For some of this Jugoslav material see Dedijer, *Op. cit.* chapter 17 and *On Economic Relations between Socialist States.* By Milentije Popovic, Jugoslav Information Bureau, London, 1950.

munist Parties of the satellite states apparently directed against
any leaders suspected of possible sympathies with Titoism, who
may have wished to defend national independence and interests
against the Soviet Union and to develop Communism in their
countries on lines that might differ from that followed in the
U.S.S.R. It is probably not necessary to discuss the trials through
which this purge was conducted. The posthumous rehabilitation
of such leaders as Kostov and Rajk seems to show that Communists would not now dispute the conclusions which were
reached at the time by most non-Communists who examined the
evidence. But when the spurious charges have been eliminated
it becomes more likely that the only real case against the accused was lack of subservience to the Soviet Government.

These purges were accompanied by shifts in policy. Up to
1948 the satellite governments seem to have made real efforts
to obtain popular support. After 1948 there was a shift towards
rapid "Gleichschaltung" with the Soviet Union which involved
policies unpopular with both workers and peasants, the concentration on rapid development of heavy industry and the collectivization of agriculture. This last point may be illustrated by the
conclusions of an English expert on agrarian problems whose
general standpoint was extremely sympathetic to Communism.
". . . there was certainly no popular demand for collectivization
and, at that time, no pressing economic need to begin it. . . .
The east-west conflict had entered into what seemed a very
dangerous phase. The Soviet Government needed to test the
loyalty of the Communist Parties to consolidate the revolution;
and the decision to collectivize was the supreme test, the *credo
quia impossibile*. That this was so is proved by the dissension
it caused; it meant throwing away the support which the Communist Parties had gained by the middle way conception, the
half-revolution on national lines."[1]

This is only a very brief summary of some of the main points
in the evidence which has led non-Communist opinion to certain conclusions about the countries which they consider to
be "satellite states" of the Soviet Union. The conclusions are,

---

1. *Revolution in Eastern Europe*. By Doreen Warriner, London,
Turnstile Press, 1950, pp. 62-3.

firstly, that in all these countries Communist governments were not based on majority popular support but obtained power through terrorism and fraud with Soviet intervention exerting, in most cases, a decisive influence; secondly, that these Communist governments have been subservient to the government of the Soviet Union which was able to secure the liquidation of any leaders suspected of desiring some measure of genuine national independence; thirdly, that the satellite states have been subjected to economic exploitation by the Soviet Union. Most non-Communist opinion would also consider that, although there is some evidence that Soviet control has been relaxed since the death of Stalin, it is still doubtful whether the satellite regimes are genuinely independent and even more doubtful whether they have any genuine claim to represent the people. This last point involves some fundamental and controversial issues of principle and is considered in a later subsection.

To refute these three conclusions defenders of the Communist position would need to go through a mass of rather detailed evidence from a wide variety of sources and show that in all cases the facts had been inaccurately reported or could be given a different interpretation. *Would Communists now seriously maintain that these conclusions were quite unfounded? If so, could they examine the non-Communist material on at least one of the countries involved and try to give a refutation of the non-Communist case?*

These non-Communist conclusions about the satellite states obviously imply very serious suspicions about Soviet policies. It appears that the Soviet Government has been determined to impose Communist governments on other states which would be kept subservient to the Soviet Government and which would allow the economic exploitation of their countries by the Soviet Union. If Soviet policy in the past is taken as a precedent for Soviet policy in the future it follows that no country without adequate military strength and adequate security precautions against any local Communist minority can reasonably feel secure against similar attempts to impose a Communist government.

Except for people with contacts in the policy making circles of the Soviet Government, the precise motives behind Soviet action can only be a matter for speculation. Many non-Communists have explained Soviet policy towards the satellite states as the first stages in a program of world domination. On the other hand some Western observers who had close Soviet contacts in the immediate post-war period, such as Earl Browder and Koni Zillisacus, have reported that Soviet leaders at the time disclaimed any objective of imposing satellite Communist regimes on neighboring states and have argued that actual Soviet policy was a reaction to a fear of the West.

To the writer a plausible hypothesis would seem to be the following:—The Soviet leaders were afraid of the Western powers, even though their fears were largely irrational. Because of this they were determined to secure friendly governments in all neighboring states. However, the previous policies of the Soviet Government especially during the period of the Nazi-Soviet Pact and the failure to maintain discipline in the Soviet Army had produced a situation in which the Communists were the only group in Eastern Europe on whose friendship the Soviet Government could completely rely. The demand for security therefore, led inevitably to the imposition of satellite Communist regimes even though this may not have been the explicit intention of the Soviet Government. It is usually true that people in a false position tend to behave badly and, having started on a policy of producing satellite states which it officially disclaimed, it was natural for the Soviet Government to abuse its powers for such purposes as economic exploitation.

This is probably the kindest explanation of Soviet policy which is compatible with the evidence, but, even if it is true, it does not remove grounds for non-Communist suspicions of the Soviet Union. It implies that Soviet policy has always operated in terms of pure power politics,—trying to base security entirely on a balance of power and rejecting any attempts at basing security on mutual confidence. And one power can only increase its security in this way at the expense of lessening the security of other powers. Even if the motive behind Soviet policy has been the desire for security and not ambitions of expansion this gives no guarantee against future attempts to extend the system of satellite states if the situation allowed it. A non-Communist country would only be secure against Soviet expansion if it were quite certain that the Soviet leaders would not consider that their security could be increased if the non-Communist government were replaced by a satellite Communist government.

In 1940 the Soviet Government suggested that, "the area south of Batum and Baku in the general direction of the Persian Gulf is recognized as the center of aspirations of the Soviet Union,"[1] which would seem to imply a policy of Soviet expansion into the Middle East. And Soviet policies in 1946 seemed to show that only a balance of power against it prevented the Soviet Government from expanding its control into Iran and Turkey. It is also possible that the Soviet Government would feel more secure if the whole of Europe were under Communist control.

Again, even if the Soviet Government has acted from motives of security and not from motives of aggression this is little consolation to the people who have satellite Communist regimes imposed on them.

Thus, whatever the motives behind Soviet actions, the policy of creating satellite regimes had given the remaining non-Communist powers very strong motives for trying to build up a balance of power against the Soviet Union which could resist any attempts at the further expansion of Soviet control.

Postscript

This section was written before the formation of the Gomulka government in Poland or the Soviet intervention in Hungary and these developments seem greatly to have strengthened its general arguments.

The visit of Soviet leaders to Warsaw during the events which led to the formation of the Gomulka government would be hard to explain if the Polish regime had really been an independent one with which the Soviet Union did not interfere.

---

1. *Nazi-Soviet Relations,* pp. 255-8.

The Soviet intervention was easily understandable if Poland
was, in fact, a Soviet satellite. Equally, developments since 1956
can easily be explained in terms of an uneasy balance between
a desire of the Polish people to throw off Russian control and
the fear of provoking Soviet military intervention if satellite
status were completely renounced.

The Hungarian incident seemed to show that the Soviet
Union is prepared to resort to military intervention in order
to maintain satellite status in another country. It also illustrates
the complete disagreement between Communist and non-Communist versions of the facts. Both versions have been set out at
length in a number of publications and it is not worth while
trying to discuss them in detail here. Only two points are worth
making. Firstly, when there were discussions of the issue, for
example in the correspondence columns of the *New Statesman*,
the claims made on the Communist side were nearly always
challenged by people who had been in Hungary and able to
make direct observations. Secondly, the Communist refusal to
allow their claims to be investigated is strong *prima facie* evidence that they would not have stood investigation. Communists
have strongly challenged the United Nations report and some of
the neutralist representatives have objected to it on the grounds
that the United Nations Commission did not obtain evidence
from the Communist side. But this failure to obtain evidence
from the Communist side was entirely due to the refusal to
allow the United Nations representatives the opportunity to
visit Hungary to secure direct evidence. It is not reasonable
to complain that the United Nations report is unfair to the Communists because it does not include information which the
Communists themselves prevented it from including.

Some statements by the Gomulka government gave strong additional evidence of economic exploitation by the Soviet Union.
It was admitted, for example, that Poland had been supplying
coal to the Soviet Union for a price which only covered the
cost of transport.

There is evidence that this Soviet exploitation has lessened
since 1956, but this does not prove an ending of satellite status

in the countries of Eastern Europe. Soviet policy can, in fact, be explained by a determination to maintain satellite status for political and strategic reasons which would rationally lead to a willingness to reduce economic exploitation which increases the risk of a popular revolt.

3

"World Communism"

"World Communism" was another subject which the Western leaders proposed for the agenda of the Geneva meeting but again they did not press their proposal when the Soviet leaders objected. Another issue of major importance in producing non-Communist suspicions of the Communist powers was therefore not considered.

The issue of the satellite states has already provided a number of instances to show the falsity of Communist claims that the Soviet authorities have never tried to "export revolution" and that Communists have never used conspiratorial methods. And these are only a small sample of the total number of cases.

Almost from the beginnings of Soviet rule in Russia one can find cases of local Communist parties using conspiratorial methods and trying to seize power by coups d'état; and doing this under the direction and with the assistance of the Soviet authorities.[1]

Admittedly the Soviet authorities might argue that in such cases they had been acting in their capacity as leaders of the Comintern and not as leaders of the Soviet Government but this is a very subtle distinction. Non-Communist opinion would certainly maintain that the Comintern was an organization effectively controlled by the Soviet authorities and it is very doubtful whether this could be disproved.

This Soviet direction of local Communist parties may often have weakened rather than strengthened them. There is, for example, a very strong case for believing that the Chinese Communist Party attained power in spite of and not because of Soviet influence.[2]

1. For a summary of this with more detailed references see *The Pattern of Communist Revolution*. By Hugh Seton-Watson, London, Methuen, 1953.

2. In 1945 the Chinese Communists ignored Soviet advice to disband their armies and come to terms with the Kuomintang and in 1948 they

For Germany there is a good deal of evidence to show that leadership from the Comintern made the Communists miss their opportunity in the early 1920's and that the Comintern policy of treating the Social Democrats as the main enemy played an appreciable part in assisting Hitler to power.[1]

However, non-Communists can hardly be expected to tolerate Soviet attempts to "export revolution" simply because such attempts have often been ineptly conducted in the past.

There is a mass of literature on the methods employed by Communists in non-Communist countries. Some of this can be dismissed as irresponsible and propagandist but a great deal remains, from both non-Communist and ex-Communist sources, which appears to be quite reliable and circumstantial. In countries where a Communist party operates legally this published material can easily be checked against the accounts of people who have had the experience of trying to work with Communists in trade unions, student associations, and many other organizations. (The writer could cite a good many instances from his own personal experience.)

The conclusion which seems to follow fairly definitely from this material is that Communists have an inveterate preference for conspiratorial methods. The claim that Communists reject conspiratorial tactics seems to be the exact contrary to the truth.

It may be worth giving a few examples of the types of Com-

---

ignored Soviet advice against changing over from guerilla and mobile warfare to positional battles and attacks on cities.

As late as 1946 the Chinese Communist leaders attributed the loss in the 1930's of their bases in South China to the mistakes committed by Moscow trained leaders. (See *Dawn out of China*. By Anna Louise Strong, Bombay, People's Publishing House, 1948, p. 18.) Before this Mao Tse-tung's successful strategy of basing a revolutionary movement on peasant support had been opposed by the Comintern; and Comintern advisers and Soviet instructions had played a large part in producing the Communist defeat in 1927. (See, *Moscow and the Chinese Communists*, by R. C. North, Stanford U.P. 1953 and *The Tragedy of the Chinese Revolution* by H. R. Isaacs, London, Secker & Warburg, 1938.

1. For a summary of this, see the section "The German Communists and the Rise of Hitler," by Alan Bullock in *The Third Reich*, by various authors, London, Weidenfeld & Nicolson, 1955.

munist behavior which have produced a very widespread conviction that Communists cannot be trusted to observe the conventions which make the working of a democratic system possible. The least objectionable are probably the cases in which a disciplined Communist minority tries to obtain control of an organization in which the non-Communist majority is disunited or simply unwilling to take the trouble of attending meetings and thus commit the organization to policies with which the majority do not really agree. In many cases, however, Communists use methods which most non-Communists would condemn as clearly dishonest. There is the very large subject of "front" organizations which are in fact under Communist control but claim, quite falsely, to be non-party. Once in control of some organization Communists are normally quite unscrupulous about the methods they will use to retain control. The history of Australian trade unions provides many instances in which Communist officials have tried to retain power by grossly fraudulent elections, the use of violence against opponents, or other undemocratic stratagems and these instances can be matched from many other countries and other organizations. There are many instances to show that Communists in any organization cannot be trusted to carry out the duties of their position. These range from the serious cases in which Communists in government employment have betrayed official secrets to the comparatively unimportant cases in which the Communist secretary of some voluntary organization deliberately fails in his duties. (In one organization to which the writer belonged non-Communist committee members would receive notice of important meetings too late to allow them to attend.) Organizations in which Communists have failed to obtain control are subjected to violent Communist attacks often based on deliberately false accusations.

This is only a very small sample of the Communist methods which have led many non-Communists to believe that Communists are people who cannot be trusted, that Communists in any organization which they do not control are likely to be working for sabotage and disruption, and that Communists will normally subordinate the objective of winning popular support to the objective of getting power by any methods.[1]

It has quite often happened that non-Communists have agreed with the policies advocated by particular Communist parties at particular times but people who have made some study of Communist methods are usually reluctant to cooperate with Communists even for agreed objectives. Many instances seem to show that someone who once accepts an organizational alliance with Communists will either find himself the victim of Communist conspiratorial tactics or else be forced to continue the alliance under increasing Communist control for new objectives with which he may not agree.

The generalization that Communists will use any methods to get power is not merely an empirical generalization from Communist behavior. It can also be confirmed from some Communist statements. For example, "The only scientific criterion of morality is the defense of the interests of the victory of communism,"[2] or, "In our time only what furthers the destruction of capitalism and the victory of communism is moral."[3] The logical implications of such definitions of morality are that Communists are likely to abandon any standards of good faith or morality which they profess to share with non-Communists whenever they consider this expedient for the cause of Communism.

There is also very strong evidence for holding that Communist Parties outside the Soviet Union have almost always been subservient to the C.P.S.U. The history of Communist parties in many countries provides numerous instances of local leaders who have been denounced by representatives of the C.P.S.U. because they held views about Communist strategy which differed from the Soviet line of the moment and who have almost always been removed from office and expelled from the Party

---

1. For a detailed analysis, mainly illustrated from American cases, see *The Organizational Weapon: A Study of Bolshevik Strategy and Tactics.* By P. Selznick, New York, McGraw-Hill, 1952.

2. "Communist Morality" in *Bol'shaia Sovetskai Entsiklopediia*, 2nd. Edition, Vol. 30, 1954, p. 207. (Quoted in Annals of the American Academy, Jan. 1956, p. 134.)

3. "Politics and Morals," *Voprosy Filosofii*, 1951, No. 4, p. 67.

if they persisted in their disagreement. In some cases the judgment of the C.P.S.U. may have been right and that of the dissident local leaders wrong but it is extremely unlikely that this
was always true. One clear test case was provided by China after
1927 where the policies followed by the Central Committee supported by the Comintern failed and the unorthodox policies
followed by Mao Tse-tung succeeded. In other cases the evidence is not so clear but one can point to a number of cases in
which later developments, including changes in Soviet policy,
suggested that the dissident local leaders had been right and
the C.P.S.U. wrong in their analyses of the situation.

Further evidence is provided by the record of Communist
parties in following changes in the Soviet line. Here the clearest
test cases are provided by the Nazi-Soviet Pact and by the expulsion of Jugoslavia from the Cominform. Within a very short
period after the signing of the Nazi-Soviet Pact every Communist
Party, which had previously been calling for a united front to
resist Nazism and Fascism, reversed its line. (In England and
some other countries Communist leaders first gave qualified
support to the war against Germany and hastily changed their
position when the Soviet line became clear.) While the Pact
remained in force all Communists denounced the governments
fighting Nazism and Fascism with extreme violence and seldom
went beyond mild expressions of disapproval for the Nazis. In
every country they called for acceptance of Nazi peace proposals.[1]

In America the Communists cooperated with the extreme
rightwing Republicans in opposing Roosevelt in the 1940 elections. The German invasion of the Soviet Union produced another abrupt change to full support for the allied war effort
even where, as in India, this involved a break with other parties
struggling against colonialism.

It is possible to suggest some excuses for the Nazi-Soviet Pact
itself as a stratagem in Soviet foreign policy. It is not really
possible to believe that Communists all over the world, reasoning independently from general Communist principles, came to

---

1. For a detailed study see *Betrayal of the Left*, by Victor Gollancz,
London, Gollancz, 1941, and *The Russo-German Alliance*, by A. Rossi,
London, Chapman & Hall, 1950.

identical conclusions about the correct attitude towards Soviet-Nazi collaboration. The facts are much more simply and adequately explained by supposing that Communists normally follow any directive from the C.P.S.U.

In this case it is worth pointing out that Communist policy would almost certainly have been disastrous for the Soviet Union if it had succeeded. Assertions about what might have happened are unsatisfactory because they can never be verified. However, insofar as one can make this type of judgment, it is reasonable to believe that Hitler would have won the war against the Soviet Union if the workers of Britian and America had been foolish enough to follow Communist leadership in 1940. If Britian had accepted Nazi peace terms and the isolationists had come to power in America, which Communists worked for at the time, it is extremely probable that German occupation troops would now be in Moscow and Japanese occupation troops still in Peking.

Again, immediately after the Soviet-Jugoslav split in 1948 all Communists parties denounced the Jugoslav leaders, in some cases almost certainly before they had had any opportunity of studying the evidence. All Communists defended the extreme accusations made at the Rajk trial, that Tito had been a British and American agent long before 1948. A specially clear illustration of the Communist attitude was provided by a controversy in the *New Statesman* which was started by a critical review of a book by a British Communist entitled *Tito's Plot Against Europe*.[1]

The Communists made no attempt to reply to the evidence showing that some of Rajk's confession must have been false because the Jugoslav leaders allegedly contacted in French internment camps were actually in Jugoslavia at the time. (One letter offered direct evidence on this point.) A Communist who had been closely associated with the Maclean mission during the war and had worked in Jugoslavia after the war at first supported the charges made in Rajk's confession and reproduced in the book, that the Maclean mission had recruited Tito as a

---

1. *Tito's Plot Against Europe.* By Derek Kartun, London, Lawrence & Wishart, 1950. *New Statesman,* 28th. January, 4th February, 18th March, 1st April, 8th April, and 22nd. April, 1950.

British agent. When it was pointed out that this could hardly have happened with his knowing it at the time, he then alleged that it must have been done through some other, highly secret mission. It was clear that no Communist was prepared to admit that Soviet charges against Tito could be false even if he had good evidence, including his own personal experience, to show that some of them were false. Now, of course, the present Soviet leaders have admitted that the charges against the Jugoslav leaders were fabrication. This leaves no doubt whatever that non-Communists were right in the conclusions they drew at the time and that Communists refused to form a rational judgment on the evidence because the results would have conflicted with a Soviet directive.

These are only two of the clearest issues which show that Communists have not been willing to base their judgments on the evidence available to them but have accepted quite uncritically any judgment coming from the C.P.S.U.

It is true that Communists will deny that they take orders from Moscow. Even if such denials are subjectively sincere they only show that directives from Moscow do not take the form of simple imperatives, "Do X!" or "Believe Y!" but are expressed in the form, "X is the correct policy." or "Y is the correct analysis of the situation." For the study of Communist psychology this distinction is of some interest; for most other purposes it is irrelevant. The form in which a directive is expressed does not alter its result, that Communists all over the world will uncritically accept and follow a Soviet directive whatever it may be.

To many non-Communists this uncritical acceptance of authority seems the most sinister aspect of Communism. It is a feature that can be found in many organizations which Communists would agree in condemning. Himmler once said, "We teach the members of the SS that many things in this world may be forgiven, but one thing never: disobedience to orders." An SS-Obergruppenführer summed up the principles of SS training even more simply, "Believe, obey, fight; full stop, that's all."[1] "The

---

1. Quoted from "The Reign of the Black order." Chapter by K. O. Paetel in *The Third Reich*, London, Weidenfeld & Nicolson, 1955, pp. 652 & 657.

Duce is always right" was a slogan of Italian Fascism and in
China the "Blue Shirt" organization and such leaders as Ch'en
Li-fu and Tai Li tried, though less successfully, to produce un-
critical obedience to the Kuomintang leadership.

The differences between Soviet leadership and Nazi leadership
do not remove the danger. Many Communists would now agree
that Stalin became a psychopath at some point in his career,
that he ordered the torture and execution of thousands of loyal
Communists, that he made serious mistakes both during and
after the war, and so on. But, so long as he lived, Communists
all over the world gave uncritical support to his leadership and
his actions. *What security is there that Communists would not
give equally uncritical support to any new leader who managed
to obtain power in the Soviet Union, even if he showed still
more marked symptoms of paraphrenia?*

Admittedly Communists now denounce "the cult of the individual" and call for "collective leadership", but, in most cases,
they only started to do so after it had become the official Soviet
line. Such cases offer no reasons for believing that they have
given up the tradition of following the Soviet line whatever it
may be, or that they would not return to their former beliefs
if the Soviet line changed again. To show that Communism
had abandoned uncritical acceptance of authority it would
be necessary to find cases in which Communists had made statements not in accordance with the official Soviet line without
being compelled to retract on pain of expulsion from the Party.
Quite recently there have been a few cases of fairly independent
statements but it is still too early to say whether or not they represent a real and lasting change.

The same point can be put in a quite general way. An organization whose members retain the right to express individual
judgments will no longer follow its leaders if they depart from
the accepted common purposes of the organization. An organization which has established the tradition of uncritical acceptance of authority has lost an important defense mechanism
against degeneration in its leadership; it will continue to follow
almost any policies which its leaders may order. And because
"Power tends to corrupt and absolute power corrupts absolutely,"
it is extremely likely that this type of organization will sooner

or later have a degenerate leadership. It is also likely that an organization in which there is an uncritical acceptance of authority will be unscrupulous in its methods. Someone who has subordinated his individual judgment to some outside authority over the choice of policies is not likely to revive his individual judgment over the choice of methods by which these policies are implemented. And this deduction seems to be confirmed by empirical evidence. The doctrine that the end justifies the means has usually been associated with authoritarian organizations. The Nazi SS was only an extreme case both of emphasis on unquestioning obedience and also of complete disregard for any other moral standards in its actions.

To sum up, most non-Communists opinion would consider that there are good reasons for holding the following conclusions about "world communism":—firstly, all Communists have been, in effect, controlled from the Soviet Union. This control may not take the form of a definite chain of command, though there have been cases in which agents sent from the Soviet Union have directed the policies of other Communist Parties. In general Soviet control has been maintained by ensuring that Communists will uncritically accept any policies or analyses of the situation put forward by the Soviet authorities. Local Communist leaders who have tried to use their independent judgment have been attacked by the Soviet authorities and almost always removed from power.

Secondly, Communists have in general shown a preference for deception and conspiratorial tactics as a means to power. They have often won some measure of popular support by taking the lead in voicing dissatisfaction with existing institutions or in protest against particular abuses but in most cases it is clear that this has been simply a tactical maneuver to increase Communist power and weaken any non-Communist society. They have in general tried to sabotage any reform measures which did not increase the chances of a Communist seizure of power.[1] In every

1. Cf. the comments of a recent book on France, "Since 1948 the Communist Party has counted in the political life of France only as a dead weight which . . . has sterilized the votes, wishes, demands, and dissatisfactions of five million Frenchmen. True, most of these five millions had only a very unclear idea of what they were voting for.

case where a Communist Party has come to power it has followed policies extremely different from those which it advocated to gain popular support before it came to power. For example, no Communist Party has advocated the collectivization of agriculture before coming to power and, while Communists out of power have often claimed to be strong supporters of civil liberties, once in power they have invariably suppressed them.[1] In countries where Communism is weak the tendency to work through deception and conspiracy has been strongest and the main objectives of Communist policy have often appeared to be economic sabotage and the disruption of democratic institutions.

If these conclusions are correct it is clear that non-Communists have strong grounds for suspecting and taking defense measures against an organization controlled from the Soviet Union, showing a preference for conspiratorial tactics, and working for the disruption of any organization it cannot control. *Could defenders of the Communist position show that such suspicions and precautions are unjustified?*

This view of world Communism as predominantly a conspiracy for power directed from the Soviet Union differs very widely from the accounts Communists give of themselves.[2] They claim to be leaders of the masses in their struggle against oppres-

---

But they had an exceedingly clear idea of what they were voting against. However, the weight of their votes, which in a healthy democracy might have turned the scales in favor of economic and social reform, henceforward counted for as little as if they had left their voting papers unmarked or had stayed away from the polls. . . . These five million were represented at the Palais Bourbon, not by deputies concerned with their interests, but by an obstruction and sabotage group which kept up a continual barrage against any sound policy whatever." (*The State of France*. By Herbert Lüthy, Secker & Warburg, London, 1955, p. 159.)

1. It might be argued that China was an exception to the generalization that no Communist Party has obtained power with popular support, but even here it is fairly certain that the Communists would have been weakened if they had advocated before 1949 many of the policies they have actually followed since 1950.

2. For example, in *On the Party*. By Liu Shao-ch'i, Foreign Language Press, Peking, 1950.

sion and towards a better society. The writer would maintain that the view of world Communism as nothing but a conscious conspiracy for power is a very confusing over-simplification and that the behavior of most Communists can only be explained by an analysis which allows for a subjectively sincere devotion to the interests of the masses distorted and confused by faith in an unsatisfactory theoretical system and by psychological tensions.[1] But such an analysis of Communist motivation does not alter the empirical evidence about actual Communist behavior in most countries or the case for holding that "world communism" has been in general an influence working against social, economic or political reforms. By trying to divert every dissatisfaction with non-Communist social systems towards the establishment of a Communist ruled society the Communists have usually divided what they themselves would call the "progressive" forces and strengthen those whom they themselves would call "reactionaries."

1. This analysis is worked out in *China and the Cold War*. By Michael Lindsay, Melbourne University Press, 1955, especially in Chapter 5, (An Analysis of Communism.), and Chapter 13, (Psychological Influences.)

(4)

German re-armament

The Soviet Union and the non-Communist powers have been having disputes about German problems ever since 1945 and the German problem as a whole is one of the issues which have become too complicated for convenient discussion. German re-armament, however, is one aspect of the problem which provides a fairly simple issue which is worth discussing.

Any study of Communist publications and statements or material issued by such organizations as the World Council of Peace will show that great emphasis has been placed on opposition to German re-armament. The various plans and agreements which finally led to the organization of an army in West Germany were repeatedly denounced in the most violent terms—as a revival of German militarism, as a breach of international agreements, and so on. When the East German Government on 18th. January, 1956 decided to establish a regular army *International Affairs* commented, "The German Democratic Republic is a sovereign state, enjoying an indisputable right to have armed forces of its own."[1] Before this, however, Communist or pro-Communist sources were always silent or evasive on the subject of re-armament in Eastern Germany.

In fact, until quite recently German re-armament was almost entirely confined to East Germany. As early as 1948 the organization of armed forces in the Soviet Zone of Germany was commented on in British official statements and at the end of May, 1950 the governments of the Western powers sent notes of protest to the Soviet Government. The British note of May 23rd said, "In that part of Germany subject to Soviet control a police force has been created which, by reason of its organization, training, and equipment, has the character of an army. No informa-

---

1. *International Affairs,* 1956, No. 2, p. 125.

tion regarding this militarized force has been communicated to H. M. Government by the Soviet Government. It is known, however, to be organized on the basis of *Bereitschaften* (alert squads) under the control of the *Hauptverwaltung für Ausbildung* (training department), and to consist of nearly 50,000 men. They are embodied in military formations which include artillery, tank and infantry battalions. They receive basic military training and are not employed on normal police duties. They are equipped with military weapons including, in some units, machine-guns, howitzers, anti-tank guns, A.A. guns, mortars and tanks. A number of former high-ranking German army officers are employed in this force.

"The creation of this military force directly violates a number of inter-allied agreements to which the Soviet Government is a party." (The British note then gives quotations from the joint statement of 11th. February, 1945 after the Yalta Conference, the declaration on the defeat of Germany signed by the military chiefs of the American, Soviet, British and French armies, the joint report of 2nd. August, 1945 after the Potsdam Conference, and an agreement of 20th. September, 1945 between the U.K., the U.S.A., the U.S.S.R. and France. The last agreement stated that, "1), All German land, naval and air forces . . . and all other military and quasi-military organizations . . . shall be completely and finally abolished in accordance with the methods and procedures to be laid down by the Allied representatives; 2) All forms of military training, military propaganda, and military activities of whatever nature on the part of the German people are prohibited. . . .")

The British note then continues, "It is clear that, whereas the U.S., U.K. and French Governments have adhered to the principles laid down in the agreements quoted above and have carried out the demilitarization of their zones of occupation, the Soviet Government, by promoting and encouraging the creation of a German quasi-military organization in contravention of its international obligations, is fostering in the Soviet zone of Germany the revival of the militaristic and aggressive system which the four occupying powers fought together to destroy. . . ."

The Soviet Government did not reply to these notes until

20th. October, 1950 and it was only during this interval of five months that the Western powers modified their policy of complete German demilitarization. (The change was almost certainly influenced by the Korean war.) On the 21st. November, 1949 the British Government had stated that it, "has not contemplated and does not contemplate" the re-armament of West Germany and similar statements were made on the 16th. and 17th. of November by the American President and Secretary of State. As late as 22nd. July, 1950 the U.S. High Commissioner in Germany declared that he was opposed to the creation of a German army and in a parliamentary debate on 26th. July the British Minister for War opposed suggestions that Germans should participate in Western defense. It was not until August, 1950 that proposals for West German forces began to be seriously discussed. The Foreign Ministers meeting at New York in September issued a statement saying, "They recognize the fact that outright military units have been created in the Soviet zone of occupation," and authorized the creation of mobile police and frontier guards in West Germany, and on 26th. September the NATO Council agreed that Germany should be "enabled to contribute to western defense."

The Soviet reply in October was very evasive and largely concerned with countercharges based on the authorization of the mobile police and frontier guards in West Germany, though this was only a response to the threat produced by previous East German militarization.

The actual development of plans for West German armed forces was very slow and they only took final form at the beginning of 1955. Meanwhile there was a steady development in the East German forces. A British White Paper of 13th. July, 1954 gave the following figures for forces in the two parts of Germany:—
In East Germany a military force of 80 to 90,000 men, who since October, 1952 had worn military uniform and not police uniform, had about 1,300 tanks and self-propelled guns and the same number of pieces of field artillery, anti-tank and A.A. guns. *Seepolizei* of about 6,000 men had some 30 vessels, and an air force, organized in 1952, had about 7,500 men and some 75 planes, admittedly of obsolescent types. In addition to these

military forces there were about 55,000 civil police, 12,000 security police and 25,000 frontier guards. The total ratio of armed forces and police to population was approximately 1:100. In West Germany there were slightly over 10,000 frontier guards with pistols, rifles, light machine-guns, 50 armored cars and some mortars. Mobile police also totalled about 10,000 equipped with pistols, rifles and light machine-guns, and there was a marine police organization with about 700 men. These units had no tanks, artillery or aircraft. In addition there was a civil police force of 90,000 the total ratio of police and frontier guards to population being approximately 1:450.

Since then there have been further developments in East German militarization including the training of youth in paramilitary organizations.

It is clear from all this that the creation of military forces started in the Soviet zone of Germany long before the Western powers had even accepted in principle that West Germany should be re-armed and that these actual East German forces were steadily expanded throughout the period during which any West German re-armament remained at the state of plans for the future.

The obvious conclusion is that the strong objections to German re-armament expressed by all Communist and pro-Communist organizations were completely hypocritical. The World Council of Peace, for example, declared that it had, "specifically expressed its opposition to the re-arming of Germany in any form or under any pretext" but its record of refusal to comment on the East German forces shows that it had no objection to the creation of German armed forces, with many officers from the Nazi Reichswehr, provided only that this was done by Communists with Soviet approval.

Could defenders of the Communist position give any good reasons for judging re-armament in East Germany by entirely different standards from re-armament in West Germany?

It is true that, until January, 1956, the East German forces did not call themselves an army but it is hardly worth discussing this purely verbal distinction except as an instance of a Communist tendency to attach immense importance to names. It could also be argued, with slightly more reason, that the East German forces have been too small to be an important factor in the general balance of power while the West German forces may become one. This assumes that the East German forces will not be increased and it also leaves out of account a possible motive for their creation. Though the East German forces may not be strong in relation to the regular army of any of the important powers they have, for the past eight years, been very strong in relation to any West German forces and are quite likely to remain so for several years to come. The Soviet government has repeatedly proposed the withdrawal of all foreign forces from Germany and, if any of these proposals had been accepted, it would have left an internal balance of military power completely on the Communist side.

The Reichswehr played a very important role in the politics of the Weimar Republic. From 1919 on German governments were dependent on the support of the Reichswehr and Reichswehr leaders, such as von Seekt, often used their power to influence government policy,—to prevent, for example, any effective action by left-wing governments against the extreme right-wing terrorist organizations. By 1954 the East German armed forces were already almost as large as the Reichswehr of the Weimar period and were much more strongly equipped. Any of the Soviet proposals which involved the withdrawal of Western forces from Germany and left unification to be discussed between the East and West German governments would produce a situation in which West Germany could make no effective resistance to any demands which the East German regime chose to back by a threat of military force. In the long run the military balance of power in Germany may shift to the West with its much larger population but is is likely to take some time for West Germany to overtake the lead which East Germany has obtained by starting re-armament and military training much earlier and by creating a reserve partially trained in para-military youth organizations.

Soviet policy over German re-armament can, therefore, be explained by the hypothesis that it has been working to produce a situation in which the whole of Germany could be brought under Communist control by the use or threat of military force. *Could defenders of the Communist position give a more satisfactory explanation?* The writer would not maintain that there has been nothing wrong with the policies of the Western powers. Having decided, after considerable delay, that re-armament in Western Germany was a necessary response to Soviet policy, which had included the re-armament of Eastern Germany, they have been unduly reluctant to explore alternatives. The writer has argued in publications and broadcasts that the Western powers should have been willing to consider the alternative of a genuinely neutral and demilitarized Germany. It is unlikely that the Soviet Government would have accepted this alternative because it would have involved the liquidation of the East German armed forces and the setting up of some body with effective powers of inspection and control in East Germany to ensure that they were not reconstituted. The Soviet Government would probably have insisted on an agreement with no effective sanctions for its enforcement and this would have been worthless because the original creation of the East German forces showed that the Soviet Government had not been willing to observe previous agreements on demilitarization. However, if the Western powers had offered the alternative of a genuinely demilitarized Germany, and if this offer had been rejected by the Soviet Union, it would have placed the onus of responsibility for German re-armament quite clearly on the Soviet Government.

(A somewhat similar issue showing the worthlessness of Soviet obligations was provided by the states which were German satellites and are now Soviet satellites. The peace treaties limited the Bulgarian army to 65,000 men, the Hungarian to 70,000 and the Roumanian to 120,000. According to a report by the Jugoslav Government to the National Assembly in January 1954, their actual strengths had been increased to 240,000, 220,000 and 500,000 respectively. It is reasonably certain that this illegal re-armament could not have taken place without the approval and assistance of the Soviet authorities.)

(5)

The Korean War

It has been suggested above that a probable motive for Soviet policy over German re-armament was to work for a situation in which the whole of Germany could be brought under Communist control by building up a superiority of military force in the part of a divided Germany where the Communists were already in power. To most non-Communist opinion it would appear that Korea provided a case in which such a strategy was actually tried. And the Korean war is important as a case in which the "cold war" developed into fairly large scale fighting.

Developments in Korea from 1945 to 1950 form a very complicated subject. Few people would argue that the record of the American occupation authorities in South Korea or that of the South Korean Government were entirely defensible and many would argue that they were bad. Very little reliable information is available in non-Communist countries about the record of the Soviet occupation authorities or the North Korean Government but there is one piece of evidence which seems fairly clearly to disprove the Communist contention that conditions were very much better in the North. The American authorities reported that between October, 1945 and April, 1948, 829,886 refugees from North Korea entered South Korea through official refugee entry stations. This is known to be an underestimate of the total number of refugees and some estimates have put the total between 1945 and the Korean war as high as two million. Thus at least a tenth and perhaps over a quarter of the entire population of North Korea abandoned their homes in order to reach the admittedly poor conditions of the South.

The exact origin of the war is a matter of dispute. The United Nations Commission on the second day of the war reported that, "The Commission's view is that the Northern regime is carrying out a well planned, concerted and full-scale invasion of South

Korea; second that South Korean forces were deployed on a wholly defensive basis in all sectors of the parallel; and third that they were taken completely by surprise." Just before the outbreak of war the United Nations Field Observers reported to the United Nations Commission on the results of an observation trip along the parallel which had started on 9th. June. They said, "Principal impression left with observers after their field tour is that South Korean army is organized entirely for defense and is in no condition to carry out attack on large scale against forces of North." The report then goes on to give, under seven headings, the observations on which this impression was based. These show that the disposition of the South Korean forces was purely defensive with no signs of concentrations, building up of supplies or other preparations for attack and that "fourth, so far as equipment of South Korean forces is concerned, in absence of armour, air support, and heavy artillery, any action with object of invasion would, by any military standards, be impossible."[1] Another heading reported that North Korean forces had occupied several salients South of the 38th parallel and that the South Korean army showed no sign of trying to drive them back.

If one accepts the good faith of the United Nations Commission, which had an Indian chairman, these reports would seem to be very clear evidence that the war was started by a North Korean attack.

However, defenders of the Communist position have maintained that the war was started by a South Korean attack. Vyshinski, in his speech to the Political Committee of the United Nations on 2nd. October, 1950, supported this view by citing statements and letters by the South Korean leaders referring to plans for an attack on the North and a map showing plans for an attack which the Communists claim to have found in the South Korean archives after the capture of Seoul. He also cited some statements made by Americans promising support for South Korea though the only evidence that any of these ex-

---

1. Quotations from British White Paper, *Summary of Events relating to Korea* 1950. Cmd. 8078.

tended to support for an attack on the North was from declarations by two Koreans who, presumably, were in Communist hands when they made their statements. This would seem to be good evidence that the South Korean leaders had considered an attack on the North and very doubtful evidence that some Americans may have approved of these plans. It certainly does not prove that an attack was actually made by South Korea. While the actual date of the North Korean attack was a surprise there had been reports for some months of North Korean preparations for a possible attack. Nothing in Vyshinski's speech provides evidence against the conclusion that, whatever the South Korean Government may have been planning for the future, it was the North Korean Government which actually attacked.

Others have produced more complicated hypotheses of a plot to start a war in Korea by the South Korean Government, John Foster Dulles, and some American military leaders.[1]

The clearest evidence against the Communist view was provided by developments after the outbreak of war. The course of the fighting until U.N. intervention became effective showed that North Korea had overwhelming military superiority, based mainly on a great superiority in equipment. It was quite clear that the Soviet Government had supplied the North Korean Army with tanks and other equipment suitable for the invasion and conquest of South Korea while the American Government had not supplied the South Korean army with similar equipment, that the South Korean army was equipped for little more than action against guerilla forces. If the American authorities had really planned to assist a South Korean invasion of North Korea it is extremely unlikely that they would have failed to give the South Korean army equipment at least comparable to that of the North Korean army.

Defenders of the Communist position always evade the issue raised by developments after June 25th. Since the withdrawal of Soviet and American forces there had been a series of clashes along the 38th parallel which previously had not led to general

---

1. The most elaborately worked out of these is probably *The Hidden History of the Korean War.* By I. F. Stone, London, Turnstile, 1952.

hostilities. Even if it could be shown that South Korean forces had attacked on June 25th, it would still need to be explained why the North Korean Government chose to make this particular incident the occasion for a general offensive aimed at conquering the whole of South Korea, which would certainly have succeeded but for U.N. intervention. Consider, for example, the very naive account given by Sir John Pratt, "At dawn on Sunday, June 25, Syngman Rhee launched a sudden attack which took the North Koreans by surprise. His forces crossed the 38th parallel at several places and captured Haeju some miles to the North on the road to Pyongyang. The North Koreans staged a counter-offensive and the South Koreans threw down their arms and fled. The North Koreans then drove on across the parallel and staged a full-scale invasion of South Korea."[1] The North Korean invasion is presented as if it did not need any explanation. But if the North Korean Government had wanted peace and did not have aggressive intentions why did it not accept the demands of the Security Council Resolution of 25th. June?[2] If the North Korean army had withdrawn to the 38th parallel it would have removed any pretext for U.N. intervention on behalf of South Korea; and, if it had been possible to prove a South Korean attack, the South Korean Government would have been revealed as the aggressor.

The case against all theories of an anti-Communist plot to start a war in Korea is that such a plot could only hope to succeed with the cooperation of the North Korean Government. Suppose that South Korean forces had launched an attack and that the North Korean army had remained on the defensive along the frontier. (And with its great military superiority the North Korean army could then have done this without risk.) Any anti-Communist plot to start a war in Korea would then have ended in a fiasco highly discreditable to those engaged

---

1. *Korea, The Lie that Led to War.* By Sir John Pratt, London, Britain-China Friendship Association, 1951, p. 3.
2. THE SECURITY COUNCIL . . . I. *Calls* for the immediate cessation of hostilities; and *Calls upon* the authorities of North Korea to withdraw forthwith their armed forces to the 38th parallel; . . .

in it. Thus the theories of an anti-Communist plot to start the
war in Korea would only be plausible if it could be shown that
the plotters had assurances from the North Korean leaders
that any South Korean attack would be taken as the occasion
for full-scale hostilities by the North Korean army. Neither Mr.
I. F. Stone nor Sir John Pratt have made any attempt to supply
this essential link in their theories, nor, so far as the writer is
aware, has anyone else.

To sum up, the Communist case as stated by Vyshinski proves,
at the most, that the South Korean leaders had been considering
plans for an attack on the North and, much more doubtfully,
that some individual Americans may have encouraged them.
It does nothing to rebut the evidence that the actual attack on
the 25th. June, 1950 was launched by the North Koreans. Even
if other defenders of the Communist position could prove their
allegations of an original South Korean attack it would still be
clear that the Soviet Government had given the North Korean
army equipment suitable for a conquest of the South while the
American Government had not given the South Korean army
equipment suitable for a conquest of the North; it would still be
clear that, whatever happened on June 25th, the North Korean
Government did not try to limit hostilities or to reach a peaceful
settlement but went ahead in an attempt to conquer South
Korea. Finally, the theories that the Korean war was started by
an anti-Communist plot would only make sense on the fantastic
assumption that the North Korean Communist leaders were involved in the plot. Thus, the arguments so far advanced by defenders of the Communist position, even if their allegations of
fact could be proved, would only show that North Korean
aggression had some mitigating circumstances of provocation.

*Could defenders of the Communist position now state any
better case against the conclusion that the general war in Korea
was the result of aggression by the North Korean Government?*

The next subject of controversy is the actions of the United
Nations. It has been argued by defenders of the Communist
position that the actions of the Security Council were illegal,
because the Soviet representative was absent, because China was
represented by a representative of the Taipei Government and

not of the Peking Government, and because the Korean war was a civil war in which the U.N. had no jurisdiction.[1] The case against these arguments is:—firstly, that previous cases with which the Soviet Government had concurred had established the precedent that a resolution of the Security Council was not invalidated when a permanent member abstained from voting; secondly, that, whatever the rights and wrongs of Chinese representation, the actual Chinese representative had been appointed in accordance with the rules and practices of the U.N.; and thirdly, that a civil war is war in which two rival governments fight for control of a state which had previously had one government, whereas in this case the South Korean Government had never had jurisdiction over North Korea nor the North Korean Government over South Korea.[2] (If the non-Communist powers had accepted this Communist argument about civil war it would have provided a precedent which would have allowed the invasion of West Germany by the East German forces.)

The only argument which appears to have some substance is that North Korea was not invited to send a representative in accordance with Article 32 of the U.N. Charter.[3] However, the Security Council could have put itself entirely in the right by making an invitation to North Korea dependent on the withdrawal of the North Korean forces behind the 38th parallel.

Thus, the arguments against the U.N. action used by Vyshinski and other Communist spokesmen seem, at the best, to be technical legal points and even at this level their validity seems to be very doubtful. Their reliance on this type of technical objection to U.N. action gives some additional reason for sup-

---

1. These points are made by Vyshinski in the speech of October 2nd referred to above.

2. For a more detailed statement see the British White Paper cited above. Pp. 14-16.

3. "Any Member of the United Nations which is not a member of the Security Council or any state which is not a Member of the United Nations, if it is a party to a dispute under consideration by the Security Council, shall be invited to participate, without vote, in the discussion relating to the dispute. The Security Council shall lay down such conditions as it deems just for the participation of a state which is not a member of the United Nations."

posing that they could not produce any good argument against the basic non-Communist view, that the U.N. action was an instance of collective security against aggression,—the type of action which might have prevented the second world war if the League of Nations had shown a similar willingness to resist aggression in the 1930's.

The first phase of the Korean war provided interesting evidence about the nature of the Communist inspired "peace campaign." There was violent criticism of the United Nations both for intervening in the conflict at all and for acting before going through the procedures of Article 33 of the U.N. Charter.[1] On the other hand no one from the Communist side criticized the North Korean Government for its use of military force. No one suggested that, whatever had happened on June 25th, the North Korean Government should not have launched a full scale invasion of South Korea. No one suggested that, in order to secure a peaceful settlement, the North Korean army should withdraw to its own side of the frontier or at least halt its advance into South Korea.

It was clear, therefore, that the Communist "peace campaign" did not imply any disapproval of the use of military force by Communists. It seemed that, for the Communists and their supporters, no threat to "peace" was involved when a Communist army undertook the conquest of non-Communist territory, but that "peace" was threatened by any measures which tried to prevent such a conquest. The implications of this were that Communist professions of desire for "peace" were not incompatible with the use of military force to extend Communist power.

On the evidence now available one can only speculate on the motives behind the Korean war. It is not certain whether the decision to attempt the conquest of South Korea came from the

---

1. "1: The parties to any dispute, the continuance of which is likely to endanger the maintenance of international peace and security, shall, first of all, seek a solution by negotiation, enquiry, mediation, conciliation, arbitration, judicial settlement, resort to regional agencies or arrangements, or other peaceful means of their own choice.

"2: The Security Council shall, when it deems necessary, call upon the parties to settle their dispute by such means."

North Korean or the Soviet authorities though it is unlikely that the North Korean Government would have launched its offensive without reasonable assurance of Soviet support, if only because its army was dependent on Soviet supplies. It is possible that the North Koreans decided to launch a preventive war to anticipate a possible attack from South Korea. It seems more likely that the war was the result of a Communist misjudgment about the probable reactions of America and the United Nations. There was, at the time, some evidence that the American authorities were doubtful about including South Korea in the area they considered it essential to defend and the Communist leaders may well have thought that it would be possible to expand Communist power by military force without producing intervention by the non-Communist powers.

To a great deal of non-Communist opinion the Korean war seemed to show that the Communist leadership was prepared to use military force to extend Communist power whenever it seemed that this could be done without too serious risk of producing a general war. And it would follow from this that if Communist action had not been resisted in Korea it would have provided a precedent for similar military adventures in other parts of the world.

On this point it is worth citing the evidence of a German doctor who was in a Soviet concentration camp for political prisoners where he had the opportunity of meeting men who had held fairly responsible positions in the Soviet Union. He reports that in private discussions among the prisoners it was considered that the Berlin blockade and the Korean war had been test cases on the readiness of the non-Communist powers to resist Communist expansion and that a failure to intervene in Korea would have led to similar attempts to expand Communist power in other parts of the world.[1]

Thus the Korean war, and the attitude of Communists towards it, gave non-Communists reasons for believing that Communist professions of desire for peace did not rule out the use of military

---

1. *Grenzen der Sowjetmacht.* By Wilhelm Starlinger, Würzburg, Holzner-Verlag, 1955, pp. 112-3.

force to extend Communist power and that the non-Communist
sector of the world could only be secure if it built up a balance
of military power which could resist any such Communist expansion.

In the latter phase of the Korean war the issues became less
clear. In the first phase the objective of U.N. intervention was
simple, to apply collective security in resistance to an aggressive
attack, but there was considerable disagreement about what
should be done in the next phase when this attack had been re-
pelled. Some people argued that the U.N. forces should stop
when they had reached the 38th parallel; others argued that
this would leave the aggressor unpunished and free to launch
another attack if an opportunity appeared.

This indecision of the U.N. leadership about the ultimate objectives of U.N. action in Korea left a very undesirable degree
of responsibility in the hands of the U.N. commander on the spot,
General MacArthur. And his recommendations and appraisal of
the situation probably had considerable influence in securing the
decision of the U.N. General Assembly on 7th. October, 1950,
that the objective of the U.N. forces should be to establish a
"unified independent and democratic Government of Korea."
—which implied the conquest of North Korea.

Many non-Communists, including the writer, criticized the
policies of the U.N. during this phase of the war and argued
that the U.N. forces should not have crossed the 38th parallel
unless the North Korean Government had rejected proposals
for a settlement which established the principles of collective
security. The Secretary General of the U.N. did prepare a draft
of proposals on these lines which, unfortunately, was discarded.[1]
It is likely that the North Korean Government would have rejected Mr. Lie's suggested terms or even any milder terms which
met the essential conditions of penalizing aggression and providing effective guarantees against its renewal. But if the U.N.
had proposed a settlement and the North Korean Government
had rejected it the U.N. forces would then have had a clear
case for entering North Korea.

---

1. *In the Cause of Peace.* By Trygve Lie, New York, Macmillan, 1954,
pp. 344-5.

The U.N. should also be criticized for its failure to restrain the South Korean Government. There is much evidence to show that the Communists behaved with great brutality to suspected political opponents during their occupation of South Korean territory, but the U.N. forces, fighting to resist totalitarian aggression, should not have been willing to tolerate the use of similar totalitarian methods by a government which owed its continued existence to U.N. help. Later the U.N. could be criticized for tolerating the use of illegal methods by Syngman Rhee to secure his re-election.

Finally, many people argued that the U.N. forces should have stopped their advance at the narrow point of the Korean peninsula north of Pyongyang. This would have left a buffer zone between the U.N. forces and the Chinese border. It would also have satisfied the requirements of collective security. The North Korean regime would have been punished for its aggression by the loss of half its territory; and with greatly reduced resources and population it would have found it hard to launch another invasion over a shorter and more easily defensible frontier.

It is not certain that a decision to halt the U.N. advance at this point would have prevented the Chinese intervention which led to the third phase of the war, but it might have done so. It would at least have made it absolutely clear that Chinese intervention was not a response to any threat to Chinese territory but came simply from determination to support an aggressive Communist regime in Korea.

The actual decision to attempt a complete conquest of Korea was an act of folly. General MacArthur ignored every warning of impending Chinese intervention. Chinese official statements mixed their warnings with so many wild and exaggerated assertions that a failure to take them seriously is understandable. But these warnings were confirmed by reports from Indian representatives in Peking and by American and British intelligence reports. A British correspondent in Korea referred to "MacArthur's megalomania and delusions of grandeur" and argued that he lived "in a dream world, isolated and insulated against the facts and general opinions by his clique of sycophants." President Truman's memoirs and the reports of the inquiry after General

MacArthur's dismissal confirm the substantial accuracy of these opinions.

Though the failings of U.N. policy must bear part of the responsibility for the continuation and expansion of the Korean war into its third phase the failings of Chinese policy were at least as serious. Many non-Communists would agree that the Chinese had some genuine grievances against the U.N. and still more against the U.S.A. (The American decision to neutralize Formosa was criticized by many people who supported U.N. actions in Korea.) They would admit that General MacArthur's behavior was often dangerously provocative, considering the extreme suspicion of the U.S.A. which dominated Chinese thinking. Many people have argued that China probably entered the war because the Chinese leaders really believed their own propaganda and were afraid that the U.N. forces would not stop at the Chinese border but would go on to invade China.[1] But, if the Chinese leaders really believed this, it is clear that, even more than General MacArthur, they lived "in a dream world, isolated and insulated from the facts"; isolated, in this case, by their dogmatism and refusal to establish contacts with the non-Communist world. This does not mean that the Chinese fears had no real basis at all. What it does mean is that the Chinese leaders vastly exaggerated their reasons for fear. If they had been willing to acquire more direct knowledge about the non-Communist world they would have found that General MacArthur or those Americans who might have liked to invade China did not have the power to control U.N. policy or even U.S. policy, and that the dangers of an invasion of China over the Korean border were almost entirely imaginary. Throughout the period the Chinese Government showed the psycopathic attitude of people who prefer a continuing grievance to any settlement which does not give them everything they want. They denounced frontier violations and bombings on Chinese territory by American aircraft but refused to consider an American offer to accept responsibility and pay compensation for any incidents which could be substantiated by a neutral Indian-Swedish investi-

---

1. For example see *Spotlight on Asia,* by Guy Wint. London, Penguin, 1955, p. 185.

gating commission.[1] The account given by Mr. Trygve Lie shows that the Chinese Government refused U.N. invitations to discuss measures to provide guarantees against any violations of the Chinese frontier and to safeguard their interests in the frontier zone of Korea and that the Wu Hsiu-ch'uan mission refused to negotiate for a cease-fire in Korea.[2]

An adequate explanation of Chinese policy at this period could only be provided from China. And it would be valuable if Chinese scholars working in the field of international relations could produce a serious study of Chinese policy. At present people outside the Chinese ruling group can only speculate on the motives which led China to enter the Korean war. Such evidence as is available suggests that there was a difference between Chinese and North Korean behavior. The most likely explanation of the original North Korean attack seems to be a calculated decision to use military aggression to extend Communist power and to secure the unification of Korea on Communist terms. The most likely explanation of Chinese intervention seems to be that the Chinese leaders were victims of their own propaganda who had deluded themselves into believing that intervention was an essential measure of self defense.[3] If this explanation is true it provides some excuses for Chinese policy but does not make it defensible.

The resolution passed by the U.N. General Assembly branding China as an aggressor could have been justified in terms of the definition of aggression given by the Second World Congress of Defenders of Peace at Warsaw in November 1950:—

"1. The aggressor is that state which first uses armed force, under any pretext, against another state.

---

1. Chinese statements alleged that the American air force was acting deliberately, but this is something which would need to be proved. Incidents during the world war showed that bombing of neutral territory was quite likely to happen through a genuine mistake; (The Allies dropped bombs in Switzerland and the Germans in Eire). These incidents had been settled by the payment of compensation and the question of a neutral investigating commission did not arise because there were diplomatic representatives who could check any claims.

2. *Op. cit.,* pp. 350-7.

3. For a fuller discussion of these points see the writer's *China and the Cold War,* Melbourne University Press, 1955.

"2. No political, economic or strategic consideration, no pretext based on the internal situation of a state, can justify armed intervention."

It might be argued that the first use of armed force was against China through the American neutralization of Formosa but there are several strong objections to this argument as a justification for Chinese intervention in Korea. It was not clear that the neutralization of Formosa could be classified as the use of armed force against China. Formosa was certainly not under the *de facto* control of the Peking Government and its exact legal status was doubtful, especially at this period before the signing of the Japanese Peace Treaty. At any rate, the neutralization of Formosa was an action by the United States while the Chinese attack was against forces of the United Nations and included the invasion of South Korea. Finally, both Chinese official statements and the sequence of events show that Chinese intervention in Korea was a reaction to the advance of U.N. forces towards the Chinese border rather than to the neutralization of Formosa.

The second clause of the definition quite explicitly rules out the justification usually given for Chinese action, that the "strategic consideration" of preventing Korea from coming under the control of forces which the Chinese Government considered to be hostile justified "armed intervention" as a measure of self defense.

Could defenders of the Communist position state a case against the conclusion that China was an aggressor, in terms of this definition of aggression given by a Communist dominated "Peace Congress"?

Chinese behavior during the war raised several issues on which Chinese policy was neither defensible nor excuseable. One such issue was the treatment of U.N. prisoners of war. The evidence on the treatment of British prisoners is summed up in an official British pamphlet.[1] The Chinese did not observe the Geneva Convention although they later claimed that its provisions should

---

1. *Treatment of British Prisoners of War in Korea,* Ministry of Defense, London, H.M.S.O., 1955.

be strictly and legalistically interpreted when it suited their case. "For referring to the convention men were struck, threatened and made to stand to attention for long periods."[1] The authorities in charge of P.O.W. camps told the prisoners that they had been engaged in an unjust war and were, therefore, war criminals so that their captors had the right to kill them. However, the Chinese argument continued, a "Lenient Policy" would be applied to those prisoners who used the opportunities provided for re-education and expressed remorse and repentance for their crimes. In accordance with this "Lenient Policy" better treatment was given to those prisoners who co-operated with Communist indoctrination and allowed themselves to be used for the purposes of Communist propaganda. The majority of prisoners who were reluctant to do this were very badly treated and, in many cases, tortured. "Torture and ill treatment were carried out quite cold-bloodedly for the purpose of breaking a man's resistance."[2]

Most accounts agree that the North Koreans were considerably worse than the Chinese in ill treatment and torture of prisoners of war and that American prisoners were treated even worse than British prisoners.

This issue is of some importance as showing that Communists cannot be trusted to observe the ordinary rules of international law or civilized behavior in dealing with politcal opponents. It also illustrates the bad faith of Communist propaganda. Communist publicity claimed that the general treatment of prisoners of war was good. The actions favorable for Communist propaganda, extorted by the use or threat of ill treatment and torture, were presented as evidence of voluntary support by prisoners for the Communist case.

There are, of course, Communist countercharges that the U.N. forces ill treated prisoners of war and forced them to join in anti-Communist activities. Even if these countercharges were true they would not excuse Communist action and it seems fairly certain that they were greatly exaggerated. The administration of the Koje Island camps was widely criticized by non-Com-

1. *Op. cit.,* p. 31.
2. *Op. cit.,* p. 22.

munists, but one of the most disgraceful episodes was the failure
of the camp authorities to act when they could repeatedly hear
the screams of prisoners being killed by the Communist groups
which had established control within the camps. The final
exchange of prisoners took place, with neutral supervision,
under conditions which tried to offer each prisoner the free
choice between accepting or refusing repatriation. Under these
conditions only one British, 21 American and 325 South Korean
prisoners refused repatriation while over two thirds of the 21,000
Chinese prisoners refused. It is extremely unlikely that the
Chinese prisoners would have acted in this way if their anti-Communist activities in the P.O.W. camps had simply been the result
of pressures similar to those applied by the Communists to the
prisoners which they held.

Another issue is the charges of germ warfare. Communist supporters still claim that these charges were true but there is very
strong evidence against this which can be summarized briefly
here. The Americans who had made confessions of using germ
warfare all repudiated their confessions when released and
claimed that they had been made under duress, in most cases
under torture. The Communist countercharge that the repudi-
ations were made under duress is seriously discredited by the
evidence of a much larger number of released American prisoners who reported that unsuccessful attempts had been made,
through pressure and torture, to induce them to make similar
confessions.

The American and the United Nations forces always professed
themselves ready to allow a full investigation of the charges by a
commission from organizations such as the International Red
Cross or the World Health Organization, which would have been
a very risky offer to make if the charges had been true. The Communists, on the other hand, refused to allow investigation except
by commissions appointed by Communist controlled organizations which were only able to operate on the Communist side
of the front and to which, therefore, the presentation of evidence
was controlled by the Communists. This Communist behavior
is simply explained by the hypothesis that the charges were
fraudulent and would not stand examination by any reasonably

impartial experts able to get evidence from both sides. It was extremely stupid behavior if it had been likely that such an investigation would have confirmed the Communist charges.

The alleged methods of germ warfare were inherently improbable. If the Americans had decided to use germ warfare it is very unlikely that they would have used techniques which were certainly obsolete, if indeed they had ever been considered effective, and used them moreover under conditions likely to minimize their results, (such as dropping insects under severe winter conditions). On the other hand, if some Communist secret service organization had wanted to fake evidence to support the Communist charges, they would have had strong reasons for using such methods which could appear to give striking support to Communist claims while only producing a small number of casualties on their own side. This hypothesis that evidence was planted by some Communist organization would explain the reports of Chinese scientists and members of the International Scientific Commission on purely technical scientific points, a field in which their professional standards would be directly involved. The Report of the International Scientific Commission, which was appointed by the World Peace Council, devotes hundreds of pages to questions involving bacteriology, entomological ecology, etc. but never considers the possibility that the basis of their technical investigations might have originated from the activities of some Communist agency and not from those of American aircraft.

The evidence so far available may not be absolutely conclusive but it is very strongly against the hypothesis that the charges of germ warfare were true and in favor of the hypothesis that they were deliberately faked. There is no way of telling how far the charges were genuinely believed even among the Communist leadership but it would seem that some Communists at least deliberately tried to rouse international hatred by false charges and that, to support such charges, they were prepared to torture prisoners of war into false confessions. If the International Scientific Commission was right in its technical findings it would appear that they deliberately sacrificed a number of lives among people on their own side in order to produce faked evidence that might appear convincing.

A final phase of the Korean war started with the armistice negotiations. The main issues centered on the conduct of the negotiations and are considered in a later sub-section. However, the events of the period which has been briefly discussed provided a number of grounds for suspicion of the Communist powers. They seemed to show that Communist leaders were prepared to resort to military invasion in order to extend Communist power. Followers of the Communist inspired "peace movement" did not, apparently, see any incompatibility between such Communist use of military force and their definition of the term "peace." The Chinese leaders rejected the opportunities for discussion and negotiation with the non-Communist world which could, almost certainly, have kept their country out of the war. Some issues which arose during the war appeared to show that Communists acted on the principle that "The only scientific criterion of morality is the defense of the interests of the victory of communism" and were, consequently, completely unscrupulous about the methods they used in support of Communism. The treatment of U.N. prisoners of war was an absolutely clear issue and the "germ warfare" publicity an almost certain one.

Though Communist policy may have changed since 1953 the policies of the Korean war period have never been repudiated. Soviet publications in 1956 still repeat the arguments used in 1950.[1] And fairly recent Chinese statements still refer to the germ warfare charges.[2]

Do defenders of the Communist position still maintain that Communist policies during the Korean war were entirely correct and offered no grounds for suspicion of the Communist powers?

---

1. "The Korean Question" by G. Tavrov, *International Affairs,* 1956, No. 2.

2. For example, a statement by Kuo Mo-jo to the Chinese Academy of Science reported in the *Jen Min Jih Pao* of 12th. June, 1955. (Still more recent statements have been made in connection with the Powell trial in the United States.)

6

Colonialism

Communists claim to be leaders in the struggle against colonialism. Communist statements express sympathy for all subject and oppressed peoples in their struggle against alien control and claim to support the right of all peoples to self-determination and independence. Soviet representatives in the United Nations demand rapid development towards self-government and independence for even the most primitive races in Trust Territories. Communist statements not only express quite uncompromising opposition to colonialism, they also imply an extremely wide definition of "colonialism". The term is interpreted to include not only formal political control but also cases in which one government is able to influence another through its stronger economic power.[1]

This Communist suport of "anti-colonialism" has had considerable influence, especially in countries which have recently gained their independence from a former colonial status. To many non-Communists, however, the Communist position appears to be completely hypocritical. They would argue that Communist countries are, in fact, among the leading imperial powers and that, whereas non-Communist colonialism has greatly diminished since the war, Communist colonialism has been expanding. While Communists claim to give almost unqualified support to the principle of self-determination, they always abandon this principle when it might be applied against Communist rule.

In terms of the very wide definition of "colonialism" which

1. For example, ". . . N. S. Khrushchev said in the report of the Central Committee to the 20th Congress of the Communist Party of the Soviet Union that the colonialists now use new forms of colonial enslavement in the shape of 'aid' to underdeveloped countries." *International Affairs,* 1956, No. 4, p. 79.

is implied by Communist statements about the non-Communist section of the world the satellite states should be classed as instances of colonialism. The evidence summarized in section (2) of this part indicates that the satellite states have been controlled by, and for the benefit of, the Soviet Union and that the degree both of control and of exploitation has been greater than that involved in many relationships between non-Communist states which Communist publicity denounces as instances of colonialism.

The degree of control and exploitation involved in the Soviet relationship with a nominally independent satellite country, such as Roumania, may be less than was involved in the Japanese relationship with the nominally independent Manchukuo; but it is almost certainly greater than the control exercised by foreign powers in China. If pre-1949 China is classified as a "semi-colonial" country, which is the normal Communist description, then the satellite states should be classified as at least "¾-colonial" countries. *Could defenders of the Communist position state a case against such classification?*

When people speak of Communist colonialism they are often thinking primarily of the satellite states. (At the Bandung Conference Mr. Nehru criticized the attacks on Communist colonialism with the argument that the areas involved were independent states, in some cases members of the U.N.). However, both the U.S.S.R. and China could be classified as imperial powers even under a narrower and more generally accepted definition "of colonialism", which would, in present usage, imply something like the following:—Colonialism is a system under which the government of the imperial power controls an area inhabited wholly or mainly by people of a different race or culture and prevents them from acting to secure independence or to join another country should they so desire. It usually has a connotation of relationship between an economically advanced imperial power and an economically backward colonial area. This definition would rule out the cases in which the less advanced racial group has no real possibility of changing its status because the areas it inhabits are too small, too scattered or otherwise incapable of existing as an independent or even semi-independent state.[1] It is often hard to draw the line and the problem gives rise to real controversies, such as the claim for "Pushtustan" by the tribes on the Pakistan-Afghan border. Colonialism is often used with implications that the imperial power exploits the colony but it is also used by people who would deny this implication.[2]

Communists might want to dispute this sort of definition. They sometimes argue that imperialism is the highest stage of capitalism so that Communist countries cannot be imperialist because they are not capitalist. There is, of course, nothing to prevent Communists from using "imperialism" or "colonialism" in a special sense defined in the context of Marx-Leninism, but this should not prevent other people from using these terms in a wider sense. If Communists insist on using "imperialism" and "colonialism" only as Marx-Leninist technical terms they should, if they were honest about it, make this clear and explain that when they talk of opposing "imperialism" and "colonialism" they mean only to oppose what non-Communists would call "capitalist imperialism" or "capitalist colonialism" and not other forms. In the ordinary wider usage of these terms there is no implied restriction to capitalism. Most people would apply the terms "empire" and "colony" to non-capitalist systems. Thirteenth century Mongolia was certainly not a capitalistic society but Chingiz Khan and his successors established a Mongol Empire which ruled subject peoples. Sixteenth century Spain would probably be classified by Marxists as a feudal society, capitalism was certainly at a very early stage of development, but it is usual to refer to the Spanish colonies in South and Central

---

1. The Soviet Union at one time recognized this distinction by reserving the status of Soviet Republic for areas which would be able to use their theoretical right of secession.

2. This definition is, of course, widely different from the earlier meaning. The *Shorter Oxford Dictionary* defines "Colony" as, "a settlement in a new country; a body of settlers, forming a community politically connected with their parent states; the community so formed, as long as the connection lasts," and relates "colonialism" to this. This earlier meaning is still used, but for a long time the term "colony" has been extended to areas in which settlement from the imperial power was negligible.

America. In the 19th and early 20th centuries only capitalist powers were strong enough to practice imperialism but this is no logical reason for a permanent association of imperialism with capitalism.[1]

The literature on Communist colonialism is much less voluminous than that on the satellite states. The following summary of the case for considering that the Soviet Union is an imperial power controlling colonial areas is based mainly on two books, *Soviet Empire* by Olaf Caroe[2] and *Russia and her Colonies* by Walter Kolarz.[3] Both seem to be scholarly works with documentation very largely from Soviet sources.

The clearest case of Communist colonialism is the Soviet position in Central Asia,—the area now forming the Soviet Republics of Kazakistan, Uzbekistan, Turkemenia, Tajikstan and Kirghizia.

Russian penetration into the northern part of what is now Kazakistan started in the 18th century but the southern part of Kazakistan and the rest of the area was only conquered between 1850 and the end of the century. In a series of campaigns against nomad tribes and native states Russian rule was established over territory inhabited by various Muslin Asian races. The Russian conquest was often brutal. General Kaufmann in the 1870's gave orders for the extermination of tribes which made any resistance to the Russians. Later, General Skobelev declared, "I hold it a principle that in Asia the duration of peace is in direct proportion to the slaughter you inflict on the enemy," and his campaigns were marked by several fairly large scale massacres of civilian population.

Under the Tsarist regime Bukhara and Khiva were left as protectorates and the rest of the area was under direct Russian

---

1. The Communist theory of imperialism is derived, through Lenin, from J. A. Hobson's *Imperialism*. Hobson, writing at the beginning of this century, was quite explicitly dealing with the situation of his time and the immediate preceding period. He mentions other and earlier types of imperialism only to dismiss them as of no present importance which, in 1902, was quite correct.

2. Macmillan, London, 1953.

3. Philip, London, 1952.

administration. There was a considerable amount of coloniza-
tion in the original sense. A great deal of land was given to
Russian peasant settlers, often dispossessing the former native
owners, and Russian communities developed in the towns.
There were revolts against Russian rule in 1898 and in 1916
which were suppressed with considerable brutality.[1]

For some time after 1917 many Soviet historians would have
agreed that this conquest by Tsarist Russia of non-Russian territory was an instance of imperialism. However, by 1937, Pokrov-
sky, who had been the leading exponent of such views, was
condemned as anti-Marxist. Since then official Soviet history has
maintained that the Tsarist conquest was a favorable development for the area because it associated it with Russia and so
enabled it to join in the development to socialism, and because
it prevented possible absorption by Turkish or British imperialism. Native literature praising leaders of resistance to Russian
conquest, tolerated in the 1920's, was later suppressed as reactionary.

For some years after 1917 the situation was confused. Many
of the native leaders were impressed by Lenin's promises of freedom for subject peoples and took the Communist side in the
civil war. Local regimes tried to recover some of the land which
had been alienated to Russian settlers and to work for closer
union between the different native races which mostly had a common Turkish background. When it appeared that Communist
promises of freedom did not mean a lessening of Russian control
there were rebellions against Soviet rule which were not finally
suppressed until about 1930.

The real Soviet position was summed up by Stalin, "There are
instances when the right of self-determination comes into conflict with the other, the higher right—the right of the working
class . . . In such cases, this must be said bluntly, the right to
self-determination cannot and must not serve as an obstacle to
the exercise by the working class of its right to dictatorship. The

---

1. "It is estimated that 150,000 Kirghiz were killed either by Tzarist
punitive expeditions or by Russian colonists." (*Russia and her Colonies*, p. 271.)

former must give way to the latter.[1] In these colonial areas the natives were mostly peasants or nomads while the very small working class in the towns was almost entirely Russian. The desire of the colonial peoples for self-determination was, therefore, suppressed in the interests of the small Russian proletariat.

The policies enforced during the First Five Year Plan produced widespread opposition. This was suppressed by measures which involved the extermination of more than a fifth of one of the more important native races. Between the 1926 census and the 1939 census the total number of Kazaks in the U.S.S.R. fell from 3,968,000 to 3,099,000 although the total Soviet population rose by 15.9% during this period. No census figures are available after 1939 but calculations based on voting in the 1946 elections suggest that the total population of Kazakistan may have fallen by nearly a quarter million since 1939 in spite of the imigration of about two hundred thousand people from other parts of the Soviet Union. The 1950 election, however, indicates a large rise in population.

The migration of Russian population to the colonial areas continued throughout the period of Soviet rule and became very rapid with the development of industrialization. Russians are now the largest single racial group in Kazakistan and since 1926 the proportion of Kirghiz population in Kirghizia has fallen from two thirds to under half.

The old protectorates of Bukhara and Khiva were abolished by the Soviet Government and the area is now divided into five Soviet Republics. Nominally the Soviet Republics of the U.S.S.R. have a considerable degree of autonomy but there is little to suggest that this is more than nominal. The actual degree of autonomy is less than that enjoyed by the states in Australia or the U.S.A., the cantons in Switzerland, or even the provinces in India or Canada.[2]

---

1. *Marxism and the National and Colonial Question.* By J. Stalin, Lawrence & Wishart, London, 1942, pp. 168-9.

2. "The highest form of Soviet autonomy is enjoyed by the sixteen constituent Soviet Republics. According to Soviet legal theory these sixteen Republics are fully fledged sovereign states, . . .

"The sovereignty of the Soviet Republics is, however, a mere consti-

Even in the field of culture the degree of autonomy has been very limited. A series of purges have been conducted against "nationalist deviations" with the apparent aim of suppressing any tendency for the races of Central Asia to think in terms of local patriotism rather than as citizens of the U.S.S.R. The Soviet authorities have been specially concerned to suppress pan-Turkish tendencies which might lead to a feeling of unity among the native races and to prevent links with peoples of similar race and culture outside the Soviet Union. Most of the Muslim peoples in the Soviet Union had used Arabic script or modified versions of it but in the late 1920's they were compelled to change to the use of the Latin alphabet. This may have been a useful reform in some ways but it was opposed even by the local Communists among many races so long as discussion of the issue was allowed. And the change obviously served the purpose of cutting off the native peoples both from the Muslim world outside the Soviet Union and from their traditional literature, except insofar as the Soviet authorities allowed republications in the new form. In the late 1930's the Latin alphabet was replaced by the Cyrillic alphabet. This obviously helped assimilation to Russian culture but two changes of script in such a short

---

tutional fiction, because in reality they have no say in questions of internal security, high-level economic planning, transport, or higher education, not to speak of foreign policy or defense. . . .

"Even from the merely legal point of view the constituent Soviet Republics do not own the natural riches on their soil. . . .

"The sovereignty of the Union Republics is also rendered fictitious by the existence of the 'Prokuratura', the strongly centralized office of the all-Union Attorney-General. . . . Republican governments cannot interfere in the least with the work of the 'Prokuratura' nor can they influence the composition of its local staff. The Attorney-General of a Union Republic, on instructions from the all-Union Attorney-General, can rescind any local laws and decrees if they contradict the so-called 'revolutionary legality'." (*Russia and her Colonies*, pp. 20-21.) Following pages discuss the subject in more detail.

It may be worth comparing the position of a Soviet Republic and that of an Australian State under the headings given by Kolarz. An Australian State controls police and internal security except for a small Commonwealth Security Service. High-level economic planning requires, in most fields, the cooperation of the State and Commonwealth

period must have produced some set back in education. Another object of the change may have been to cut off the Central Asian peoples from Turkey which had adopted the Latin alphabet.[1]

All this adds up to a general picture of colonialism with similarities to French colonialism in North Africa. In both cases native Muslim population with a considerable nomad element was conquered by a European power within the last 150 years. In both cases foreign rule has been accompanied by quite large scale immigration from the ruling race. In both cases the ruling power has tried to produce assimilation to the culture of the ruling race. An important difference is that Soviet colonialism has been much more thorough and much more ruthless. In North Africa the native races have increased faster than the immigrant population during the last few decades, while in Central Asia the proportion of immigrant population has rapidly increased and, in some cases, the native population has decreased in absolute numbers as the result of Soviet action. Measures to produce assimilation of the native peoples to the culture and social structure of the ruling race have been pushed much further under Soviet rule than under French rule.

Of course there have been favorable aspects of Russian rule. Though Central Asia had been the scene of highly developed civilization in earlier centuries it had become a backward area before the Russian conquest. The native states were oppressive and obscurantist. The nomad tribes enjoyed more freedom but lived at a primitive level. The Russian conquest brought eco-

---

governments. Intra-state transport and education at all levels are State responsibilities. Only foreign policy and defense are purely Commonwealth responsibilities. Land and minerals are under State control. The legal powers of the States are restricted by the constitution, but so are those of the Commonwealth Government, both in theory and practice and under the constitution the States have all powers not explicitly given to the Commonwealth. Since the war the States have been financially dependent on the Commonwealth which has taken over the collection of Income Tax but this situation may be changed.

Even with this Commonwealth control of Income Tax the real powers of an Australian State are considerably greater than those of a Soviet Republic.

1. See *Russia and her Colonies,* pp. 34-38.

nomic development which was accelerated in the Soviet period. Soviet rule has brought popular education and provided opportunities to participate in a wider culture. It has raised the status of women and eliminated injustices of the old social systems. It has provided public health services and other technical amenities of modern civilization.

Such considerations provide an entirely valid case for holding that Soviet rule has conferred some real benefits on the peoples of Central Asia. But similar considerations provide equally valid arguments for holding that non-Communist colonialism has often conferred some real benefits on the peoples of colonial areas. To continue the comparison with French North Africa; before the French conquest Algeria was a backward area supporting less than a quarter of its present population at a very low average standard of living. Most of the interior was in a state of tribal anarchy. The native government at Algiers was oppressive in the area it controlled and had maintained itself largely by organized piracy. French rule has provided quite genuine benefits by establishing law and order, by producing great economic development, by extending education and public health measures, and so on. One could point to many other cases in which non-Communist colonialism has produced very great economic and social progress.

The only valid conclusion which can be drawn from the favorable side of the Russian record in Central Asia is that colonialism is not an unmixed evil whether Communist or non-Communist. The balance sheets of Communist and non-Communist colonialism are compared later in this section.

While Central Asia is the most important Soviet colonial area it is not the only one. The Caucasian and Transcaucasian areas are largely inhabited by non-Russian peoples. After the 1917 revolution Georgia tried to take advantage of the right of secession proclaimed by the Soviet leaders and established an independent Social Democratic Republic, which was conquered by the Soviet Union in 1921. The peoples of the Caucasus had resisted Russian conquest during the 19th century and large numbers of Circassians and Chechens emigrated to Turkey rather than submit to Russian rule. Some resistance to Soviet rule continued after 1917 and, after 1945, four races, the

Chechens, the Ingush, the Balkara and the Karachy were deported en masse for having assisted the Germans during the war.

Similar mass deportation was carried out for the non-Russian communities of the Crimean A.S.S.R., the Kalmuck A.S.S.R. and the Volga German A.S.S.R. and, as mentioned in an earlier section, there were large deportations from the Baltic States. In this respect the Soviet Government has reverted to practices of much earlier imperialisms, such as the Assyrian which deported the Hebrew population of Palestine.

The Ukraine is another area where a movement for separation from Russia has at times shown itself to be fairly strong. The Baltic States did actually secede after 1917 and were only reincorporated by force in 1940. In *Russia and her Colonies* Kolarz lists a number of other parts of the Soviet Union with some characteristics of colonial areas though some of them would not be capable of maintaining an independent existence and would not, therefore, be classed as colonies under the definition given at the beginning of this section.

The following are some of the questions which defenders of the Communist position would have to answer if they wished to refute the cast for holding that colonialism can be found in the Soviet Union.

How would they describe the Russian conquests of areas inhabited by non-Russian peoples during the Tsarist period? If they wish to maintain that these were not instances of imperialism what criteria could they give for distinguishing them from apparently similar cases of conquest by other powers which they do denounce as imperialism?

Could they refute the evidence summarized briefly here and at greater length by such writers as Caroe and Kolarz for holding that the Soviet Government has opposed and suppressed the efforts of non-Russian peoples in the U.S.S.R. to work for freedom and independence or even for a greater degree of autonomy under Russian rule?

If they wish to defend the Soviet record in such areas as Central Asia by citing the economic and social progress made under Soviet rule, could they show why similar considerations should not be cited to defend the record of non-Communist imperial powers in many colonial areas?

Tibet would seem to be an instance of Chinese colonialism. At one time Tibet was a fairly powerful independent country. It was first conquered by China under the Yuan dynasty. Under the Ming dynasty it again became practically independent though China retained some vague claims of suzerainty. The next Chinese invasion was in the early part of the 18th century. A Chinese expedition in 1718 was defeated but another in 1720 captured Lhasa. Chinese troops were withdrawn in 1723 but a civil war in Tibet led to another Chinese occupation in 1728. From then on there were Chinese residents at Lhasa but the degree of Chinese control was at times very small. By the middle of the 18th century there were only a hundred Chinese troops in Lhasa. Towards the end of the century Chinese forces took the main part in repelling Gurkha invasions. Chinese authority at Lhasa was strengthened and exerted to put through a program of reforms. When the Chinese Government was weakened by the T'ai-p'ing rebellion, Tibet again asserted practical independence. Chinese suzerainty was never definitely renounced but Chinese influence was largely replaced by British influence through India. Chinese troops in Tibet were expelled in 1913 and all remaining Chinese officials in 1949.

The invasion and conquest of 1951 were justified by claims that Tibet was a part of China and that Tibet had belonged to China for 700 years. It is true that Chinese claims of suzerainty have existed for a very long time and that, under international law, the Chinese Government was acting within its rights in reasserting sovereignty over Tibet. But this is really irrelevant to the issue of colonialism. Under international law non-Communist colonial powers have had at least as good claims to sovereignty over their colonial territories, claims which in some cases go back for several centuries. The claim that Tibet is part of China is more doubtful. Chinese authority was usually exerted for strategic purposes, to prevent Tibet coming under the control of other peoples who might threaten China. Except for a short period under Ch'ien Lung, Chinese control before 1951 was never more than a protectorate involving little interference with Tibetan internal affairs. It had disappeared almost completely during the Ming dynasty. And though it was reasserted by the Ch'ing dynasty it practically disappeared again when the imperial power became weak in the latter part of the 19th century. The general historical picture shows intermittent assertion of Chinese authority in an area of strategic importance to China which always retained a large degree of practical independence and always tended to move towards greater independence when Chinese authority was relaxed.

There were close similarities between the Chinese relationship with Tibet and the Chinese relationship with Korea. Korea was conquered by China during the T'ang dynasty, several centuries earlier than Tibet, and similar claims of suzerainty remained. At the end of the 19th century, when Tibet had reasserted practical independence, Korea still acknowledged Chinese suzerainty and, as Chinese Resident in Korea, Yuan Shih-k'ai exerted a considerable degree of control over the Korean government.

What is directly relevant for the issue of colonialism is that Tibet is inhabited by people who are non-Chinese in race, language and culture. They have been brought under Chinese rule by the use of military force and, if reports of rebellions during 1956 are correct, it would appear that many of them do not want to be under Chinese rule.

The claims of reforms and progress under Chinese rule might possibly show that this was a case in which colonialism was likely, on balance, to benefit the people of the colonial area. They would not show that Chinese rule over Tibet is not an instance of colonialism.

It is worth pointing out that the colonial status of Tibet was, at one time, admitted by the Kuomintang Government. In a speech to the Supreme National Defense Council Chiang Kai-shek said, "When the Tibetans should have attained the stage of complete self-reliance in political and economic conditions, the Chinese Government would like to take the same attitude as it did towards Outer Mongolia, by supporting their independence. However, Tibet should be able to maintain and preserve its own independent position in order that the historical tragedy of Korea might not be repeated."[1]

---

1. Reported in *Ta Kung Pao* of 28th, August, 1945 and in the *New York Times* of the same date.

If defenders of the Communist position maintain that long standing claims of suzerainty justify the establishment of Chinese rule over an area with non-Chinese population, by what standards do they reject the validity of similar claims by other powers? (Portuguese control of Goa, for example, goes back for more than four centuries.)

If the Chinese conquest of Tibet was justified, what is there to prevent even stronger historical claims of suzerainty over Korea from being used as a justification for the conquest of Korea, or rather vaguer historical claims as a justification for the conquest of several other parts of Asia.

There are other parts of China which might be classified as colonial areas. Chinese penetration of Sinkiang dates back to the Han dynasty and the area has several times been conquered by strong Chinese dynasties and lost at periods when the Chinese Empire was weak. But in large parts of the province the population is still predominantly non-Chinese and there has been a long series of rebellions against Chinese rule continuing to quite modern times. In the 1870's Jakub Beg's rebellion tried to establish an independent state until it was suppressed with great slaughter by Tso Tsung-t'ang. In the 1930's Sheng Shih-ts'ai, the Chinese Governor; was only able to suppress a rebellion by calling in Soviet assistance, and rebel movements on a smaller scale have continued since then.

Mongolia is a similar area. The present Chinese control only dates back to the Ch'ing dynasty and the Mongols tried to reassert their independence after the 1911 revolution. Outer Mongolia has now gained at least nominal independence, and real independence from China, but there are other areas with a predominantly Mongol population that are still under Chinese rule. These have now been granted the status of autonomous areas but there is no clear evidence available in non-Communist countries to show whether or not the autonomy is more real than that of the Soviet Republics.

In Southwest China there are considerable areas inhabited by primitive non-Chinese tribes, but these are probably too scattered to be classed as colonial.

The argument so far has only tried to show that the Com-

munist claims to oppose colonialism are hypocritical because
both the Soviet Union and China must be classed as imperial
powers controlling colonial territories if their position and that
of non-Communist powers are judged by the same standards.[1]
The rights and wrongs of colonialism are a much more complicated problem involving several issues.

Firstly, there is the question of whether colonialism may not
be desirable or necessary for certain areas. The clearest case for
colonial rule is in really primitive areas of which New Guinea
is a good modern illustration. In this case a large area is inhabited by numerous tribes with mutually unintelligible languages and mostly at a Stone Age level of technical development.

Some people might argue that it would be desirable to preserve this primitive society, but it is not worth discussing this
here as Communists would almost certainly not support such
arguments. At any rate, primitive society could only be pre-
served if some outside authority undertook responsibility for
preserving isolation from the rest of the world. Without such
isolation the most probable development would be that the
tribes with most contacts with the outside world would acquire
modern weapons and proceed to enslave or exterminate their
neighbors.

(Central Africa a century ago was a similar area though
native society was rather less primitive. Here the establishment

---

1. An argument advanced to justify the Indian refusal to criticize
Communist colonialism is that colonialism should only apply to rule
from overseas and should not apply to cases where the two territories involved have a common land frontier. Such a definition would,
of course, rule out Russian and Chinese colonialism, for both Communist and pre-Communist regimes. It is, however, a very queer definition. Those who defend it would have to show that the relationship
between two societies becomes quite different when contacts between
them have to cross salt water, even though sea communications may be
easier than land communications. (The short sea passages which separate France from North Africa or which separated Japan from Formosa,
Korea and Manchuria are smaller natural obstacles than the moun-
tains or desert which separate Russia from the Central Asian Republics
or China from Tibet and Sinkiang.) It is true that India has ex-

of colonial rule put an end to the growing power of Arab slave traders.)

The natives of such an area may dislike the establishment of colonial rule but they themselves will be quite incapable of providing even a rudimentary general administration or of producing economic and social progress except over a period measured in generations. Assuming that economic and social progress is desirable, it can only be secured by a period of tutelage under colonial rule. The only open question is what outside power should exercise this tutelage,—whether, for example, West New Guinea should be a colony of Holland or of Indonesia.

The less primitive and backward the original native society the weaker the case for colonialism. For less primitive societies there will be alternatives of rapid economic and social progress under colonial rule or slower progress under native rule. A judgment as to whether colonialism is justified in particular cases must depend on the relative weighting attached to progress and to independence.

Secondly, there is the question of whether colonial rule is exercised for the benefit of the people of the colonial area or to exploit them for the benefit of the imperial power. This is an entirely separate issue from the first question. For example, there was a very strong case for colonial rule in tropical Africa in the 19th century but the record of the Congo Free State was quite indefensible because it was primarily concerned with exploitation of the natives.

In this respect the record of colonialism varies very greatly. At one extreme there are cases of colonialism in which the imperial power has been entirely concerned with exploitation. It is doubtful whether there have been any cases of the other ex-

---

perienced colonialism from overseas while conquests of India by land have led to new regimes in India, largely because the mountain barrier made it impossible to administer Indian territory as part of a Central Asian empire. This can explain an Indian emotional feeling which associates colonialism with rule from overseas but it does not provide a basis for rational argument. To give an analogy, someone who has been bitten by a black dog many have emotional associations about black dogs but has no rational grounds for arguing that dogs of other colors do not bite.

treme, a purely altruistic colonialism, especially if one allows
for the fact that imperial powers have acquired and held colonies from strategic as well as economic motives. But there are
many cases where some exploitation has been combined with a
considerable degree of concern for the native population.

The concept of benefit to the population of a colony is ambiguous and produces further issues. How far do the people of a
colony benefit by changing their original culture and social
structure for one based partly or wholly on the culture of the
imperial power? What price in economic and political progress
is worth paying to avoid the difficulties caused by a rapid change
in culture pattern? And so on.

Thirdly, complicated questions arise when colonialism is accompanied by large scale immigration. The natives may become
a minority group in their own country. Even if this does not
happen the immigrants will be a large minority group creating
the special problems of a plural society unless racial mixture is
exceptionally rapid. Most independent countries try to prevent
immigration on a scale likely to create such problems. But what
should be done when large scale immigration has already happened? The original immigration may have involved injustice
to the natives, but the removal of the immigrant community
would involve even greater injustice to the immigrants or their
descendants. "America for the Indians" or "Australia for the
Aborigines" are not really possible policies because descendants
of the immigrants have completely replaced the natives over
most of the country. But in other areas immigration on a scale
likely to swamp the original native races has only taken place
during the present generation. There is no obvious and simple
way of reconciling the claim of the original population to be
allowed to continue their way of life in their native country
with the claim of the immigrant group to continue their way of
life in what has become their native country. Assimilation between natives and immigrants is probably the best way out of the
difficulty but this still leaves open the question of whether immigration should continue.

This is only a very brief review of a very complicated subject but enough has perhaps been said to show that colonialism

is a very complex question. A comparison between Communist and non-Communist colonialism is also complicated.

Communist colonialism has been superior in producing rapid economic development. Few non-Communist colonial areas have a record of economic development comparable to Central Asia under Soviet rule.

Communist rule has been more effective in producing rapid changes in colonial societies. Some aspects of this would command general approval. Most people would agree that the rapid spread of education and the rapid improvement in the status of women in the Muslim colonial areas were real benefits to the population. For other aspects the benefit is more doubtful. Communist policy has been based on the assumption that there is a universal optimum type of social and economic organization which is known to the Communist elite. It has, therefore, tried to produce everywhere the same basic type of social structure. Policy in the colonial areas has differed from policy in the imperial areas only over questions of timing and tactics and in aspects which Communist theory would classify as "superstructure". It is clear that some social changes forced through by Communist policy have been bitterly opposed by large sections of the colonial peoples and would appear to most non-Communists as a very doubtful benefit to them.

The slower rate of social change under non-Communist colonialism is, no doubt, partly the result of the lack of any clear and consistent system of social objectives and partly the lack of interest in the welfare of colonial peoples. It has also been the result of a belief that no one type of culture can claim to be superior to all others, from which it follows that to impose a new culture on a colonial people may not necessarily be a benefit to them. The more thoughtful exponents of non-Communist colonialism would argue that, while cultural change is necessary, each colonial people should be allowed to work out its own new pattern and preserve what is of value in its traditions.

Absence of purely racial discrimination has been a feature of Communist colonialism. But this could also be found in Tsarist colonialism and exists to a considerable extent in French and Portuguese colonialism.

The exploitation of colonial areas under Communist rule is almost certainly less than in the worse types of non-Communist colonialism but may well be greater than in the best types. Policies denounced by Communist writers as methods of colonial exploitation can often be found in a more extreme form in Soviet colonial areas. For example, a Soviet writer recently criticized non-Communist colonial rule in Asia for destroying the economic self-sufficiency of the colonial countries and encourging concentration on a few agricultural or mining products.[1] But, in Soviet colonial areas, there has been a policy of forcing the extension of cotton growing, against strong local opposition, thereby producing dependence on Russia for food supplies.[2]

Large scale immigration from the ruling race has been a characteristic of Communist colonialism in most areas. During the last thirty years the native races of several Soviet colonial areas have become minorities in their own native countries and Russian immigration is still continuing. Similar developments have taken place in the past under non-Communist colonialism but they are not occurring now.

The issue on which the difference between Communist and non-Communist colonialism is most marked is that of self-determination. Most non-Communist imperial powers now accept self-determination at least as a general principle. (Belgium and Portugal are exceptions.) The acceptance is not complete even for Britain where it has gone furthest. Considerations of strategy, as in Cyprus, or the problems of plural societies, as in East Africa, are taken as reasons for refusing or postponing the application of self-determination. For other powers the acceptance of self-determination has been even more reluctant. However, though non-Communist imperial powers may have been somewhat half-hearted in accepting the right of self-determination in their colonies they have, in practice, moved a long way towards accepting it. A large number of former British colonies have now been granted full independence while others have attained a large measure of autonomy and have been

---

1. Y. Shvedkov in *International Affairs*, 1956, No. 6, p. 83.
2. *Russia and her Colonies*, pp. 243 & 276-8.

promised future independence. Former French and Dutch colonies have in fact attained independence or substantial autonomy though against greater resistance from the imperial power.

The Communists have made all sorts of high-sounding claims
about self-determination. For example, the Republics of the
Soviet Union were given the theoretical right of secession. For
the first few years after 1917 Communist policy had some relation to Communist claims but, while the claims have remained,
actual policy was soon completely reversed. Of the areas which
tried to exercise the right of secession from the Russian Empire
only Finland now remains independent, with reduced boundaries. Georgia was reconquered as early as 1921 and the Baltic
States in 1940. Elsewhere every movement for independence or
even for greater local autonomy has been suppressed, and suppressed with extreme ruthlessness. The Soviet record in liquidat-
ing entire racial communities for disloyalty to the imperial
power could be matched in the record of Fascist colonialism,
e.g. Mussolini's treatment of rebellious North African tribes.
It is much more ruthless than the recent record of the democratic
non-Communist imperial powers.

Similarly, a new Chinese conquest destroyed the practical
independence of Tibet in 1951 and Chinese authority has been
strengthened in Sinkiang.

This refusal to allow self-determination has no relation to any
real case for continued colonialism. Compare, for instance, the
British record in tropical Africa with the Soviet record in Central
Asia. British colonial administration and Russian administration
were established during approximately the same period. The
original native society in most of the British colonial areas was
more primitive than in Central Asia and might, therefore, have
justified a longer period under colonial rule. In fact, by 1956
the Sudan had become independent, Nigeria and the Gold
Coast have a very large measure of autonomy and the latter
has been promised independence very soon. In Central Asia,
on the other hand, there are no signs of any relaxation of
effective Russian control.

This comparison between Communist and non-Communist
colonialism is a very brief summary of a large subject. It does,

however, indicate that Communist colonialism does not have any obvious superiority over non-Communist colonialism.

The whole issue of colonialism produces suspicions of the Communist powers in a number of ways. Firstly, governments committed to holding down subject races will find difficulties in accepting genuine peaceful co-existence. The reasons for this are discussed in a later section.

Secondly, the Communist refusal to allow their actions and those of non-Communist powers to be judged by the same standards seems to show a degree of either dishonesty or else of lack of objectivity which must make any peaceful agreement with Communists very difficult.

Thirdly, the Communist record over colonialism seems to fit the hypothesis that Communism is a system which gives absolute priority to maintaining and extending its power. The proclaimed principles through which Communists try to win non-Communist support are at once abandoned where they might conflict with the maintenance or extension of Communist power. Equally, the Communist criticism of non-Communist colonialism is completely irresponsible and appears to have the main objective of rousing hatreds and causing confusion likely to weaken and disrupt the non-Communist section of the world.

Non-Communist criticism of Communist colonialism is often much more responsible. In *Russia and her Colonies* Kolarz gives a highly critical account of Soviet colonialism but in his concluding chapter he says, "The emergence of a multitude of small national States in Eastern Europe, in the Caucasus and Central Asia, in the territory of what today is the U.S.S.R. would increase the anarchy in the world and would not even benefit the nationalities concerned. . . . What both the interests of the peoples of Russia and the maintenance of world peace really require is the transformation of the mock federation, which is the U.S.S.R., into a genuine federal union." He argues that some territories, such as the Baltic States, should be allowed to secede and that internal adjustment of boundaries might be desirable and goes on to say, "The problem of Russia's Moslem border republics will be the most difficult to solve, but political reason demands that they should not be separated altogether from the Russian body. The case for the present Soviet Central

Asia remaining within the framework of a Russian federation is at least as strong as the French case for the retention of Algeria within the French Union."[1] If Communist criticism of non-Communist colonialism were to become equally responsible it might make a contribution to solving the real and serious problems of colonialism which, at present, it only exacerbates.

The problem of Taiwan is not a case of colonialism but it does very directly involve the issue of self-determination. A good deal of non-Communist opinion, especially British opinion, considers that the most just and reasonable solution of the Formosan question would be to allow the future of the island to be determined by the wishes of its inhabitants. It is argued that the legal claims of the Kuomintang to rule the island are doubtful.[2] And at any rate the Kuomintang had a record of scandalous misgovernment and exploitation in Taiwan between 1945 and 1949 even though it may have improved since then. It was wrong after the war to impose on the people of Taiwan a government which they clearly did not want; and past injustice should not form a precedent for future injustice. The people of Taiwan have a just claim to the right of choosing the form of government they desire. This right may have been denied them in the past but it should not be withheld from them now. They should be allowed to decide their own future through a plebiscite or free elections. (And to secure free voting it would probably be necessary to have some form of international supervision.)[3]

---

1. *Russia and her Colonies,* pp. 316-7.

2. There was a long discussion of the legal position in the English press at the beginning of 1955. The general consensus of opinion among experts in international law seemed to be that the exact legal status of Taiwan was uncertain. Japan had clearly renounced sovereignty but no one else had clearly acquired it. The Kuomintang government could only claim to be administering the island on behalf of the war time allied powers or the powers which had signed the Japanese Peace Treaty. (It seemed to be agreed that the Cairo Declaration was only a statement of intention and did not produce a transfer of sovereignty.) There was, however, agreement that the off-shore islands were clearly Chinese territory.

3. It would, of course, be a difficult problem to devise and implement any satisfactory scheme to secure free voting and the requirements of such a scheme would need considerable discussion. However, it is not

If the people of Taiwan really want to rejoin the mainland they should not be prevented from doing so. If they would prefer an independent Republic of Taiwan they should also be allowed to have it.

A Republic of Taiwan would have as large a population as some Asian states that are now independent, e.g. Ceylon, and would be economically viable. It is argued that the Chinese People's Government has reasonable grounds for objecting to a rival Chinese government at T'aipeh which tries to blockade Chinese ports and to interfere on the Chinese mainland and proclaims its intention of reconquering the whole of China. On the other hand an independent Republic of Taiwan, with the off-shore islands restored to China, would not be a threat to Chinese security or harmful to Chinese interests. The question of U.N. representation could be settled by giving the Chinese seat to the Peking Government and admitting the Republic of Taiwan as a new member.

A solution of the Taiwan problem through self-determination has not yet been officially proposed by any government but it has been supported by a great deal of serious non-Communist opinion.

Unfortunately, such a solution is at present opposed by all three main parties to the dispute, the American Government, the Chinese Communist Party, and the Kuomintang, (though there are some indications that the more reasonable people in the Kuomintang realize that the reconquest of the mainland is impossible and are coming to accept the idea of an independent Taiwan.) The writer has strongly criticized the American position in a number of articles, broadcasts and lectures on the grounds that the Americans are betraying the democratic principles they claim to support for rather short sighted considerations of expediency and strategy and through a purely sentimental regard for Chiang K'ai-shek. However, in this statement intended primarily for Communist readers it is the position of the Chinese Communist Party which needs to be discussed.

---

worthwhile going into this problem while the basic issue of principle—whether or not self-determination is desirable—is still strongly contested.

Chinese Communist statements on Taiwan claim that the people of the island are longing for union with the mainland. If these claims were true any fairly conducted plebiscite or elections would lead to union. However, the same Chinese Communist statements also denounce any proposals for allowing the people of Taiwan to decide their own future. A good illustration was a speech to the National People's Congress on 27th. June, 1955 by the Vice-President of the Taiwan Democratic Self Government League. He said, in the same paragraph, that, "The compatriots of Taiwan support all the policies of the motherland for the liberation of Taiwan, and night after day are looking forward to the day of liberation," and that, "Such ridiculous views of 'Taiwan independence', 'neutrality', 'trusteeship', and 'plebiscite' all come from the schemes of the imperialists, and are serious insults to the people of Taiwan."

Such Chinese Communist statements do not simply object to particular proposals for a plebiscite or free elections on the grounds that they might not be fairly conducted and would not allow the people of Taiwan to express their real wishes. They object to the whole principles of allowing the future of Taiwan to be decided by the free choice of its inhabitants; in effect, they reject the principle of self-determination as applied to Taiwan.

The only reason given for this attitude is simply that, "Taiwan is a part of China." This is often supported by the argument that proposals for a plebiscite in Taiwan are just as unreasonable as similar proposals would be for a part of the United Kingdom.[1] In fact, this analogy proves the opposite of what is intended. The argument that "Ireland is part of the United Kingdom" had a longer historical basis than the argument that "Taiwan is part of China." And this argument was used by the British conservatives who opposed Irish Home Rule. However, after 1886, the majority of the British Liberal Party supported Irish Home Rule, in favor of which the Irish electorate had shown a clear majority. In 1914 a Liberal government carried a Home Rule

1. This argument was used by Chou En-lai in an interview with a British party reported in *The Listener* of 10th. November, 1955 (p. 772) and has appeared several times in the Chinese press.

Bill through the House of Commons against violent opposition which nearly led to civil war on the eve of the first world war. After the war the Irish Free State was granted the effective independence of Dominion Status and in the 1930's was allowed, by a British Conservative government, to choose complete independence. There is, therefore, a clear instance to show that the British government has been prepared to allow the secession of a part of the United Kingdom in which the majority of the population have shown their desire for independence. The analogy chosen by the Chinese Communists shows that, on the issue of self-determination, their attitude is identical with that of British conservatives of forty or fifty years ago.

Other parts of the British Empire have been like Taiwan in being populated almost entirely by immigrants from the mother country and these obtained effective self-determination much earlier. Responsible government was granted to New Zealand and the eastern Australian States in the 1850's. If these cases are taken as an analogy, the Chinese Communist attitude would appear reactionary in comparison with the standards of the British ruling class a century ago.

The Chinese Communists appear to think in terms of pure nationalism. They seem to believe that a Chinese government has a self evident right to rule over all territory within certain frontiers regardless of the wishes of the inhabitants of any parts of the territory.[1]

Other people would consider this sort of unqualified nationalism is a principle likely to endanger world peace. They would hold that nationalism should be qualified in some cases by the democratic principle of self-determination. And British policy has shown a willingness to accept this qualification.

If the Chinese Communist claims about public opinion in Taiwan are correct their opposition to self-determination would seem to be a rather pedantic insistence on principle. They not

---

1. It is not very clear on what principles these frontiers are decided. At the moment Chinese nationalist sentiment seems to be attached to the frontiers of about 1890 minus certain areas ceded to the Soviet sphere of influence and this attachment seems to have an emotional rather than a rational basis.

only want Taiwan but also want it to be given them in a particular way. In fact nearly all other evidence about Taiwan opinion is contrary to the Chinese Communist claims.

Under present conditions the inhabitants of Taiwan do not have any decisive way of showing what form of government they would prefer. There have been, however, a great many reports by outside observers, including many with good opportunities to study conditions, and there is very close agreement between a large number of independent reports from a wide variety of people. There is almost unanimous agreement that the last thing the people of Taiwan want is to come under the present government of the mainland. There is fairly general agreement that the natives of Taiwan would prefer independence to the present Kuomintang government. And there is some evidence, though less decisive, for believing that the natives of Taiwan would give second preference after independence to Japanese rule rather than rule by either mainland Chinese party.

The situation among the refugees is rather more complex, though except at the top and the bottom of the social scale, the distinctions between refugees and natives of Taiwan seem to be disappearing fairly rapidly. The official first preference of the refugees is for the impossible alternative of unification by a reconquest of the mainland from Taiwan. Insofar as they face the real alternatives of independence or absorption by the mainland they have conflicting motives of a desire for unification and a dislike of coming under Communist rule which they fled from China to avoid. Though the evidence is less clear it seems probable that the only groups likely to favor unification are at the top of the social scale, consisting of people who feel that their opportunities for a career are restricted in a small territory or who have very strong nationalist sentiment, and at the bottom of the social scale, among the refugees who have not managed to find a satisfactory place in the economy of Taiwan and who may regret having left China.

An Australian party recently visited Taiwan and some members of this party certainly did their best to obtain evidence and to form an impartial picture. Their reports confirm the conclusions given above. They considered that the only group likely to favor union with the mainland was among the higher ranking officials and army officers from the mainland. The only possibility of union with the mainland, apart from conquest by the mainland, seemed to be a coup d'etat by this group. And such a coup d'etat would be strongly opposed by the natives of Taiwan.

The basis for the feelings of the people of Taiwan seems to be the success of a reformist land policy similar to that followed by the Chinese Communist Party between 1937 and 1946. This has been combined with technical improvements in agriculture started by the Japanese and now continued through the Joint Commission on Rural Reconstruction. The result has been to make the general standard of living in Taiwan much higher than in other Asian countries. While the higher levels of government are controlled by the Kuomintang, the natives of Taiwan have considerable control of local government and almost complete control of the co-operative organizations. They might prefer to get rid of the burden of a large army and top-heavy administration and to have full control of their country through independence, but they have good reasons for not wanting to come under a regime which would be likely to destroy their control of local government and co-operatives and force through radical changes in the existing land system.

This account of public opinion and conditions in Taiwan is, of course, very different from that given in the Chinese Communist press. It is, however, based on the evidence of a number of people with good opportunities for observing the facts and no obvious motives for distorting them. The Chinese Communist press, on the other hand, has obvious motives for presenting a picture of Taiwan favorable to the claims of the People's Government; and its record in reporting conditions in Australia, Britain and other countries suggests that its standards of accuracy and objectivity are very low.

While a Republic of Taiwan would be viable it would probably gain through association with mainland China provided it retained really effective local autonomy. Something like Dominion Status which would offer natives of Taiwan an opportunity for careers on the mainland could be a real advantage. It is, however, extremely unlikely that a Communist government would tolerate a degree of autonomy remotely approaching that of the Dominion Status.

Could defenders of the Communist position make clear their attitude towards conflicts between the principle of nationalism and the principle of self-determination?

If they believe that a potentially independent or autonomous territory should have the right of self-determination, why are they unwilling to apply this principle to Taiwan?

If they believe that the argument that "Taiwan is part of China" provides an unqualified claim for Chinese sovereignty, why are they unwilling to apply the same principle in other cases? (The Japanese claim that at least the Southern Kuriles are "part of Japan" would appear to be quite as strong as the Chinese claim that Taiwan is "part of China". And the principle would produce strong claims for some frontier revisions in Europe.)

Chinese Communist statements have often promised autonomy to Taiwan after "liberation". Would this autonomy allow the natives of Taiwan to retain an economic and social organiza-tion widely different from that of the mainland, in particular, to retain something like their existing land system as opposed to collectivization?

Postscript on the Taiwan situation

I have not changed the text of this section as sent to Peking and Moscow. However this section was written at the end of 1956 and based on information from earlier periods. In 1958 I had the opportunity to visit Taiwan and lived there for nearly seven months and the information obtained during this period has led me to modify my views on a number of points.

The case for holding that the people of Taiwan do not want to come under Communist rule is now even stronger than was suggested in my original argument. During the period of liberali-zation on the Mainland from 1954 to the middle of 1957 the idea of unification had some power of attraction among the refugees on Taiwan. It seemed that Communist rule was becoming more tolerable and unification would have made possible the re-uniting of families divided since 1949, return to a familiar climate and environment, and possibly wider opportunities for a career. But this power of attraction was completely destroyed by the anti-rightest campaign which started in June, 1957 and by subsequent developments such as the communes program. It became clear that non-Communists associated with the Peking regime had no independence or security. While the Peking authorities have continued to offer good treatment and high positions to leaders from Taiwan who might go over to them, such offers are not attractive when it is clear that the Chinese Communist Party demands complete subservience from everyone associated with it, that a high nominal position would carry no real independence or authority and that anyone who went over to the Communists would be ruthlessly discarded when the Communists no longer considered him useful. At lower levels, while many refugees were dissatisfied with their situation in Taiwan, it became clear that they enjoyed a far greater degree of freedom and security than they could expect on the Mainland.

It was also clear that the great majority of people on Taiwan were far better off economically than people on the mainland. A comparison of studies of farm incomes prepared by the Joint Commission on Rural Reconstruction with figures published in Peking indicated that the average peasant on Taiwan had nearly twice the real income of the average peasant on the mainland. The available figures were for 1956 but there seems little reason to suppose that the differential has decreased since then. The continued campaign in the Mainland press for increased consumption of sweet potatoes suggests a trend in the diet of peasants on the Mainland exactly the opposite of that in Taiwan where peasants have been eating more rice and using sweet potatoes increasingly for feeding pigs. And there is an obvious contrast between the strict rationing of many commodities on the Mainland and the unrationed supply of cheap food and locally produced consumers' goods in Taiwan.

Taiwan, in fact, seems to show that a reformist economic program can be more successful under Asian conditions than the Communist one. National income has been increasing about as fast as on the Mainland without the same degree of enforced austerity, and economic development has included a great deal of industrialization in both heavy and light industry. American aid has, of course, played an important part in all this but American aid seems to have been of the same order of magnitude as military expenditure which has been extremely high for a society with a population of only ten million. If the 600,000 men in the armed forces could be shifted into productive employment the Taiwan economy might still be very prosperous by Asian standards without American aid.

In the long run, the high rate of population increase is likely to produce increasingly serious economic difficulties. But the same problem exists on the Mainland so that it is still true that the incorporation of Taiwan in the Mainland economy would almost certainly greatly worsen the economic situation for most of the population of Taiwan.

It also seemed clear that, while independence might have had majority support from 1946 to 1949 and perhaps for some years after, it has become increasingly doubtful whether any freely conducted election or plebiscite would show a majority in favor of an independent Republic of Taiwan. While there is still some bad feeling and tension between the native Taiwanese and the refugees from the Mainland all informants agreed that it had been steadily decreasing especially among the younger age groups. The education system, which gives elementary education to about 95% of school age children, is based on standard Chinese and so provides a common language between the native Taiwanese speaking South China dialects and the Mainland refugees who mostly come from North or Central China. And the whole emphasis of the educational system is on the Chinese character of Taiwan.

Popular reaction to the Quemoy crisis of August 1958, (reported by my wife who was still living in Taichung), seemed to show a genuine solidarity in support of the government's stand and against any idea of evacuating the off-shore islands.

An interesting development has been the growth of Kuomintang organization among the Taiwanese. This showed very clearly in the elections to local government councils in January, 1958. In most areas outside Taipei city with its large Mainland refugee population a majority of the candidates and a larger proportional majority of those elected were both members of the Kuomintang and natives of Taiwan. And even informants critical of the Kuomintang considered that the voting had been secret and fairly conducted. This suggests that, even if some election or plebsicite were held under international supervision, the result would quite likely be to confirm the Kuomintang in power.

There are obviously disagreements on policy between the neo-Confucian and the more liberal groups in the Kuomintang, and a good many people are obviously critical of some aspects of the regime. But it is equally obvious that the government in Taiwan is much more responsive to public opinion than the government on the Mainland and that the restrictions on discussion or criticism of government policies are very much less on Taiwan than on the Mainland.

Nothing in this postscript weakens the main point of my original argument, that the Chinese Communists are demanding control of ten million people who quite clearly do not want to come under Communist rule. However, it suggests that there is little hope of obtaining an agreed peaceful solution of the Taiwan problem through a "two China" policy. It also suggests that the motives behind the Chinese Communist demand for control of Taiwan may not be purely nationalistic. A comparison between Taiwan and the Mainland is obviously embarrassing for the Peking regime. It shows that a Chinese regime can secure rapid economic development without serious forced austerity and with a far higher degree of freedom than exists on the Mainland. And the increasing proportion of Overseas Chinese students going to universities in Taiwan shows effective competition from Taiwan in a field which the Peking leaders consider important. Finally Taiwan could, under some conditions, be a real military danger to the Peking regime. Most responsible opinion in Taiwan rules out the possibility of a successful invasion of the Mainland, but forces from Taiwan might be decisive if they could move in to support any fairly large scale revolt on the Mainland. A revolt aided by some trained military leadership and technical personnel and supported by some well trained forces from outside would be a far greater danger to the regime than a revolt without outside support. If, therefore, the Peking leaders have any reason to fear that their policies might produce a peasant revolt they would have understandable reasons for being determined to eliminate Taiwan.

The only obvious means to a peaceful solution would be such far-reaching changes in the Peking regime that unification became attractive to the population of Taiwan and the Chinese Communist attitude to "revisionism" makes this extremely unlikely. In this particular case, therefore, the chances of reaching peaceful co-existence seem to be small and the chances of avoiding hostilities seem to depend on continuing a precarious balance of power.

POSTSCRIPT ON OTHER POINTS.

Developments since 1956 have strengthened the argument of this section on several points. Many more non-Communist colonial areas have been granted independence, thus intensifying the contrast between Communist and non-Communist colonialism, and leaving, I think, Portugal as the only non-Communist imperial power which still opposes the principle of allowing colonial areas to develop towards independence. And the Tibetan revolt of 1959 greatly strengthens the evidence for holding that Chinese rule of Tibet has been imposed against the wishes of the Tibetan people.

7

Negotiation

Negotiation is another theme which figures very prominently in Communist publicity. It is repeatedly claimed that the Communist powers demonstrate their peace-loving intentions by willingness to settle all disputes by negotiation and discussion and that international tension could be lessened by top level meetings to deal with outstanding issues of importance.

When negotiations have taken place the results have seldom been encouraging. Only too often there have been interminable disputes about the agenda before real discussion even started. Negotiations have been deadlocked for months over some single issue. Conferences have often broken up without settling any of the issues they were called to deal with. When agreement has been reached it has often been an unsatisfactory compromise which merely postponed any real settlement or a form of words to which Communists and non-Communists have attached completely different meanings.

The last top level meeting at Geneva in 1955 seemed to offer hopes of an improvement but subsequent developments showed that any agreement was only apparent and the subsequent Foreign Ministers Conference failed to settle any of the issues entrusted to it. It only recorded complete failure with less waste of time and less rudeness than previous conferences.

There is, of course, nothing new in failure to settle disputes by negotiation or even in extremely long delay over preliminaries. (The conference which finally produced the Peace of Westphalia in 1648 spent its first six months in disputing the order in which the delegates should enter the conference hall, with the war still going on.) Even in recent years negotiation has failed to settle some important disputes in which the Communist powers were not involved.

Nevertheless, in the period since 1945 negotiations between

non-Communist powers have been, on the average, far more expeditious and far more successful than negotiations between Communist and non-Communist powers.

Many non-Communists would argue that, while talking about negotiations, the Communist powers have actually very seldom been willing to negotiate in any meaningful sense of the word. To discuss this it is necessary to begin with some general remarks about negotiation.

Negotiation usually involves a mixture of two rather different processes—bargaining and attempt to reach agreement. In the case of bargaining each party considers only its own interests and tries to get as much as possible from the other party while giving as little as possible in return. In an attempt to reach agreement the parties are trying to find some way of co-operating for a common objective and, if the attempt is successful, it will often resolve a previous conflict of interests.

Situations of almost pure bargaining are fairly common. It is uncommon to find situations in which the element of bargaining is entirely absent. Even when both parties are trying to co-operate for a common objective there will usually be room for bargaining about relative contributions and so on, but there are situations in which the bargaining element is comparatively small. At the international level trade negotiations are often examples of almost pure bargaining. At the other extreme the element of bargaining is often small in international agreements for technical objectives, such as locust control, or in such organizations as the International Postal Union. The clearest cases of negotiation resolving previous conflicts of interest are those which result in the setting up of new organizations commanding new common loyalties.

The problem is to consider the conditions under which different types of negotiation can succeed and whether such conditions exist between the Communist and non-Communist powers.

Pure bargaining is the simplest case and one which has been analyzed theoretically in the theory of barter in economics. This analysis shows that there will normally be a range within which exchange will benefit both parties. At one extreme the benefit will be almost entirely to one party and at the other extreme almost entirely to the other party. The exact terms on which exchange will take place are indeterminate on general theory and will depend on the relative bargaining strength and skill of the two parties. This general analysis will apply to bargaining in international negotiations though the situation will be more complicated than the simple barter case in economics because the things to be exchanged will seldom be definitely measurable, except in commercial negotiation, and because bargaining will depend on threats as well as on inducements.

If country A has greater military strength than country B, then A can try to obtain what it wants from B, not only by offering something in exchange but also by the threat of military action to support its demands. B's bargaining strength will depend on the losses which A would incur by resorting to military action, both materially and in prestige. Similarly, if country B is economically dependent on country A, then A can enforce its demands by the threat of economic pressure. B's bargaining strength will depend on its willingness if necessary to accept the economic losses which A could produce and on the cost to A of exerting this economic pressure.

However, these complications do not alter the essential features of a bargaining situation. There will normally be a limited range within which both parties can gain by making a bargain and the actual terms of the bargain within this range will depend on the relative strength and bargaining skill of the parties.

The conditions under which negotiations can lead to a successful bargain for simultaneous performance are fairly simple. Each party must be willing to keep its proposed terms within the range which the other party would be willing to accept. This is likely to happen when both parties have fairly objective estimates of their relative bargaining strength and of the limits beyond which the other party would not be willing to make a bargain. Negotiations are likely to fail when one or both parties have seriously inaccurate estimates of their bargaining strength and of the terms which the other party would be willing to accept. The chances of reaching agreement will be higher if the parties really wish to reach an agreement to the extent of being willing to accept slightly less good terms than the other party might have been induced to grant. If both parties are determined to drive as hard a bargain as possible negotiations are likely to . be very protracted and will fail if either party even slightly overestimates its bargaining strength.

The situation changes when the two sides of a bargain are not simultaneous because this introduces the extra factor of confidence. Both sides may agree on what would be a reasonable bargain, but negotiations will fail unless the party that is to perform first has confidence that the other party will carry out its side of the bargain later. This situation is not of much importance in economic theory because commercial contracts are usually enforceable. International agreements, however, are usually not enforceable and without a certain degree of mutual confidence bargaining involving future performance may become practically impossible. The point was put very clearly by Hobbes three hundred years ago, "If a Covenant be made, wherein neither of the parties performs presently but trust one another; in the condition of meer nature, (which is a condition of Warre of every man against every man,) upon any reasonable suspition, it is Voyd: But if there be a common Power set over them both, with right and force sufficient to compell performance; it is not Voyd. For he that performeth first, has no assurance that the other will performe after; because the bonds of words are too weak to bridle men's ambition, avarice, anger and other Passions, without the fear of some coercive Power, which in the condition of meer Nature, where all men are equal, and judges of the justness of their own fears, cannot possibly be supposed. And therefore, he that performeth first, does but betray himselfe to his enemy; contrary to the Right (he never can abandon) of defending his life and means of living."[1]

In fact the international situation is not entirely Hobbes' "condition of meer Nature" even though there is no international authority with "coercive Power" to compel the performance of treaty obligations. The advantages of being able to make bargains are so obvious that most countries, for their own

---

1. *Leviathan.* By Thomas Hobbes, Andrew Crooke, London, 1651, p. 68.

long term interests, wish to maintain a reputation for keeping their promises. The value of a treaty obligation will not be as high as that of a contract which could be legally enforced but it will not be entirely worthless. A bargain which exchanges a future performance for a present performance will not be "Voyd" as in Hobbes' "condition of meer Nature" but the value of the promised future performance will be discounted by some allowance for the possibility of repudiation. The extent of this discount will depend on the reputation of the country concerned, because it is the loss of reputation which provides the sanction against repudiation. It will become extremely difficult to negotiate a bargain involving future performance with a country whose reputation for observing its obligations is poor.

A moderate discount on the value of the future part of a bargain to allow for the possibility of repudiation does not make agreement impossible, because even the discounted value of the future part may still be great enough to make the bargain worthwhile. If A agrees to give X now in exchange for B giving Y in the future and the chances of repudiation by B are estimated at $z\%$, then the contract will still be worth making for both parties, provided that the exchange of X for a certainty of Y ($1-z/100$) is an exchange which A would consider worth making, even though less favorable than the nominal terms of the bargain. However, if z is large it is very unlikely that agreement can be reached. To allow for a considerable risk of repudiation A would need to insist on very favorable nominal terms which would probably be outside the range within which B considered the bargain worthwhile.

In practice, when there is a serious lack of confidence about future performance the negotiations for a bargain usually turn on questions of possible guarantees for performance or possible schemes for dividing the total bargain into sections for each of which simultaneous performance is possible.

People who have acted as non-Communist representatives in negotiations with Communists agree that negotiations for a bargain with simultaneous performance are often successful, though usually more difficult and much more protracted than similar negotiations with non-Communists. They are apt to be difficult and protracted for two reasons. Communist negotiators usually try to drive a hard bargain and are less ready than most non-Communist negotiators to make concessions for the sake of securing rapid agreement. A more important factor is the unwillingness of a Communist organization to delegate authority. It is the usual non-Communist practice to allow negotiators a considerable range of discretion over concessions which they can make on their own initiative if the course of negotiations shows that such concessions are necessary to secure agreement. Communist negotiators, unless they come from the very top levels of leadership, are seldom given such discretion. If agreement cannot be reached on their original terms and some concessions prove to be necessary, the negotiations usually have to be interrupted while the issue is referred back to the higher authorities.[1]

People with experience of negotiating with Communists are much more doubtful about the possibility of reaching worthwhile agreements involving future performance from the Communist side. The general reputation of Communist governments for observing their agreements is extremely poor, whenever political considerations are involved. It is only in purely commercial transactions that Communist organizations have a fairly good reputation for observing their contracts. There is nothing unusual about such a duality of standards. It can often

---

1. Cf. an account of war time negotiations by General John R. Deane. "As usual, there was a representative of the N.K.V.D. prepared to take notes of everything that transpired. This Soviet practice is, in itself, sufficient reason why negotiation with Soviet leaders is so difficult, if not to say futile. They dare not agree with any argument that is advanced by the other party no matter how sound it may be, if it is not in accord with the instructions received prior to the conference. Hence, it is impossible to come to an agreement at a first meeting if any differences of opinion develop. It is best not to press for agreement under such circumstances, since there is no chance of obtaining it and it evokes fantastic argument from the Soviet official, from which it is difficult and embarrassing for him to recede at a later meeting if he is permitted to do so after reporting to his superiors." (*Negotiating with the Russians,* World Peace Foundation, Boston, 1951, p. 13.)

be found in capitalist business. Many businessmen will be completely scrupulous about observing some types of contract and may consider themselves to be bound even by a verbal agreement without witnesses while they have no scruples about resorting to sharp practice to evade other types of obligation.

This communist reluctance to honor agreements is not simply a feature of the Cold War period but can be found even in inter-allied relations from 1941 to 1945 which Communist apologists continue to cite as evidence that the Soviet Government has proved itself willing to join in friendly co-operation with the Western powers. The books written by men who were allied representatives in Russia during the war cite a number of cases in which agreements made at the highest levels of the Soviet leadership were later evaded or repudiated by the Soviet authorities. These include agreements in which the political content was comparatively small, such as the arrangements for handling allied prisoners liberated from German prisoner of war camps by the Soviet forces. The conclusion which most of these writers draw even from their experience during the period of inter-allied co-operation is that the only type of bargain that can usefully be made with the Soviet authorities is one involving simultaneous performance.

Earlier sections of this statement have described a number of much more important cases in which Communist powers have repudiated their obligations. A good many of these cases go back to the period when Stalin was in power in the Soviet Union but there are a number of more recent instances. There is, for example, strong evidence that the Communists have not observed the terms of the Korean armistice about the build-up of military forces and air field construction in North Korea while the Soviet intervention in Hungary appeared to be in contradiction not only with the general Soviet undertakings about non-interference with the internal affairs of other countries but also with the assurances given very shortly before by the Soviet Government through its representatives at the United Nations. The seizure of Mr. Nagy after he had left the Yugoslav Embassy under safe conduct seems to be a completely cynical breach of good faith.

Admittedly the record of the non-Communist powers over observing agreements is not perfect but there is still an important difference of degree. The rate of discount which it would be reasonable to apply to non-Communist promises of future performance is much lower than the rate which it would be reasonable to apply to Communist promises.

If negotiations between the Communist and non-Communist powers are limited to trying to reach bargaining agreements involving simultaneous performance one cannot expect them to produce results likely to have any very great influence in settling outstanding disputes and reducing world tension. To show that negotiations are not subject to this limitation defenders of the Communist position would have to explain, *How is it possible to negotiate any useful agreement involving future performance by Communist powers without some guarantee that their future record over observing agreements will be different from their past record? And how can the Communist powers give such a guarantee?*

It was suggested in the first section of this statement that it would not be possible to obtain a really satisfactory answer to the second question until the Communist powers are willing to admit that their record in the past over observing agreements has not been good. So long as the Communists insist on maintaining their doctrine of Party infallibility and refuse to admit that Communist Governments have ever broken agreements in the past it is not possible to attach anything like its face value to a future agreement by a Communist Government, except insofar as the agreement contains provisions for some enforceable system of sanctions against evasion or repudiation.

It may be unrealistic to expect that the Communist powers could explicitly admit that their past record over observing agreements has been bad. In the present international system few governments would be willing to incur the loss of face involved in such an admission. It would, however, be possible for the Communist powers, (if they are sincere in wanting negotiations to reduce world tension), to admit implicitly that there is a lack of trust in the value of promises of future performance and to work for agreements which would go as far as possible in providing guarantees for performance. This would not involve any particular loss of face as the guarantees would apply equally to both sides. In fact an important obstacle in negotiations has been the unwillingness of the Communist powers to accept agreements containing any effective system of guarantees that they would be observed. The negotiations on disarmament are an obvious illustration.

Disarmament is a good example of a bargaining situation. Both parties can make a clear gain if they can agree to make reductions in armament expenditure which will leave their relative strength unchanged. In this bargaining a considerable proportion of Soviet proposals have been for schemes depending entirely on mutual trust whereas the non-Communist powers have repeatedly stressed the importance of guarantees of performance by an adequate inspection system.

For years the Soviet Government persisted in proposals for a general reduction of one third in the numbers in the armed forces of the major powers without providing any machinery for establishing the actual size of these armed forces, though even from internal evidence it is clear that some of the statements of the Soviet Government about the size of its armed forces must have been untrue. Some years ago the Soviet Government replied to allegations that the Soviet Union was maintaining far larger armed forces than any of the non-Communist powers by claiming that the total number was only two and a half million. Since then the Soviet authorities have announced two reductions in the size of the armed forces of 650,000 and 1,200,000 which, subtracted from 2,500,000 leaves only 650,000. This is not only a very improbably small figure but also inconsistent with other statements by the Soviet authorities about their willingness to consider proposals under which the armed forces of both the Soviet Union and the United States would be limited to 1,500,000 men.

During the last few years the Soviet Government has moved some way towards accepting the need for an inspection system to secure the observance of any agreement on disarmament or the limitation of atomic tests. But a large part of the gap between Communist and non-Communist proposals is still that Communist proposals imply a considerable reliance on mutual trust while non-Communist proposals emphasize machinery for inspection and procedures to deal with possible breaches of agreement. There is, of course, a real problem that effective inspection measures would weaken the relative position of the Communist powers by destroying the advantage they enjoy at present from the greater degree of secrecy with which they operate. But this should not be a very serious obstacle to agreement if it were introduced explicitly as a factor in the bargaining. What is likely to make agreement impossible is a refusal to admit that any acceptable scheme must go as far as possible in providing for an effective machinery for inspection and an effective procedure for dealing with breaches of the agreement.

There seem to be still greater difficulties in the way of negotiations which are not simply bargaining but which are an attempt to reach agreement about the best way to attain some common objective. If such negotiations are to succeed there must be some measure of agreement about the objectives to be attained and about the standards by which various possible means of attaining these objectives should be judged. These conditions may be satisfied when the common objective is basically technical, such as co-operation in research for the International Geophysical Year. It is doubtful whether they exist over political questions.

It is true that some negotiations in recent years have done something to settle political questions. The Berlin blockade was finally lifted, an armistice was finally reached in Korea, and the Geneva Conference produced some sort of settlement in Indo-China. However, all these agreements were bargains involving simultaneous or nearly simultaneous performance. Both sides wanted to withdraw from an uncomfortable or dangerous position but to do so in a way which did not give too much advantage to the other side. The negotiations were successful insofar as they struck a bargain about conditions for mutual withdrawal. Insofar as they tried to reach agreement about how to settle the underlying issues they were a complete failure.

Communists often cite the period of inter-allied conferences from 1941 to 1945 as evidence that Communist and non-Communist powers can reach agreements for co-operation. However, subsequent developments seem to show that a large part of the agreement which seemed to have been reached at these conferences was simply misunderstanding. As soon as questions of implementation arose it became clear that the meaning attached to the agreements by the Communist powers was quite different from the meaning attached to them by the non-Communist powers.

The main uncertainty about the possibility of finding common objectives comes from the Communist statements which seem to imply that Communists give an absolute priority to the objective of socialism, and define socialism in terms of Communist power. For example, an article on "Independent Thinking" in the Chinese periodical *Hsueh Hsi* of 3rd. October, 1957 said, "We should say that like democracy, independent thinking is a means and the building of socialism is an end." An article on "Party Leadership in Journalism" in the Peking *Jen Min Jih Pao* of 4th. January, 1958 began by saying, "Socialism can be built only under the leadership of the Party. There will be no socialism without Party leadership."

The statement that democracy is only a means towards the building of socialism seems to show that the Communist objective is not limited by whether or not people want it. A great many non-Communists would say that the people of any country have the right to try any social system they like, if democratic procedures show that they really want to try it. They would also say that the people of any country have the right to resist any attempt to impose the Communist form of socialism if they do not like it.

So long as Communists give an absolute priority to the building of socialism, as they define it, any other objective they accept must always be limited by the implicit qualification "insofar as this can be realized without hindrance to the building of socialism", and this qualification must raise doubts about how far the Communists really accept the other objective.

On a common sense view, an obvious common objective for Communists and non-Communists is the maintenance of peace, but Communist statements never face the contingency that there may be a conflict between the maintenance of peace and the building of socialism. *How far would Communists be prepared to co-operate with non-Communists in the maintenance of peace if this co-operation involved some restriction on the expansion or consolidation of the Communist form of socialism?* Until Communists have committed themselves on this question, which their statements so far have always evaded, the extent of possible co-operation must remain doubtful.

More serious doubts about the possibility of negotiations producing co-operation arise from the difference between Communist and non-Communist standards of judgment. One fundamental question which defenders of the Communist position need to answer is this:—*How can Communists and non-Communists agree if all thinking has a class character?* Assertions that all thinking has a class character are very frequent in Communist publications of the more theoretical kind. It is argued that the class standpoint of an observer is a fundamental factor in determining his judgment about any situation, (or at least about any situation with a political content), that it is impossible for anyone to form an objective judgment which abstracts from his class standpoint. Communists would also claim that the Communist and non-Communist representatives in negotiations will normally have different class standpoints. If these premises are granted how can Communist and non-Communist representatives possibly agree about anything?

The problem is raised in a slightly different form by Communist statements which claim that "truth is that which serves the interests of the masses." This definition is never combined with an attempt to answer the question: By what standards can it be determined what is or is not in the interests of the masses? On the contrary it is usually clear from the context that it is combined with the claim that the Communist Party represents the interests of the masses, which makes this definition of truth equivalent to saying that truth is what is asserted by the Communist Party. It would follow from this that the only cases in which negotiation can produce agreement between Communists and non-Communists is one in which the non-Communists end by accepting the Communist position.

Many non-Communists would agree that such factors as class

standpoint have an influence on judgment and would admit that Marx's work was important in calling attention to this influence which previous thinkers has tended to neglect. But there is a vital difference between holding that judgment is influenced by some factor and holding that judgment is determined by this factor. The possibility of reaching agreement through negotiation and discussion, as distinct from pure bargaining, depends on the assumption that judgment can be influenced by objective standards. People who start by disagreeing can end by agreeing if their views can be changed by rational argument and production of evidence. Insofar as they accept the common standards of scientific method they will tend to agree about the judgment which is justified by the available evidence. A purely objective judgment determined entirely by the standards of scientific method may be a theoretical limiting case unattainable in practice, but it is only insofar as both parties accept these standards and allow them to have influence on their judgment that a process of discussion can serve any useful purpose in lessening disagreements. If differing views are entirely determined by some factor, such as class standpoint, which is not changeable by discussion, then it is futile to hope that a process of discussion can do anything to produce agreement. Insofar as one party to a dispute consistently maintains a position which implies that their judgment of the dispute cannot be changed by rational argument or the production of evidence, the dispute becomes one of which no agreed solution is possible. The most that can be hoped for under these conditions is some limited bargain on particular points whose terms will depend on the balance of bargaining strength.

The Communist theories which maintain that judgment is determined by class standpoint or that truth is what is asserted by the Communist Party are theories which must make futile any attempt to reach agreement between Communists and non-Communists, insofar as Communists act consistently in terms of these theories. Communists must show that they are in fact ready to act in a way which makes it possible for negotiations to reach agreement if they want to demonstrate the good faith of their proclaimed willingness to settle disputes by negotiation and if

they want to refute the non-Communist argument that negotiations are only possible from "positions of strength". *Are Communists willing to allow the truth or falsity of Communist assertions to be tested by the scientific procedure of experiment or
examination of the evidence? If they are not, can they explain
how any negotiations can be expected to reach agreement?*

Of course, Communists are not the only people who state views
which must make negotiations futile, insofar as they are consistently followed. A very simple and common illustration of a
basically similar attitude among non-Communists can be found
in bureaucratic organizations. People argue that they cannot
modify their policy in response to criticism because this would be
"yielding to pressure" and create a precedent subversive of proper
administration. This argument implies that policy cannot be
changed by discussion or negotiation. The only way in which
policy can be changed is by creating a balance of power situation
which will compel the bureaucrats to yield to pressure. (And in
fact situations in which obstinate bureaucrats face determined
critics often build up to large-scale power struggles.) The implicit basic assumptions behind this bureaucratic refusal to negotiate have some similarity with the position stated more explicitly
by Communists. The Communist claim that truth is what is asserted by the Communist Party is similar to the implicit claim
that the right policy is what is decided by the proper authorities.
In both cases there is a refusal to admit that judgment may be determined by objective rational standards. (The argument that
yielding to criticism creates a dangerous precedent is only valid
on the assumption that no distinction can be drawn between
justified and unjustified criticism so that yielding to one would
create a precedent for yielding to the other.)

This particular case is interesting because the theoretical basis
for refusing to negotiate is so simple. In more general terms one
can say that it is not normally possible to reach agreement by
discussion with anyone whose basic assumptions are irrational,
who does not admit that there are objective standards of rational
judgment which should influence his judgment of the issue in
dispute. And it does not matter very much whether this basic
irrationalism is fanatical or sceptical. It would be hard to better

Hume's formulation of this point;—"Disputes with men pertin-
aciously obstinate in their principles are of all others the most
irksome, except perhaps those with persons entirely disingenuous
who really do not believe the opinions they defend but engage
in the controversy from affectation, from a spirit of opposition, or
from a desire of showing wit and ingenuity superior to the rest
of mankind. The same blind adherence to their own arguments
is to be expected in both; the same contempt of their antagonists;
and the same passionate vehemence in inforcing sophistry and
falsehood. And as reasoning is not the source whence either dis-
putant derives his tenets; it is vain to expect that any logic which
speaks not to the affections will ever engage him to embrace
sounder opinions."[1]

All this may seem rather abstract and philosophical, but it has
had very important practical implications. One good illustration
was the negotiations for an armistice in Korea which were protracted for two years by the dispute over the repatriation of prisoners of war. The dispute involved a fairly simple and definite
question of fact, whether or not certain prisoners wanted to be
repatriated. And this question was unusual among political questions because it could be settled with a high degree of certainty by
an experimental procedure, by allowing the prisoners to express
their wishes under conditions which guaranteed that their choice
was made with freedom from pressure and on the basis of adequate information. There was room for argument about the exact
form of experimental procedure which could best provide these
conditions but discussion on this point played a very small part
in delaying agreement. For a long time the Communists asserted
that all expressions of desire to refuse repatriation were made
under duress but refused to allow the truth or falsity of this assertion to be tested by any sort of experimental procedure. Admittedly, the Communists finally accepted the experimental procedure of the Indian proposals but even then they did their best
to make it unworkable by taking advantage of the failure to
specify any time limit on the period allowed for explanation before prisoners made their choice.

---

1. David Hume. *An Inquiry Concerning The Principles of Morals.*
(Opening Paragraph).

The Communist attitude on this question seemed to show that they were acting consistently in terms of the principle that truth is what is asserted by the Communist Party and refused to allow this definition of truth to be tested by any scientific objective standards. By contrast the attitude of the United Nations side was based on scientific principles. The assertion that many prisoners wished to refuse repatriation was presented as a reasonable deduction from the evidence already available and not as an unchallengeable certainty. It was accompanied by the offer to allow the issue of fact to be tested by any scientific experimental procedure which could provide really clear evidence, which implied a willingness to modify the original view of the United Nations side if new evidence showed it to be incorrect.

The Communist position on Hungary seems to be another clear illustration. This was summarized in a form short enough to be quoted here in an article by Chen Chih in *Hsueh Hsi* of 3rd. November, 1957 entitled "The Attitude towards the Soviet Union is the Attitude towards Revolution." "The so-called 'interference with internal affairs' (by the Soviet Union in Hungary) referred to by the rightests is a thorough bourgeois lie. Under this statement they are selling the bourgeois reactionary, hypocritical conception of nationalism. When the insurrection created by the imperialists and bourgeois counter-revolutionaries reached the stage at which it threatened the socialist cause of Hungary, threatened the basic interests of the working people of Hungary, and when the Hungarian Workers' and Peasants' Revolutionary Government officially applied to the Soviet Union for armed assistance, the only correct stand that the Soviet proletariat could adopt was resolutely to support and help the Hungarian working people to repulse the attack of the counter-revolution, to preserve the fruits of the revolution of the Hungarian working class, so that the independence and sovereignty of the socialist state of Hungary would escape the oppression of the imperialists. The Soviet Union acted accordingly, and this once more proves the powerful united strength of the international socialist camp headed by the Soviet Union, and inflicted on the imperialists a deserved lesson."

The obvious criticism of this statement is that its main assertions of fact are directly contrary to the weight of the evidence.

The very great majority of observers on the spot, (including the correspondent of the London *Daily Worker*), agreed in reporting that the insurrection had general support from the "Hungarian working people" and that it was the working class districts of Budapest which were most determined in resistance to the Soviet forces; that the part played in the insurrection by supporters of the pre-Communist regime or people with foreign connections was very small; and that the proclaimed aims of the insurrection were not opposed to socialism but only to the Communist form of socialism. It is also clear that the request for Soviet armed intervention was not an "official" request from the legitimate Hungarian Government of Prime Minister Nagy but came from a rival regime set up by Janos Kadar who was only one of the ministers in the official government. (It is interesting that the accounts given in the Peking press during the first days of the insurrection were markedly different from the version summarized in this later statement and that a sudden change in the line taken by the Chinese press occurred immediately after a visit of the Soviet Ambassador to Chou En-lai.)

It is also clear that the Communists are not prepared to allow their factual assertions to be subject to any sort of test. The communique issued by Khrushchev and Kadar on 9th. April, 1958 declared that a discussion of the affairs of Communist ruled countries at an international conference would be "incompatible with the principles of the United Nations charter and a flagrant interference in the internal affairs of sovereign states," and that, "The U.S.S.R. and Hungary resolutely state that the question of the state structure of the people's democracies as of any other sovereign state cannot be a subject for discussion at an international conference since it has long been decided upon by the peoples of these countries who have firmly and finally taken the road of building Socialism."

The second section of this statement has summarized some of the evidence for holding that the regimes of many Communist ruled states were not "decided upon by the peoples of these countries" but were imposed by Soviet military intervention; and that they operate under a degree of Soviet control which makes their independent sovereignty largely formal. Thus the Khrush-

chev-Kadar communique is, in effect, a demand that any top-level
negotiations should accept without question the Communist version of the facts on one of the most important issues causing international tension in which it is precisely the facts which are a
matter of dispute.

The position taken in this Khrushchev-Kadar communique is,
therefore, a clear practical illustration of the theoretical point
made earlier in this section, that the Communist theories about
the nature of truth lead Communists to take positions which
make it impossible for any negotiations to reach agreement except through non-Communists accepting the Communist view.

The issue is so important that it is worth saying a little more
to make it quite clear. It is hard to see how negotiation and discussion at any level can do much to reduce international tension
if some of the main issues which have produced mutual suspicions between the Communist and non-Communist sections of
the world are excluded from the discussions; and Soviet policy
in Eastern Europe is one of the most important of these issues.
Equally, when disagreement depends on differing judgments
about the facts of the situation, it is hard to see how disagreement can be lessened except by discussing the evidence and trying
to find out what judgment of the facts can be substantiated.

(It is not certain that such a process would produce complete
agreement. When the facts are complicated it is often not possible
to obtain evidence which can show clearly that one particular
judgment of the situation is the most reasonable. But if both
parties co-operate in studying the evidence it is fairly certain that
the extent of their disagreement can be reduced. And a situation
in which both parties recognize that different judgments can
honestly and reasonably be held does not produce the same kind
of tension and mutual suspicion as a situation in which each
party asserts its judgment as the only one which can honestly
and reasonably be held.)

If negotiation is to produce worthwhile results it is essential
that the important issues should be discussed and also that they
should not be prejudged. It would be quite unreasonable to
insist that negotiations should be based on the non-Communist
version of the facts. It is possible that the Communist leaders

sincerely believe their own statements and they would be justified in refusing to accept a formulation of the agenda for a conference which implied the non-Communist view. To give a purely
hypothetical example, the non-Communist powers would make
negotiation impossible if they insisted on an agenda including,
"The satellite regimes established in Eastern Europe by Soviet
imperialism." In fact, of course, they have not made any such
demands. They have tried to insist that important issues should
be discussed but they have been quite willing to allow them to be
formulated for discussion in a way which does not imply that
either the Communist or the non-Communist view is correct.

As against the neutralists it is worth pointing out that the
Communist and non-Communist positions are not symmetrical.
On the one side the Communist powers insist that the Communist
view on some of the most important and controversial issues
relevant to world peace must be accepted in advance. On the
other side the non-Communist powers only insist that important
issues relevant to world peace should be discussed and are willing
to leave the final judgment on these issues to be determined by
a process of discussion and investigation. It is one thing to be
neutral in the sense of refusing to express support for either
the Communist or the non-Communist case. It is quite another
thing to refuse to draw any distinction between people who are
willing to allow their case to be tested by discussion and investigation and people who are not so willing. A refusal to draw a
distinction in the latter case is really incompatible with the neutralist claim to support the settlement of international issues by
discussion and negotiation.

To sum up, if the Communists wish to show that their claims
of readiness to solve international disputes by negotiation are
made in good faith, there are a number of basic and somewhat
theoretical points on which they should clarify their position.
They should be willing to co-operate with non-Communists in
considering how to establish the degree of mutual confidence
which will make it possible to reach bargaining settlements involving future performance. And they should be willing to co-
operate with non-Communists in reaching agreement about basic
standards of judgment without which it is futile to expect that

discussion of practical issues can produce agreement. *Are Communists willing to support their claims of desire to work for peace through negotiation by trying to work for the sort of mutual confidence and agreement on standards which could make it possible for negotiation to go beyond the very limited range of bargains for simultaneous performance?*

8

The Nature of the Communist System

It is possible that some Communists would be willing to admit that the case stated in previous sections was not entirely wrong, that the Communist powers had acted in ways that gave some grounds for suspicion about their peaceful intentions. But they would almost certainly explain any defects they admitted in Communist policy as corrigible defects in an inherently superior and inherently non-aggressive system, often as defects caused by influences remaining from the non-Communist period. They might draw a comparison with technical progress in which it often takes some time to eliminate all the defects in new equipment or new processes which, in basic principles, are clearly superior to anything used before.

The basic claims which one finds in numerous Communist statements are that:—Socialism, in its Communist form, has abolished the exploitation or oppression of man by man and is superior in every way to all other social systems; only the Communist Party can lead the transition to this new form of society; the Communist Party represents the masses and cannot have any interests of its own apart from those of the masses; the only alternatives for mankind are this Communist-led socialism and capitalism.

For example, "The socialist revolution, compared with the democratic revolution, is a liberation movement of a more comprehensive and penetrating nature, which will enable all the people finally to shake off the yoke of exploitation, oppression and poverty, for after the institution of socialism, basically speaking, there will be no class and exploitation and the phenomenon of man exploiting man or man oppressing man will be thoroughly uprooted, so that the people's status as masters will endure forever. But the strong leadership provided by the Communist party again is the guarantee of socialist construction. Without the Party, socialism cannot be built up. Only the Communist Party can take the lead in this great cause. The bourgeois political parties, soaked in exploitation thinking, are basically incapable of eliminating the exploitation system, nor are the petty bourgeois political parties in a position resolutely to eradicate the system of the private ownership of the means of production, under which the phenomena of exploitation and class division must inevitably arise and develop and socialism cannot be built up. . . .

"Sectarianism and the Communist Party are basically incompatible. To charge that the Party is the root of sectarianism is a basic distortion of the nature of the Party. The Communist Party is a political party of the working class, which is the last one exploited and oppressed in human society and must seek to liberate the whole of mankind in order to liberate themselves. . . . That the working class and the Communists stand at the forefront in all liberation struggles is because all forms of exploitation and oppression hamper the liberation of the working class and all anti-exploitation and anti-oppression struggles are conducive to the advancement of the liberation of the working class. The interests of the Communist Party, therefore, are compatible with those of the people. The Party's interests are the people's interests. Naturally the Party is fair and impartial. Such a party has not the least connection with sectarianism. The premise upon which Ch'u Anp'ing and other rightests have slandered the Communist Party as sectarian is that the Party's interests and those of the people are incongruous. Such a premise is as baseless as an air castle.

"The root of sectarianism lies in the system of private ownership, the exploitation system and the resultant clashes between man and man, group and group. Where the system of private ownership and the exploitation system exist, sectarianism cannot be overcome. The ultimate objective of the working class and the Communist Party is to lead the people to inaugurate the communist society with common ownership of the means of production, thus eradicating all the sources of sectarianism. Many progressive people in class society oppose sectarianism, but they cannot overthrow it. The Communists oppose it, and are the only people who can overthrow it. Moreover, when the world state materializes there will be no class, the foundations of political parties disappear and all parties, including the Communist Party, must disappear. . . .

"It is true that certain Communists are imbued with sectarianism, but they have been influenced by the ideology of the exploiting class, . . . The sectarianism manifested by certain members inside the Party is illegal, which is one of the objectives of the recent rectification movement."

These illustrations are taken from an article in the Chinese periodical *Hsin Chien She* of January, 1958 by Sun Ch'eng-p'ei entitled "Refutation of the Preposterous Idea of 'Party Empire'."[1] The same points could be found in statements by more eminent Communist spokesmen but this article is of special relevance as it is a reply to criticism of the Communist Party. Also it puts the Communist position more frankly than some statements.

Within this general system of ideas it is quite possible for Communists to be convinced that Communism is bound to conquer the world and also to be quite sincere in claiming the Communist regimes have no aggressive intentions and that attempts to impose Communism on other countries would be contrary to Communist doctrine. If Communist led socialism is obviously superior to any other social system it will have a very clear attraction for the masses in all non-Communist countries. It will be opposed only by capitalist or feudal ruling classes and it is unlikely that these small minorities will be able to oppose revolutionary pressure from the masses for very long. In this sort of world one could expect revolutions and there might be some risks of non-Communist governments starting a war in the hope of preserving their power at home, but the Communist powers would not need to intervene in the internal affairs of other countries to secure the ultimate victory of Communism. In fact, there are strong reasons for considering that this Communist model of the world is widely different from reality.

One of the most common criticisms is that Communist led socialism has not shown any particular superiority as an eco-

---

1. Translation from *Extracts from China Mainland Magazines,* No. 123, March 17th, 1958. American Consulate General Hongkong.

nomic system. A good deal of the controversy on this point is confused because people on both sides often overstate their case. The more extreme Communist statements try to show that the workers' standard of living has been falling in all capitalist countries, which is obviously untrue. On the other hand it does not prove very much to show that the general standard of living is considerably higher in the United States or Western Europe than in Communist ruled countries because there was already a very wide gap before the establishment of Communist rule and the gap may have been narrowing.

A fair comparison between the relative performance of different economic systems is an interesting but also a complicated and controversial subject. One can point to cases in which the masses seem to have fared badly under Communist rule as compared with other systems operating in similar circumstances. The "exploited" West German workers seem to be better off than the "unexploited" East German workers. The standards of the "unexploited" peasants on the Chinese mainland, as described in surveys published in the Peking press, seem to be considerably lower than those of the "exploited" peasants on Taiwan. And Gomulka, shortly after coming to power, admitted that the real wages of the Polish workers were lower in 1956 than they had been in 1938. On the other hand there seems to be good evidence that productivity is rising faster in some Communist ruled countries than in non-Communist countries. But this evidence can be interpreted in different ways. It can be argued that Communist regimes are acting in the long term interests of the masses in imposing temporary austerity to produce a rapid rise in national income through a high rate of investment. It can also be argued that cases of rapid economic growth under Communist rule do not prove any superiority of socialism but only that a dictatorship can enforce a diversion from consumption to investment on a scale which the people would not tolerate under a democratic system. Again, supporters of Communism can point to many instances of inefficiency in non-Communist economic systems and critics of Communism can point to many instances of inefficiency in Communist economic systems. Altogether, although the subject is extremely interesting it is too complicated to be worth discussing in this statement which has tried to select simple test cases. It is, however, clear that the Communist economic system has not got an obvious superiority.

The claim that exploitation has disappeared under Communist rule seems to be disproved by the relations between the Soviet Union and the "satellite states" which have been discussed in an earlier section. The Soviet Union has raised its national income at the expense of the national income of other Communist ruled countries. Exploitation within a country is harder to define because there is no agreed standard of how the national income should be distributed if there were no exploitation. Communists define exploitation in terms of Marxian theory as the appropriation of surplus value and it is exploitation so defined which is supposed to be impossible under socialism. In capitalist countries surplus value is appropriated by the owners of the means of production; in socialist countries workers cannot be exploited because any surplus value they produce accrues to organizations which the workers themselves own through the state which represents them. The validity of this argument, even in terms of Marxian theory, depends on the assumption that the state represents the workers.

The most fundamental criticism of Communist claims about their system questions this assumption. It is argued that the state in a Communist regime is, in fact, controlled by the Communist Party; that the Communist Party is a group which does not necessarily represent the masses and whose interests may not coincide with those of the masses; and that the Communist control of the state may be used primarily for the interests of the Communist Party which can become a new ruling and exploiting group owing its power, not to ownership of property, but to control of the apparatus of the state.

Controversy on this subject has a very long history. Even while Marx was alive he was criticized by Bakunin for advocating a type of socialism which would be "the despotism of a governing minority". And since the establishment of Communist power the same basic criticism has been formulated in a number of ways. As early as 1920 Bertrand Russell, after a visit to Russia, predicted that the Communist Party was likely to degenerate into a "bureaucratic aristocracy". Milovan Djilas, in a series of articles published in *Borba* in 1950, argued that the system of the Soviet Union was not really socialism but what he called "bureaucratic centralism" in which the Soviet Communist Party had become a new ruling group exploiting and oppressing the masses. (In my opinion, these articles put Djilas' case in a shorter and clearer form than his better known later book, *The New Class*.) Karl Wittfogel in his book *Oriental Despotism* and in a number of earlier articles argues that there have been many historical examples of societies in which the ruling class has been an official bureaucracy and that Communist ruled societies are of this type. He related his theories to passages in Marx's writings which recognize the existence of "Asiatic society" as a type which had developed in different lines from the European evolution from feudalism to capitalism, and he points out that some of the Russian Marxists at the beginning of this century noted the danger of a revolution in Russia leading to an "Asiatic restoration." George Orwell's *Animal Farm* and *Nineteen Eighty-four* put the same basic criticism in a more popular form and present the logical development of Communist rule as "oligarchical collectivism". In China, the period of comparatively free criticism in 1957 produced Ch'u An-p'ing's theory of the "Party Empire" while other critics compared the position of the Communist Party to that of the Mongols or the Manchus in earlier periods of Chinese history. This list is almost certainly incomplete and it is interesting that most of the people who have produced the same basic criticism of the Communist system seem to have done so quite independently. Djilas does not mention the theories of "Asiatic society" which would have been relevant to his case and Wittfogel's *Oriental Despotism* does not mention Djilas. It is unlikely that Ch'u An-p'ing would have had access to any material critical of Communism published since 1949.

There are really two separate issues involved, whether it is theoretically possible for a Communist Party to develop into a new exploiting and ruling group, and whether Communist Parties have actually developed in this direction. Communists usually argue that such development is theoretically impossible. In the passage quoted above, Sun Ch'eng-p'ei argues that the

Communist Party cannot be sectarian with interests of its own different from those of the masses because "The root of sectarianism lies in the system of private ownership", and that while "It is true that certain Communists are imbued with sectarianism," this is only because "they have been influenced by the ideology of the exploiting class." Another common line of argument is based on the Marx-Leninist theory of a one-to-one correspondence between parties and class interests. Each party must represent some particular class interest and the Communist Party is, by definition, the party of the workers. Such arguments are only convincing to people who are already convinced believers in orthodox Marx-Leninist theory and it seems curious that people who claim to be materialists should attach such weight to arguments which imply that the real world must conform to a certain system of ideas.

On the question of fact Communists usually resort to argument by repeated assertion. A large part of Sun Ch'eng-p'ei's article consists of variations on the theme that the Communist Party is the party of the working class which must build up socialism to liberate itself and all mankind. But repeated assertion does not prove anything. By scientific standards the question of whether or not a particular party represents certain people and serves their interests is a question of fact which can only be decided by empirical evidence. Admittedly, the Communist Party claims to represent the workers, but other organizations have made similar claims, including the National Socialist German Workers' Party. To support their case the Communists should produce evidence to show that their claim is true and others false. Admittedly, Communist regimes claim to act in the interests of the masses, but so have other ruling groups such as the Confucian bureaucracy of the old Chinese Empire. Evidence is needed to show how far such claims are true. And for the scientific confirmation or disproof of some assertion one needs to look for cases in which one kind of evidence can be expected if it is true and another kind if it is false.

In non-Communist countries where the Communist Party is legal there is direct evidence about the degree of support for Communism. There are a good many occasions when people show fairly directly whether or not they consider the Communist Party to represent them. One has information about membership of the Communist Party and associated organizations, the Communist vote in elections of various kinds, support for Communist demonstrations, expressions of pro-Communist views in public controversies or in public opinion studies, and so on. There may be evidence to suggest that the real degree of support for Communism is greater than is shown publicly because public support for Communism, though legal, is in fact penalized in various ways. Conversely, there may be evidence suggesting that the real degree of support for Communism is less than is shown publicly because some public support is a protest against existing society rather than approval of Communism and because some public support may be obtained by deception, (e.g. when people support Communist sponsored organizations because they have been told that they are non-Party.)

In this sort of situation one can make a reasoned estimate of the degree of support for Communism,—that so many people are firm supporters, so many are sympathetic and might become firm supporters, so many are unstable supporters who might switch to any other organization expressing a protest against society (e.g. the big floating vote between Communism and Nazism in Germany before 1933), and so on. There will be a considerable margin of uncertainty within which reasoned estimates may differ but parts of the evidence would become hard to reconcile with estimates going outside this range.

In most cases the evidence does not support the claim that the Communist Party is the Party which represents the workers. In France and Italy the Communist Party has large scale working class support, but these are countries which have been comparatively unsuccessful in handling their economic and social problems, and even there a good deal of the Communist vote seems to be a protest against existing society rather than positive approval for Communism. In other industrialized countries the Communist Party has only managed to obtain support from a minority of the workers, often a very small minority. In many cases it seems that Communism has been more successful in attracting support from intellectuals than from workers. This is so to some extent in England and the United States, and in some parts of the world the Party seems to represent dissatisfied intellectuals more than it represents workers.[1]

How would defenders of the Communist position explain this comparatively limited success in winning working class support by the party which, they claim, represents the workers? It is not really a satisfactory explanation to argue that the ruling classes of imperialist countries have been able to bribe the workers with the profits of colonial exploitation. This argument is controversial even where it applies and it completely fails to explain the small support for Communism in countries with no colonies, such as the Scandinavian countries, West Germany, Austria, Canada, etc.

A non-Communist can easily suggest an explanation. The Communist Party wishes to represent the workers and obtain their support, but it also wishes to use this support for objectives which many workers do not want, the revolutionary overthrow of capitalism and the setting up of socialism under Communist leadership. Communists believe that these objectives are in the workers' best interests. Many workers believe that their interests can be better served by reformist policies than by revolution and are doubtful whether they would be better off under Communist rule. There is, therefore, nearly always an element of false pretenses in the relationship between the Communist Party and the workers. The Party may have genuine support from workers who feel so frustrated under capitalism that they would accept the risks and uncertainties of revolution. In other cases the Communist Party can only obtain working class support by disguising its real objectives and tends to lose support when it reveals them; when, for example, it stages strikes to sabotage the capitalist system rather than to secure economic gains for the strikers. This hypothesis seems to give a satisfactory explanation of the evidence. *Can defenders of the Communist position suggest a better one?*

---

1. A very detailed study for one area is given in *Communism and Nationalism in the Middle East* by Walter Laqueur. (Praeger, New York, 1956).

It becomes harder to estimate the degree of support for any party in a totalitarian system. When a well organized regime suppresses political opposition, only support for the regime can be expressed publicly, (except when the system of suppression fails to work). Such indices as election results, membership of organizations, public demonstrations, public expressions of opinion, etc. no longer provide any direct evidence of support for or opposition to the regime because, so long as the regime maintains its controls, opposition cannot be expressed in these ways. Direct evidence can only come from public expressions of opposition which the regime is not able to prevent or from small scale samplings of public opinion under conditions of secrecy, and such evidence may be of rare occurrence or hard to obtain. In general, the degree of opposition to a totalitarian regime can only be estimated from indirect evidence.

Sun Ch'eng-p'ei, in the article quoted above, is quite frank in admitting that the Chinese Communist regime does not allow the free expression of opposition views. "Our government and various undertakings are by no means monolithic and exclusive, admitting co-operation between Party members and non-Party elements. But there can be one direction only; nobody is allowed to go his own way and especially no freedom is granted to oppose socialism. Stooges of imperialism have often bragged about capitalist countries granting the freedom to propagate socialism with a view to hoodwinking those who believe in 'pure democracy.' Actually the bourgeoisie has always spared no efforts to destroy the Communist party; imperialist countries have proclaimed the Party as illegal and ruthlessly slaughtered its members. But the bourgeoisie can never succeed in destroying the working class because it cannot destroy the proletarian class, whose destruction would also mean the destruction of the bourgeois class and the capitalist society. Failure to destroy the proletarian class means failure to destroy the Communist Party. In the struggle for liberation on the part of the proletarian class, the Communist Party must inevitably come into being and grow up. With the existence of the Communist Party there must be communist propaganda and struggle for Communism. The presence of the Communist Party in capitalist countries, therefore, does not

indicate genuine espousal of democracy on the part of the bourgeois class but an insurmountable contradiction within the framework of capitalism. There is also the phenomenon true in many
lands: the bourgeois party in imperialist countries always stub-
bornly refuses to form a coalition government with the Communist Party under whatever circumstances. We don't know how
Ch'u An-p'ing would explain this point.[1] From our point of view,
though the bourgeois class cannot help admitting the existence
of the Communist Party, it will not by any means allow the
latter to share its regime. The presence of the Communist
Party propagating communism in the midst of capitalist society,
therefore, is an historical 'must'. But the working class is able to
destroy the bourgeois class, with whose destruction the former
can still carry on and build up a country one thousand or ten
thousand times better than before. Moreover, the working class
must necessarily destroy the bourgeois class, failing which socialism cannot be built up. It is, therefore, also an historical 'must'
that no freedom is granted to oppose socialism in the socialist
society. That no freedom is granted in the socialist society to
propagate capitalism is not because we are afraid of capitalism
but because this will hamper socialist construction and prove
detrimental to the interests of the people." Other Chinese Communist statements have made clear that the continued existence
of the so-called "democratic parties" will only be tolerated on
condition that they transform themselves into socialist parties
and accept Communist leadership.

Other Communist regimes may be less frank than the Chinese
about their refusal to allow the expression of opposition views,
but there is no evidence to suggest that their practice is any more
liberal, except perhaps in Jugoslavia or to a lesser extent in
Poland since the Gomulka regime. This means that the actual
degree of support for the Communist Party in Communist ruled
countries can only be judged from indirect evidence.

One obvious test of the degree of support enjoyed by any

---

1. It would be interesting to know whether Ch'u An-P'ing was allowed to make the obvious reply that, in the post war period,
coalition governments between the Communist Party and "bourgeois"
parties held office in France and Italy up to 1947 and in Czechoslovakia up to 1948.

system of government is the means it uses to maintain its power. The weaker the opposition the less the system needs to rely on an apparatus of suppression and organized force. The more the system enjoys voluntary support from an informed public opinion the greater the freedom it can allow to the people without danger to its stability. Conversely, the larger and more determined the opposition the more the system has to rely on force and an apparatus of suppression to maintain itself. The smaller the minority who are convinced supporters of the system the less it can afford to allow the people freedom to express their opinions or to organize. This seems fairly obvious from general common sense and it is easy to find practical instances to illustrate the principle. Perhaps the clearest illustration is the contrast which can usually be found in the administration of colonies and of the home country by the same regime because it is fairly certain that the degree of support for the system will be less in the colonies. It is normal to find that the colonial areas have more elaborate police and security organizations with wider and more arbitrary powers and that freedom of the press, freedom of organization and other civil liberties are much more restricted in the colonial areas than in the home country.

I do not know whether Communists would dispute this general principle that there is a relation between the degree of support enjoyed by any system and the methods of control it employs. The principle is implied by Marx's argument that the state maintains an appartus of repression because it is an instrument of class domination and by the theory of the withering away of the state, (in a society where all social conflicts have disappeared the administration would not need any apparatus of suppression or control).

Communists argue that all existing regimes are class dictatorships but that Communist regimes are dictatorships by the vast majority of the population over small minorities while non-Communist regimes are dictatorships by small minorities, over the great majority.[1] If Communists like to use the word "dictator-

_____

1. For example, "All countries in the world enforce class dictatorship; the question is which class enforces dictatorship and against which class it is enforced. In all capitalist countries, the bourgeoisie enforces dictatorship, i.e. a few capitalists enforce dictatorship against

ship" to describe any regime which bases its power to some extent
on the use of force they are simply defining it as a Marx-Leninist
technical term; and they presumably have to find some other
word to use for the earlier meaning of "dictatorship", which originated from the procedure in which the Roman Republic entrusted supreme power to a single man to deal with an emer-
gency. This Communist definition may be confusing but it is
irrelevant to the relationship between the methods of government
employed by a regime and the degree of support it enjoys. Whatever different regimes are called there should be marked differences between those which are supported by the great majority of
the population and those which are opposed by the great majority.

There are very wide differences between Communist ruled
countries and many non-Communist countries but the differences are exactly the opposite of those one would expect if Communist claims were true. A regime which is strongly opposed
only by a small minority may need a large army to meet possible
attack from outside but should not need much organized force
to deal with the internal opposition. It may need organizations
to deal with foreign agents or with sedition among the minority

---

the workers, peasants and all the working people. All their policies
and decrees proceed from their dictatorship. They oppress and exploit the working people of their own countries, and the imperialist
countries also plunder and invade the weak nations and turn other
countries into their colonies. The bourgeois dictatorship means oppression of the majority by the minority, democracy for a minority and
freedom for a minority while the majority enjoy no democracy and no
freedom. This is not so in our country. Our country is a country of
the people's democratic dictatorship led by the working class and based
on the worker-peasant alliance. Our people's democratic dictatorship
is enforced by the people led by the working class against the reactionary classes, reactionaries and enemies of the socialist revolution.
Our democracy does not belong to a few but belongs to the majority,
to the workers, peasants, working people and all the patriotic people
who support socialism. Socialist China, like all the other socialist
countries, is the most democratic country in the history of mankind."
(*On Socialist Democracy and Bourgeois Democracy*, by Li Che-Jen in
Hsueh Hsi of 3rd. September, 1957. Translated in *Extracts from China
Mainland Magazines* No. 110, 9th. December, 1957)

opposition but the main work of such organizations will be investigation; they will not need semi-military sections to meet a threat of possible internal revolt. This is the sort of situation one finds in many non-Communist countries. The Commonwealth Security Service in Australia, MI-5 and the Special Branch of the Metropolitan Police in the United Kingdom, or the Federal Bureau of Investigation in the United States are comparatively small organizations primarily concerned with investigation and without any special armed forces at their disposal. And the same general position can be found in other non-Communist countries. On the other hand, all Communist regimes have very large internal security organizations mostly including considerable semi-militarized sections. (I am not sure how far comparative figures have been published as I am writing this with very little reference material available, but I can give a few illustrations.)

The figures quoted in Section (4) of this statement show that the East German regime had 1% of the total population in police forces while the West German regime had less than 1/4%. Even if one excludes what was really the East German army the ratio of police to population was still over twice as high in East Germany as in West Germany. (And these are only figures for regular uniformed police. The difference might be still bigger if other security organizations were included.)

When the British Labor Party delegation visited China in 1954, the mayor of Anshan admitted that there were about 5,000 armed security police for a population of some 600,000. He claimed that they were necessary for protection but, when pressed to explain "protection against whom?", he refused to answer the question. At that time the total police force of Hongkong, a colonial territory, was also about 5,000 for a population of over 2,500,000. In Rangoon, with a larger population than Anshan, the police force was only about 1,000 and very few of them carried arms, although the Burmese government was still fighting an armed opposition in parts of the country.

If Communist leaders really believe that they have the support of the masses and are only opposed by small minorities, why do they divert far more man power and resources into the type of organization needed to deal with the threat of internal revolt

*than regimes which they consider to be small minorities opposed
by the masses? To put it more crudely, if Communist leaders believe that they have the support of the people, why do they show
themselves to be so afraid of the people?*

There are similar wide differences in civil liberties. Here critics
of Communism often spoil their case by exaggeration. If countries are simply classified as free or not free it is easy to show that
all countries impose some restrictions on civil liberty and to argue
that class of free countries has no members so that there is really
nothing to choose between different regimes. If it is admitted that
all countries impose some restrictions on civil liberties it becomes
clear that a number of non-Communist countries impose much
smaller restrictions than any Communist ruled country. No country completely realizes what Engels called, "the first condition of
all freedom, that all functionaries should be responsible for all
their official acts to every citizen before the ordinary courts and
according to the common law."[1] But the citizens of many non-
Communist countries have a far greater degree of legal protection
against arbitrary official action than the citizens of any Communist ruled country. In all countries free speech and publication
is limited to some extent by law and, even within the law, certain
views may find it hard to secure publication; but in many non-
Communist countries the restrictions are far smaller than in any
Communist ruled country. It would be easy to cite non-Communist newspapers which give their readers less and less accurate
information than *Pravda* or the *Jen Min Jih Pao*. But in many
non-Communist countries a citizen who wishes to make a reasoned
judgment on public affairs can obtain a great deal of relevant
information and analysis, if necessary free of cost at a public
library, while in Communist ruled countries much of this information is classified and only available to those in authority.
The list of differences could be continued almost indefinitely.

It is easy to understand why a regime representing only a
minority and opposed by the majority of the population should

---

1. From letter to Bebel in 1875 criticizing the Gotha Program for its
failure to include this "first condition of all freedom. . . ." *Marx-Engels
Selected Works.* Foreign Languages Publishing House, Moscow, 1949,
p. 38.

impose great restrictions on civil liberties; they obviously weaken its powers of control. *But, if Communist regimes really have more popular support and a smaller opposition than any non-Communist regime, why should they impose much greater restrictions on civil liberty than many non-Communist regimes? Why should civil liberties under socialism be postponed to the indefinite future when the state has withered away?*

It is not at all obvious that the restrictions on civil liberty found under Communist regimes would strengthen the position of a socialist regime, if it really had popular support. They obviously weaken the attraction of Communism in other countries and they might, on balance, have internal disadvantages. For example, the press in Communist ruled countries frequently reports cases in which the higher authorities intervene to correct abuses of power by local officials and it is clear from these reports that local officials can often abuse their powers for considerable periods before corrective action is taken. Establishment of the rule of law would provide a more rapid and efficient system of correction. Misuse of power by local officials would automatically be restrained by the citizens who had suffered appealing to the courts. Again, it is not at all obvious that freedom which allowed the expression of opposition views would "hamper socialist construction and prove detrimental to the interests of the people." Many strong opponents of Communism consider that the social gains from free discussion and criticism are far greater than any loss from the resulting freedom for Communist propaganda. And the corresponding arguments would be valid for Communist ruled countries if the anti-Communist minority is no larger than the pro-Communist minority in non-Communist countries where Communism is legal.

All these features of Communist government can be found in non-Communist regimes, but not in those which non-Communists would call democratic. A good many can be found in the governments of colonial territories, such as security organizations with wide powers, considerable restrictions on freedom of speech and of organizations, etc. The closest similarities, however, are between Communist and Fascist regimes. In both there are very large internal security organizations with very wide powers, with special armed forces at their disposal and with an elaborate apparatus for surveillance and control of the population. In both there are great restrictions on civil liberty and attempted isolation of the general population from "dangerous thoughts". In both there is the single ruling Party claiming the right to exercise leadership in all aspects of social life and suppressing all opposition. In both there is the attempt to secure mass support by indoctrination in the official ideology of the regime and the building up of mass organizations controlled by the Party. And in both, the attempts to win mass support have some success. (Both German Nazism and Italian Facism clearly had some mass support if only from a minority.)

Why do Communists maintain that socialism must be combined with these totalitarian features? This is a very important question. Communist statements continually assert that opposition to the Communist form of socialism is, in fact, support for capitalism because no other alternative exists. This argument would collapse if another form of socialism were possible without the totalitarian features of Communist led socialism. Though the question is so important, Communists usually evade it and, when they do consider it, give very confused answers.[1]

---

1. For example, a Soviet commentator on international affairs, David Zaslavsky, published a rejoinder to an article and a letter of mine in which I had argued that all forms of totalitarianism, including the Communist, were neurotic responses to the problems of the modern world. ("Reply to an Australian Professor", *International Affairs,* December, 1957.) He claimed that "a society not based on the exploitation of man by man . . . has already been created in the countries which you label 'totalitarian'," and that any important social reforms in non-Communist countries might be "a substantial step towards the social system which you label totalitarianism." This would seem to imply that there is a meaningful sense in which Communist ruled countries can be called totalitarian but that totalitarianism, in this sense, may be associated with social progress. He then argued that to discuss the world situation in terms of a contrast between democracy and totalitarianism "lacks scholarship, is of no assistance theoretically and is clearly a symptom of primitive dogmatism," and that "totalitarian" was merely a term of abuse "borrowed from the gutter press". He also claimed that the Soviet Union and People's China were not totalitarian and supported this by some very disingenuous argument

For non-Communists an explanation of the situation is quite simple. Communist regimes need large and elaborate internal security organizations and impose severe restrictions on civil liberties because they are regimes controlled by small minorities carrying out policies which are often disliked by a majority of the population. They try to obtain support by propaganda and indoctrination and are afraid of free discussion or contacts with outside ideas because the support produced by indoctrination is unstable. If the official ideology which secures support for the regime had to hold its own in free discussion it might be partly or even wholly discredited. If people could check official information calculated to produce support for the regime against other sources they would find that much official information was inaccurate or biased.

It is also possible to suggest two processes which would tend to make Communism totalitarian. One can trace totalitarian tendencies back to Marx but one can also find statements in which Marx supports democracy and civil liberties, and conflicting tendencies remained in Marxism. It is doubtful whether the Communists were clearly committed to totalitarianism until after the Russian Revolution.

At the time of the revolution many Communists were altruists who did subordinate their private interests to what they believed to be the interests of the masses, though they believed that they could judge the interests of the masses better than the masses themselves. They felt that they were justified in taking power and suppressing the opposition before they had majority support because they saw this as an act of leadership which the masses would accept as soon as they had experienced the obvious superiority of the socialist society which Communist power had estab-

---

trying to show that the press in the Soviet Union was as free as in the United States.

Thus, in replying to a statement that Communist ruled countries were totalitarian, a Soviet scholar writing in a serious journal uses three mutually inconsistent arguments in less than three pages, all of them of very doubtful validity.

I wrote to Mr. Zaslavsky criticizing his arguments and challenging him to state a more defensible case. Mr. Zaslavsky did not reply.

lished. They may have genuinely expected that there would be more freedom in Communist ruled society once socialism had been established and the power of the old ruling classes destroyed.[1] In fact, because of their belief in Marx-Leninist theory Communists greatly exaggerate the importance of changes in the ownership of the means of production and greatly underestimate the difficulties of organizing a socialist system that is efficient economically. Consequently, every Communist regime faces a dilemma after a period in power. If it wishes to base its power on support from the masses it will have to follow largely reformist policies instead of pressing on to the rapid realization of socialism. (The Soviet Communist Party might have won mass support if it had continued the New Economic Policy and the Chinese Communist Party if it had been content to provide honest government and generally agreed reforms.) However, to work for socialism by a process of gradual change would be an abandonment or drastic revision of the articles of the Marx-Leninist faith to which many Communists have devoted their lives. It is much easier for them to believe that, if Communist power can only be maintained for longer, the superiority of socialism will win mass support, and to explain the difficulties of the regime as the result of continued opposition, which can be suppressed, and not of defects in the Marx-Leninist analysis of society, which they are not willing to admit.

This process tending to produce totalitarianism is reinforced by another which is likely to become increasingly powerful. The Communist Party will develop a vested interest in the continuance of its power. However much the original Communist leaders believe that the Party should use its power only in the interests

---

1. Such an expectation is a possible explanation for the Chinese Communist policy of allowing considerable freedom of criticism for a period in 1957. A number of people studying the Chinese situation have suggested that Mao Tse-tung believed that Communist rule had been generally accepted so that freedom of criticism would be an advantage to the regime and would not endanger its stability, and that he was surprised by the strong and widespread criticism which was stated even by many members of the Communist Party. This is speculative but it seems to fit the evidence better than the hypothesis of a deliberate plan to induce opponents of the regime to reveal themselves.

of the masses, they create a society in which the main road to power is through the Communist Party. And it is hard to see why Communists should have any special immunity to corruption by power. A Communist Party out of power may offer its members considerable risks and very little prospect of material reward and so attract a high proportion of genuine enthusiasts anxious to serve the masses. A Communist Party in power is bound to attract a higher proportion of careerists. There will be a very strong tendency for the Communist Party to cling to power, to use its power to expand its privileges and so turn into a new ruling and exploiting group in society. Though some Communists may try to resist this tendency it will be hard for them to do so. Communist leaders who wish the Party to base its power more on mass support face a dilemma. They have to contend with those elements in the Party who would like to continue to base the Party's power on force and can only do this with the backing of the masses. But where the Party has made itself really unpopular the masses may only be willing to support an overthrow of Communist power. The Nagy regime in Hungary chose to rely on mass support, and was overthrown by outside forces determined to maintain Communist power. Elsewhere the moves towards obtaining greater support from the masses have been followed by retreats towards Stalinism as soon as it became clear that they might endanger Communist power. At the time of writing only Tito and Gomulka maintain a precarious balance between the horns of this dilemma.

This general analysis of the Communist system is an hypothesis which seems to explain all the evidence. It explains why Communist regimes maintain large internal security forces and place severe restrictions on free discussion and other civil liberties. It explains a great deal of other evidence indicating opposition to Communist rule,—the whole series of revolts from Kronstadt in 1921 to Hungary in 1956, the flow of refugees out of Communist ruled countries in spite of efforts to prevent it as compared with the quite small movements into Communist ruled countries, the strong internal criticism which has appeared whenever the restrictions on it have been relaxed, and so on. It also explains the change within Communism from a leadership which may

have been fanatical and ruthless but which wanted power mainly
to build a new society, to a more cynical leadership more concerned with power for its own sake, a development which has
gone further in Russia than in China.[1] It can explain the anti-
equalitarian trend in Communism which has already made differences in living standards larger in many Communist ruled
societies than in some non-Communist societies; (it is natural for
a privileged ruling group to use its power to increase its
privileges).

The test of a satisfactory scientific theory is its ability to explain a wide range of phenomena and this general analysis of the
Communist system seems to pass the test. Though each particular
bit of evidence is not conclusive proof that Communist regimes
do not have the degree of popular support which they claim, the
cumulative effect creates a very strong case. It is unlikely that
Communists will agree with this case but *could they indicate
whether there is any possible sort of evidence which they would
regard as proof that a Communist regime did not have the support of the masses?* If they believe that no evidence could prove
that Communism did not have mass support, (and the Communist attitude to the Hungarian revolt suggests something like
this position), then Communists and non-Communists are talking
at cross purposes. For non-Communists, statements about support
for or opposition to a regime are statements of fact whose truth
or falsity can be judged by the ordinary standards of scientific
method; for Communists they would appear to be metaphysical
statements of *a priori* truth. It would not be possible for Communists and non-Communists to discuss a large range of important
practical questions until they have cleared up basic philosophical
disagreements.

Communists might defend their position with something like
Sun Yat-sen's theory of "political tutelage". They could argue that
Communist Parties knew what was best for the masses better than
the masses did themselves and were, therefore, justified in using whatever degree of force was necessary to maintain their

---

1. To set out the evidence for this would involve a long digression
from the main argument and the case has been stated by many writers
on the subject.

power until such time as the masses came to realize what was good for them. This, of course, assumes that the Communist Party does know what is best for the masses and the Communist claim that it does is based on the Communist knowledge of Marx-Leninist theory. If Marx-Leninism were a system certain to command agreement from those who understood it then it would be reasonable to expect that the masses would voluntarily support Communist policies after they had been educated to understand Marx-Leninism during a period of tutelage. If, however, Marx-Leninism is an unsatisfactory and on many points an incorrect system then there will never be general agreement with Communist policies, and force and suppression will always be necessary to maintain Communism.

In fact, though something like the political tutelage argument is quite often used by Communist sympathizers it is never used by the Communist regimes themselves.[1]

If the Communist regimes admitted that they were exercising political tutelage then those Communists who genuinely want to serve the masses could consider how to guard against the danger of political tutelage being misused to turn the Communist Party into a new privileged ruling group. So long as they claim that their system is the most democratic in the world and has full support from the great majority they cannot openly even admit the existence of this danger, and can, therefore, do little to guard against it.

This rather lengthy argument about the nature of the Communist system is very important for international affairs because it suggests that it is possible for a Communist system to be inherently aggressive. In fact it suggests two possible reasons for inherent aggressiveness, fanaticism and the interest of the ruling group in preserving its power.

So long as Communists believe that the masses in every country

---

1. I can recall one conversation in which a Chinese Communist admitted that the Chinese Communist Party was actually exercising something like political tutelage though they did not like to use the term and I have heard of a Soviet official in Germany similarly admitting that Soviet policy used something very like Nazi methods though for different ends. But such admissions would almost certainly be repudiated if any Communist made them publicly.

are actual or potential supporters of Communism they can com-
bine a belief that Communism is certain to dominate the world
with a belief that Communist regimes should not try to export
revolution or to intervene in other countries. But if Communism
is not able to win or even to retain mass support, then Communists must either give up, or indefinitely postpone, their expectation that Communism will dominate the world or else try to
force the actual situation to fit their beliefs. And the evidence
given in earlier sections of this statement suggests that they have
usually chosen the latter alternative.

It seems clear that the Soviet Communist leaders have never
been willing to allow people in territory under Communist rule
to reject Communism. Even in Lenin's time, when the Party
officially proclaimed the right of secession for constituent parts
of the Russian empire, Finland and the Baltic States were only
able to secede because they obtained foreign support and the
Social Democratic Republic in Georgia was conquered and re-
annexed in 1921. More recently Soviet forces suppressed the East
German revolt of 1953 and the Hungarian revolt of 1956 although
both seemed fairly clearly to have the support of the masses. And
the threat of Soviet intervention influenced developments in
Poland.

All this is directly relevant to the possibility of peaceful co-
existence. Communist statements often argue in favor of competitive co-existence. Communist and non-Communist systems
should not compete in military force but should engage in peaceful competition to see which system is best.[1] The trick in these

---

1. For example, "If you really believe your capitalist system is
superior to the socialist system, why are you afraid to abandon the
'cold war', stop the arms race and go in for peaceful competition?
The people of the socialist countries believe the socialist system is far
superior to the capitalist system. We have no aggressive intentions. We
are concerned with our peaceful labor and the building up of our own
countries and the raising of the people's material and cultural standards of life. . . . Let us see through peaceful competition which social
system is better. Is this not much better for the United States, Britain
and other Western countries than the hopeless arms race and war ven-
ture?" (*Jen Min Jih Pao* editorial, 30th. December, 1957. Translation,
Survey of China Mainland Press, No. 1686, 8th. January, 1958.)

proposals is that the Communists are only willing to compete under conditions which would allow them to gain power but not to lose it. They claim that the people under non-Communist regimes should have the right to choose Communism but refuse to allow the people under Communist regimes the right to reject it. This is not quite a proposal of, "Heads I win, tails you lose," but it is, "Heads I win, tails doesn't count." If Communists want non-Communists to accept competitive co-existence they should answer the question about what they would accept as evidence that the people of some country did not want Communism, *under what conditions would they admit that Communism had lost in some country under peaceful competition and not use military force to restore it?*

Earlier sections have given evidence suggesting that Communist regimes have, in fact, tried to export revolution. Here the difference between Communist and non-Communist policy is one of degree. One can find many historical examples in which non-Communist countries have helped revolutionary movements with which they sympathized. The battle of Navarino was a decisive British intervention in favor of a rebellion against the Turkish Empire and there are many instances of semi-official support for revolution, such as the Japanese assistance to Sun Yat-sen before 1911. In more recent times the Communists could cite military intervention by England, America, France and Japan against the Soviet Government in the period immediately after the revolution. However, since 1945, non-Communist policy has been a great deal more cautious than Communist policy.

Given the belief that all Communist Parties are parties representing the masses it is easy for Communist leaders to think of all Communist led movements as liberation struggles against oppressive regimes which deserve as much support as Communist regimes can safely give them. Whether this support might extend to military action to set up Communist regimes is a very controversial question. Some people argue that only non-Communist defense preparations have prevented such action; others argue that the danger is extremely remote. It is, however, at least possible that a Communist regime might be aggressive because of Communist fanaticism, because of a determination to realize the prediction of Communist theory that Communism must dominate the world. One could make a much better judgment of the real degree of this danger if Communists were willing to answer the sort of questions which have been raised in this statement of the non-Communist case.

Turning to the other motive, the vested interests of the Communist ruling group, it is possible that a real relaxation of international tension might be a serious danger to Communist regimes. Up to the present all Communist regimes have justified a good deal of their policy in terms of the danger of foreign aggression and have made great efforts in their internal propaganda and indoctrination to build up hostility and suspicion towards the non-Communist powers. And the appeal to solidarity against a hostile external world has undoubtedly produced internal support and has been specially important as an argument against revisionist tendencies within Communism.

Under genuine peaceful co-existence a good deal of Communist policy would become much harder to justify to the population under Communist rule. It would no longer be possible to present the non-Communist world as a danger. (If internal publicity continued to build up hostility and suspicion to the non-Communist powers there would be strong reasons for doubting Communist sincerity in accepting peaceful co-existence.) It would then be hard to give even a plausible justification for the very large security organizations, the restrictions on civil liberties, the restrictions on foreign contacts and the high degree of secrecy maintained by the regime. It would be hard to resist demands for a shift away from armaments and heavy industry to consumer goods and housing. It would be harder to obtain support through appeals to nationalist sentiment or to resist revisionist tendencies by arguing the need for solidarity against the enemies of Communism.

There is no reason to suppose that it would be impossible for a Communist regime to adjust itself to a situation of peaceful co-existence but it might well be very difficult. If the regime tried to maintain its internal system unchanged it would reveal itself much more openly as a dominant minority (to use Toynbee's term) maintaining its power by force and repression. Although the regime might still maintain its power under these conditions it would be more unstable. If the system of control and repression ever weakened, the revolutionary overthrow of Communist power would be more likely. On the other hand, the system may already be so unstable that a process of adjustment to peaceful co-existence would be dangerous to the regime.

There have been a number of instances since 1953 which suggest that it is difficult for a Communist regime to relax its control over the population without endangering its power. In some cases Communist regimes seem to have been extremely unstable. In East Germany in 1953 and in Poland and Hungary in 1956 a relaxation of control and repression very soon produced a situation in which the masses were trying to overthrow Communist power, and would almost certainly have succeeded but for the use or threat of Soviet military intervention. In other cases the instability has not been so great though it is hard to say what would have happened if the relaxation of control had not been reversed. In China some freedom of criticism produced demands for more freedom, strong criticism of various aspects of Communist policy, questioning of basic Marx-Leninist ideas, attacks on the privileged position of the Communist Party, demands for more action to raise the standard of living, criticism of the pro-Soviet line in foreign policy, and so on. Similarly when some freedom of criticism was allowed in North Vietnam the immediate result was strong criticism of Communist policies and of the Communist Party. Though the Soviet Government never seems to have gone so far as the Chinese in relaxing control of criticism and discussion, such relaxation as was allowed produced very similar results; and most of the criticism and expressions of dissatisfaction with the regime came from people who had never known anything but Communist rule, which suggests that a Communist regime does not only face opposition from the old ruling classes but continues to create its own potential opposition. All these developments provided almost no evidence to support the Communist claim that opposition to Communism means support for capitalism. The general popular demand seemed to be for a different form of socialism with much more freedom and without special powers and privileges for the Communist Party.

All this suggests that a stable socialist system would be considerably different from existing Communist systems. (By a stable system is meant one in which only a small amount of repression and control is required to prevent revolutionary change.) And the transition to a stable socialist system would upset a number of powerful vested interests in existing Communist systems. It would involve a drastic reduction in existing internal security organizations whose members now enjoy a considerable degree of power and privilege and whose special abilities would have comparatively little social value in a more stable society. It would almost certainly involve a considerable reduction in the powers and privileges of the Communist Party, and the type of person who had made a successful career in a totalitarian system might be much less successful in a system where ability to win support by persuasion was more important. In a society with more free discussion it is likely that parts of orthodox Marx-Leninism would be discredited, which would be very unwelcome to the more doctrinaire Communists. An emphasis on the efficient production of consumer goods might involve difficult economic problems; and so on.

Thus, the internal stability of existing Communist regimes has depended to some extent on being able to present the non-Communist world as a danger. The reduction in international tension which would be produced by genuine peaceful co-existence would make Communist regimes less stable unless they carried out fairly far reaching changes which would offend a number of powerful vested interests. It follows that these elements in Communist systems have an interest in continuing international tension.

Communist arguments trying to show that non-Communist systems are inherently aggressive continually stress the difficulties which they would face in adjusting themselves to a peaceful world and the vested interests opposed to such adjustment, e.g. the economic difficulties which might be caused by disarmament and the vested interests in the armament industry. It is argued that the claims of non-Communist regimes to want peace are made to satisfy the mass desire for peace and are not really sincere, that non-Communist regimes need international tension as a diversion from their internal social conflicts. What the argument given above has tried to show is that similar arguments can be applied at least as strongly to Communist regimes, though the types of vested interest involved may be different. Turning to practical illustrations, there are no cases to show that a Communist regime could survive in a peaceful environment; for the past forty years Communist regimes have always claimed that they faced imminent danger of attack from outside, sometimes with justification and sometimes, as in the Soviet war scare of 1927, with very little justification. On the other hand, there are numerous cases of non-Communist regimes showing a considerable degree of stability for long periods under conditions where the risk of external attack was negligible and admitted to be negligible.

This does not prove that Communist regimes are actually inherently aggressive but only that they have some tendencies which could make them aggressive. It does show that it is not enough for Communist regimes simply to assert their peaceful intentions. Communist leaders who wish to remove non-Communist suspicions must show themselves willing and able to resist the vested interests against peaceful co-existence in the Communist system; or else demonstrate, by the scientific standards convincing to non-Communists, that such vested interests do not exist.

Communist internal publicity could provide a good test case to show whether or not Communist regimes were willing to attempt the adjustment to peaceful co-existence. One could ask, *How do Communist regimes expect to attain peaceful co-existence so long as Communist publicity gives the people under Communist rule a highly distorted picture of the non-Communist world which seriously misrepresents the obstacles to peaceful co-existence?* At present Communist internal publicity reports an extremely biased sample of opinion in non-Communist countries. Statements by Communist leaders or the Communist press are given a very heavy weighting even for countries where the Communist Party is a small minority and its press has only a minute circulation. Neutralist statements are given considerable weighting. There is almost no reporting of public opinion expressing suspicion of the Communist powers. This weighting completely distorts the actual distribution of public opinion in many non-Communist countries as shown by public opinion surveys and other evidence.[1] The picture of non-Communist opinion implied by this reporting is one in which the great majority of the population in all non-Communist countries already sympathizes with the Communist position on international issues. If this were true it would follow that the Communist powers do not need to make any change in their statements or policies to secure mass support for peaceful co-existence in the non-Communist world.

In fact, Communist leaders who really wanted peaceful co-existence would have to take action to remove non-Communist suspicions and it is fairly certain that such action would be opposed by vested interests in the Communist system. This opposition might be overcome with the help of popular support; but popular support for the changes necessary to secure peaceful co-existence could not be organized so long as all the information given to the people is calculated to make them believe that no changes are necessary. A change in the reporting of non-Communist opinion would, therefore, be evidence of an effort to adjust to peaceful co-existence.

Given that social systems may have tendencies to aggression and vested interests against peaceful co-existence, it is not possible to maintain that the internal system of any country should be of no concern to the rest of the world. If it seems likely that the social system in some country may be inherently aggressive, other countries must take account of this in their foreign policies and defense preparations. If aggression could never be anticipated it could seldom be resisted.

It follows that a program to secure peaceful co-existence and to remove mutual suspicions must include discussion of the social systems involved. To remove suspicions it is necessary to show that any tendencies to aggression are not likely to have any important influence on policy and that the system would be

---

1. In a controversy with the New China News Agency in 1954 I was able to quote a public opinion survey showing that the views which the Chinese press quoted as if they were typical American opinion were actually held by a minority even smaller than the minority in favor of a preventive war against the Communist powers.

capable of adjusting itself to a situation of peaceful co-existence. There are obvious difficulties in carrying this type of discussion very far at the official level and this leads back to the argument of Part I, "The Case for Discussion," that discussion at the academic level is important, if not essential, to provide the foundation for discussions at the official level to reach peaceful co-existence.

PART III

Conclusion

The case for discussion restated

It does not seem worthwhile trying to suggest what the Communists might have written if they had not backed out of their original offers to cooperate in this study of the conditions of peaceful co-existence.

The questions raised in the "Statement of the non-Communist case of suspicion of the Communist powers" were designed as test questions,—questions which would yield as clear evidence as possible on aspects of the Communist position about which the present evidence of Communist statements and actions seems confused or contradictory. One set of answers would provide evidence for believing that the Communists really want peaceful co-existence, that they would be prepared to co-operate with the non-Communist powers to secure it if the non-Communist powers made clear on their side that they were willing to co-operate and to change aspects of their policies which had caused Communist suspicions. Another set of answers would provide evidence for believing that the Communists only want peace in the sense of preferring to get everything they want without fighting for it, that they would not be willing to pay for peace with any sacrifice of present or future Communist power or any modification of Communist dogma so that no co-operation is possible unless the non-Communist powers are willing to submit on Communist terms. Yet another set of answers would suggest that the Communists might go some way in co-operation for peace provided that the sacrifices of power and dogma involved were not too great.

My own opinion, based on some study of Communist statements and some personal knowledge of Communists, is that a majority of Communists could not answer these questions without a good deal of consideration because they have never been willing consciously to face the possibility that the only terms on which peace could be obtained would involve some sacrifice of Communist power and some modification of Communist dogma. An estimate of possible Communist answers would be an estimate of what answers Communists would give if they faced questions which they have so far always evaded in their public statements and may never have explicitly formulated even in their own thoughts. And it is likely that different Communists would give very different answers if they used their own judgment and did not wait until an official Party Line had been announced. Although all Communists like to preserve a façade of monolithic unity there has been a great deal of evidence of disagreements within Communism, especially during the period since the death of Stalin.

In many Communist Parties there has been disagreement between the orthodox Stalinists and those who have wanted to modify the Stalinist form of Communism towards rather more freedom and rather more concern for the actual wishes of the masses. And this disagreement has shown itself in many cases in public expressions of differing views or in struggles for power between different factions. It would be consistent for the orthodox Stalinists to answer in a way which would show that they were not really prepared to co-operate for peace and for the anti-Stalinists to show varying degrees of genuine willingness to co-operate for peace with the non-Communist powers.

An attempt to estimate what answers might have been given to my questions would, therefore, be so speculative that it would be useless as a guide to practical policy.

Given the evasiveness and contradiction of the present Communist position the only reasonable basis for non-Communist policy is to accept the fact that there is a very wide margin of uncertainty about Communist intentions. And until this uncertainty can be reduced it would not be reasonable to commit non-Communist policy to any particular line of action based on a speculative estimate of the Communist position.

If the Communists had not backed out of their offers to co-operate they should not only have answered the questions raised

by my statement of the non-Communist case for suspicion of the
Communist powers but also have produced their statement of
the Communist case for suspicion of the non-Communist powers.
It would not be difficult to produce a statement of possible
reasons for suspicion of the non-Communist powers but it would
be very hard to estimate how far any such statement written by
a non-Communist had any relation to the actual Communist case.

Many non-Communists would admit that the Communist
suspicions of the non-Communist powers have some real basis
even if they are greatly exaggerated. There have been inherently aggressive non-Communist systems in the past, and they
might revive. There are some groups in the non-Communist
countries who would like to follow aggressive policies or who
would not want to accept peaceful co-existence with Communism
even if the Communists showed themselves genuinely willing
to accept it. Even if one believes that these groups have had only
a minor influence on the policies of the major non-Communist
powers and that these powers are basically peace-loving one can
still point to a good many episodes in non-Communist policy
and a good many statements by non-Communist leaders which
could easily be misinterpreted as evidence of aggressive intentions
and which have given the Communists some reasonable grounds
for suspicion. Using such evidence one could produce a statement of a case which would justify Communist suspicions of the
non-Communist powers on grounds that would appear reasonable
to non-Communists. It might be argued that the actual degree
of Communist suspicion goes further than is really justified by
this case but the exaggeration could be explained as natural
and not unreasonable for people who look at the situation from
the standpoint of the Communist leaders. Their theories about
capitalism will incline them to believe that the non-Communist
powers are aggressive; their lack of understanding of the working of democratic systems leads them to attach undue importance
to unofficial statements; their sources of information about non-
Communist societies are seriously biased; and so on.

Such statements of a Communist case for suspicion of the non-
Communist powers have been produced by a number of non-
Communists but, as guides to policy, they are confusing rather
than helpful because it is not at all certain how far Communist

suspicions are actually based on grounds that would appear reasonable to non-Communists. It is not clear how far the Communist belief that capitalism is inherently aggressive comes from generalizations based on the actual behavior of non-Communist powers or how far it is a basic axiom of the Communist system of beliefs which cannot be changed by empirical evidence.

For planning non-Communist policy it would be extremely valuable to know what changes in policy could remove or lessen Communist suspicions of the non-Communist powers. A new situation in which the Communists were really willing to co-operate to secure genuine peaceful co-existence would be so clearly preferable to the present situation that it would be worthwhile taking considerable risks to attain it. If there were reasonable grounds for confidence that Communist suspicions could be removed by eliminating what would appear to non-Communists to be any reasonable basis for them, then it would be worthwhile making the necessary changes in policy even at the expense of some sacrifice of non-Communist security in a balance of power situation. If, on the other hand, the basis of Communist suspicions of the non-Communist powers is a firmly held theoretical belief about the inherent aggressiveness of capitalism, then the only change which could remove Communist suspicion would be the acceptance of socialism in its Communist form. So long as the non-Communist powers remain non-Communist nothing they could do would remove Communist suspicions and it would be both futile and dangerous to make any policy changes which might weaken non-Communist security in a balance of power position. These two cases are not sharply defined alternatives but extreme cases in a range of possibilities. The intermediate possibilities are those in which Communist suspicions are partly determined by grounds which would appear reasonable to non-Communists and partly by a dogmatic belief in the inherent aggressiveness of capitalism. The relative importance of the two factors would determine the extent to which it would be reasonable to modify non-Communist policies in order to remove any basis for Communist suspicions.

Differing judgments about these aspects of the Communist position are the underlying basis of the controversy over neutralism. Neutralist opinion argues that the Communists are genuinely afraid of aggression from the non-Communist powers, for which there is strong evidence, and that it would be much easier to secure co-operation for peace if this suspicion could be removed, which is quite reasonable. However, the neutralist case goes on to make the assumption, which is no more than a possible hypothesis, that Communist fears could be removed by changes in non-Communist policy, in particular by changing those aspects of non-Communist policy which are most strongly criticized by Communist publicity. As was pointed out in an earlier chapter, it is hard to distinguish preparations for defense from preparations for aggression and a misinterpretation of non-Communist defense preparations as preparations for aggression would be a possible and fairly reasonable basis for Communist fears. The main weight of neutralist criticism is, accordingly, directed against those non-Communist defense preparations which are most strongly denounced by Communist publicity,— NATO, SEATO, U.S. overseas bases, the development of atomic weapons and ballistic missiles, the re-armament of West Germany, etc. And neutralist opinion draws the conclusion that the persistence of the non-Communist powers in these defense preparations is a major obstacle to peace.

If its main assumption could be proved the neutralist case would be quite reasonable. In fact, however, it is not at all certain that the Communist powers would become willing to co-operate for peace if the non-Communist powers followed the policies advocated by the neutralists. If the main basis for Communist fears of the non-Communist powers is actually a firmly held theoretical belief that capitalism is inherently aggressive, Communist suspicion and hostility would remain and would merely be expressed in new criticisms of other aspects of non-Communist policy. If Communism is actually inherently aggressive, then the policies advocated by the neutralists would simply make war more likely by upsetting the balance of power which acts as a restraint on active aggression.

The period from 1942 to 1945 provided strong evidence against the simple neutralist assumption. The American government went fairly far in trying to avoid giving the Soviet government any reasons for suspicion. President Roosevelt believed that by showing trust in the Soviet leaders he could call forth a similar

trust from them. But this policy did not succeed in changing the
Soviet attitude of suspicion and hostility to the non-Communist
powers. The underlying suspicion remained and was justified
in Communist statements by arguments about British influence
on American policy, accusations that the Western allies were
starting separate peace negotiations with Germany, and so on.
It is, of course, not certain that the Soviet position under
Khruschev is the same as it was under Stalin, but the assumption on which the neutralist case depends is certainly not well
enough established to justify a gamble with non-Communist
security based on the balance of power.

The extreme anti-neutralist position depends equally on an
assumption that is no more than a possible hypothesis. A policy
of exclusive concentration on building up a balance of power
against possible Communist aggression would only be justified
if it were certain that Communist hostility and suspicion towards
the non-Communist powers had no relation to grounds that
would seem reasonable to non-Communists. And some aspects
of non-Communist policy seem to have been based on this assumption. One can point to a number of cases in which non-
Communist policy could have been modified in a way which
would have reduced any reasonable basis for Communist suspicions without involving any loss of strength in a balance of
power situation. In many cases the modification would have been
a matter of form rather than of substance. By using more imag-
ination non-Communist policy could have been expressed in a
way less likely to appear provocative from the Communist standpoint. Admittedly such modifications might involve a little more
trouble but the people who argue that it is not worth taking
trouble to remove possible causes of Communist suspicion would
only be justified if they could clearly prove their assumption
about the Communist position.

In fact, the extreme anti-neutralist assumption is also unlikely. Even for internal propaganda Communist regimes try
to justify their suspicions of the non-Communist powers by
arguments based on non-Communist policy. This suggests that
there must be many people in Communist ruled countries who
would not be convinced simply by theoretical arguments about

the inherent aggressiveness of capitalism and whose suspicions
of the non-Communist powers are at least partly determined
by empirical evidence based on non-Communist policies. Discussions with Communists or with people who sympathize with
the Communist position also provide strong evidence that their
suspicions of the non-Communist powers are considerably influenced by those aspects of non-Communist policy which provide some real grounds for suspicion.

These considerations suggest that a reasoned decision about
the basic principles of non-Communist policy must depend on a
judgment about the Communist position. On one judgment the
neutralist position would be reasonable. On another the only
reasonable objective for non-Communist policy is to build up
a "position of strength". On intermediate judgments it would
be worth making some sacrifices in a balance of power position
in order to remove grounds for Communist suspicions.

A good deal of present controversy is rather futile because
many people on both sides are not willing to admit that their
case depends on assumptions about the Communist position
which are no more than unproved hypotheses. For example,
some people argue that a build-up of bases for long range atomic
warfare is essential for non-Communist defense; others argue that
this is certainly provocative to the Communist powers, and that
it is not at all likely that the Communist powers would resort
to military attack. In this sort of argument it is fairly clear that
both sides are asserting speculative judgments about the Communist position with more certainty than is justified. Intelligent
and well-informed people are to be found on both sides of the
dispute, though perhaps not in the extreme positions, and this
would seem to show that no one has yet stated a fully convincing case in favor of any particular judgment about the Communist position. If people tried to adopt a scientific attitude
they should be able to agree that there is at present a real uncertainty and that the only way in which the neutralists and the
anti-neutralists can settle their dispute is by securing more evidence about the Communist position.

The present uncertainty comes from the Communist refusal
to make a clear and reasoned statement of their position. On so

many important questions actual Communist statements are inconsistent or evasive. One can find, for example, Communist statements which suggest that nothing short of a successful Communist revolution could turn the United States into a peace loving power and others which suggest that quite limited changes in American policy would make peaceful co-existence possible. What one would like to know would be what evidence would convince the Communists that the governments of the non-Communist powers really wanted peace. But Communist statements often explain the situation in terms of pressure from the masses forcing inherently aggressive ruling classes to make some moves favorable to peace. On this theory a non-Communist regime could never convince the Communists that it wanted peace because any changes in policy it might make would only prove that it was yielding to mass pressure. Similarly, Communist statements are always evasive or inconsistent about explaining the aspects of Communist policy which have caused non-Communist suspicions that Communism may be inherently aggressive.

One obvious and important source of evidence about the Communist position would be discussions with Communists. Admittedly, what people do is more important than what they say but it is possible to make experiments in a verbal form which could not be made in a practical form. To give an illustration based on the controversy about neutralism, the clearest test of neutralist policies would be to try them and observe the Communist reaction, but this would be a major and perhaps irreversible policy decision rather than an experiment. Evidence obtained through discussion about the likely Communist reaction to neutralist policies would not be so decisive but it could be obtained before any important policy decision was made. Furthermore, when it is a question of Communist intentions, Communist motives, or the basis for Communist beliefs, Communists can answer from a direct knowledge of their own mental processes while non-Communists can only make indirect deductions from circumstantial evidence. Of course, people can make false statements on such points but false statements can usually be detected if the other party to the discussion has an expert knowledge of the subject and is prepared to cross-examine by asking the right supplemen-

tary questions. If, in discussion, the Communists were prepared
to answer clearly the sort of questions I have raised in my "Statement of the non-Communist case for suspicion of the Communist
powers," it would provide a lot of evidence about the Communist
position. Equally, if they refused to give any answers that were
not evasive or if they persisted in assertions that were clearly false
this would also provide evidence about their position. It would
at least show clearly that they were not prepared to co-operate in
an attempt to settle the issues causing international tension by a
process of discussion and negotiation. It is, therefore, certain
that serious discussions between Communists and non-Communists would yield some important evidence about the Communist position. And it follows that non-Communists of all
views should do all they can to make such discussions possible.

To make this case for discussion clear it is desirable to distinguish it from a good deal of the current controversy about
contacts between the Communist and non-Communist sections
of the world. A good deal of this controversy is futile because
it is conducted by people who have already made up their minds
on the most important and most uncertain issue involved. Many
of the people who argue for more contacts accept something
like the neutralist assumption about the Communist position;
they assume that contacts, official or unofficial, will be used to
promote goodwill and for negotiation to produce co-operation
for peace. Many of the people who oppose contacts do so because they assume that it is already certain that Communism
is inherently aggressive and that contacts would simply be used
by the Communists for propaganda. Both positions are quite
different from the case for using contacts to get more evidence
about what the Communist position really is and whether or not
co-operation for peace is possible. In fact, both groups act as if
they did not really believe the opinions they defend and were
afraid that more evidence might show that their assumptions
about the Communist position were wrong.

If the neutralists really believed in their own position one
would expect them to be eager to produce more evidence in support of their views. One would expect them to say to the Communists, "We would like to persuade the rest of the non-Com-

munist world that we are right in believing that you would be willing to co-operate for peace, but it is very hard for us to do this without your help. At present a great many people do not agree with us and support their disagreement with arguments based on your actions and your statements. Will you please help us to convince the rest of the non-Communist world that the neutralist position is right by making unambiguous official statements on points where people complain that your statements so far have been evasive and by making clear the conditions under which you would be willing to modify those policies which have led many people to suspect that Communism may be inherently aggressive." In many ways the neutralists are in the strongest position for getting the Communists to provide evidence. They have closer and more frequent contacts than the rest of the non-Communist world and questions put from a friendly standpoint are more likely to be answered than the same questions put from a hostile standpoint. In fact, the neutralists never seem to make any serious attempt to get more evidence about the Communist position. They usually accept statements of peaceful intentions at their face value without asking the Communists to reconcile these statements with aspects of their policy which seem to contradict them or to make clear the Communist position on issues about which it has been evasive. Many neutralists, for example in India, are obviously sufficiently intelligent and well-informed to realize that they would have a much better chance of winning converts to their views if they could produce more evidence about the Communist position. The hypothesis which would explain their actual policy is that they themselves are not really confident that their neutralist views are right. More evidence about the Communist position might strengthen the neutralist case but also might disprove it. It is understandable that neutralists should be reluctant to make experiments if they are afraid that these might show that they had been committed to an incorrect policy, that their claims of moral superiority had no justification and that, instead of living in a world where peace could be secured by goodwill and negotiation, they were living in a much less pleasant world where, for the indefinite future, peace could only depend on an unstable balance of power. If neutralists do not like this explanation of their behavior they should be prepared to offer some alternative explanation of why they do not use their contacts with the Communists to get more definite evidence about the Communist position.

Many people who oppose contacts with the Communists take an even more illogical position. Even if they are personally convinced that Communism is inherently aggressive it is obvious that a great many people are not convinced. There are many people with considerable political influence who now sympathize with the neutralist position but who would no longer do so if the case for believing that Communism is inherently aggressive could be clearly substantiated. And contacts with the Communists could help to provide the necessary evidence if the case is, in fact, a valid one. The usual argument against contacts is that the Communists will use them for propaganda so that more contacts with the Communists will be assisting Communist propaganda. It may be true the Communists will try to use contacts for propaganda but even so there are two things badly wrong with this argument. Firstly, a refusal of contacts can also be used for propaganda. It enables the Communists to claim that they are ready to discuss the issues causing world tension and to settle disputes by negotiation while the non-Communists refuse to co-operate. This is a very effective line of propaganda which has been used on many occasions. If public opinion in the non-Communist section of the world were unanimously convinced that such Communist claims were made in bad faith, it might be quite an effective propaganda gesture to refuse contacts with the Communists until they had produced evidence to show that their offers of discussion and co-operation were serious. This is the sort of response the opponents of contacts would like to secure. In fact, however, non-Communist opinion is not unanimous. Communist offers of discussion and negotiation produce disagreements in non-Communist opinion which can plausibly be interpreted by propaganda as evidence of disagreement between the peace-loving masses and aggressive ruling classes. Insofar as governments try to use their authority to prevent unofficial contacts, for example by refusing passports, the result often seems to be an infringement of democratic freedoms even to people who are not Communist sympathizers. This again presents the Communists with a strong propaganda point to back their allegations that there is no real freedom in non-Communist countries. Furthermore, the attempt to prevent unofficial contacts is seldom completely successful simply because most non-Communist regimes do have some respect for democratic freedoms and are reluctant to apply really effective restrictions to their citizens. The actual result is often to ensure that the people who represent non-Communist countries in unofficial contacts are Communist sympathizers quite unrepresentative of general opinion.

Secondly, even if Communists try to use contacts with non-Communists to score points in propaganda it does not follow that they are bound to succeed. It is understandable that Communists should believe that they will be able to score an advantage in propaganda because they believe that the Communist case is a good one and the non-Communist case a bad one. What is curious is that many extreme anti-Communists should agree with this and base their arguments against contacts on the assumption that the Communists are bound to obtain a propaganda advantage from them. This assumption implies that Communists are bound to get the better of non-Communists in any debate, which in turn implies either that the Communist case is stronger than the non-Communist case or else that Communists are so much superior to non-Communists in debating techniques that they are bound to succeed in making the worse appear the better reason. Anyone who believes the first alternative ought logically to accept Communism. The second alternative is something which would need to be proved; it is unlikely that people who live in a totalitarian system in which there is almost no genuine discussion or debate will be more skilled in debating techniques than people who live in societies where debate and discussion are common.

It is true that Communists have often been able to derive a propaganda advantage from contacts with non-Communists but this has been the result of non-Communist ineptitude rather than of any special cogency in the Communist case or exceptional Communist ability in debate. Particularly in unofficial contacts, the Communist case has usually been stated in its strongest form by people who have been properly briefed while the non-Communist case has often been stated in an extremely weak form by people who have been too badly informed or too confused in their thinking even to raise the important questions. The remedy for this situation is not to cut off contacts but to take a little trouble to secure a proper presentation of the non-Communist case.

In official contacts there has often been no attempt at competition. In many cases the Communist representatives have clearly planned their strategy in terms of producing an effect on public opinion. The non-Communist representatives may have been well prepared for the traditional type of diplomatic negotiations but it has seemed that their whole tradition and training had made them reluctant to think in terms of an appeal to public opinion. They have obviously felt a strong sense of grievance that the Communists were not "playing the game" in terms of the conventions of traditional diplomacy but they have not been willing to react by competing in a different type of game. The whole set of concepts and strategies which might be summed up as psychological warfare has been despised as somewhat disreputable, the sort of activity which a respectable diplomatist should avoid as far as possible. Under these conditions it is not surprising that the Communists should often have been able to score successes in propaganda. The contest has been one in which wholehearted professionals have been opposed by halfhearted amateurs. Communist success might have been much greater if the general common sense of the masses had not limited the extent to which efforts in propaganda could win support for a rationally weak case. Here again the remedy for the situation is not to cut off contacts but to use them more effectively.

The non-Communist powers would have nothing to fear from contacts with the Communist powers, either official or unofficial, if they were prepared to devote to psychological warfare a small fraction of the mental and economic resources they have been ready to expend on military preparations.

On the Communist side one can find numerous official statements with claims of willingness to co-operate in discussion and negotiation, but there is a wide discrepency between these claims and the actual record of Communist behavior. An hypothesis which would explain the record of actual behavior is that the Communists try to manipulate the actual situation to fit in with their theoretical model of the world. According to ortho-

dox Communist theory the masses in all countries should be naturally sympathetic to Communist views and desirous of co-operating for peace on Communist terms though they may have been
confused by anti-Communist propaganda. On the other hand,
the ruling classes in non-Communist countries have a class standpoint which makes them inherently aggressive and opposed to
peaceful co-operation though they may be forced to act against
their natural inclinations by mass pressure. In terms of this
Marx-Leninist model of the world, Communist behavior is fairly
consistent. Official representatives of capitalist governments cannot be sincerely in favor of co-operation to secure peaceful co-
existence; if they profess themselves in favor of co-operation
for peace this is simply to appease pressure from the masses in
their own countries. Given this assumption it is quite reasonable to conduct official negotiations with a great emphasis on
publicity. *Ex hypothesi,* the representatives of capitalist powers
do not really want peace and the more their insincerity can be
exposed the greater the chance that the peace-loving masses will
finally come to realize that peace can only be secure when they
have replaced their inherently aggressive capitalist regime by an
inherently peaceful socialist one. This long term consideration
is reinforced by the short term one that the representatives
of capitalist powers will only make agreements favorable to
peace under mass pressure so that publicity designed to maintain
mass pressure will increase the chance of negotiations reaching
an agreement.

At the unofficial level the type of discussion which would be
useful for peace would be with people representative of informed
non-Communist opinion and able to make a clear statement of
the non-Communist case. In fact, this is just the type of discussion
which Communists tend to avoid. There is a very marked preference for confining discussion of international issues to people
from non-Communist countries who are already sympathetic to
Communism or who know comparatively little about the subject. A good illustration of this was provided by two episodes
in China. At the time of the Peking Peace Conference in 1952
members of the Central Committee of the Chinese Communist
Party were prepared to spend whole nights in discussion with del-

egates from non-Communist countries who were people of very little influence, but who were either sympathetic to Communism or lacking in any expert knowledge of international affairs. The visit of the British Labour Party delegation to China in 1954 offered the Chinese Communist leaders their first opportunity for unofficial discussions with representatives of one of the leading political parties in an important non-Communist country, some of whom had been members of the government and were likely to be so again in the future. But during the visit of seventeen days only two meetings were devoted to the discussion of international issues and there seemed to be no interest from the Chinese side in continuing discussion although several important and interesting questions had been raised. Other instances fit into the same general pattern.

Here again Communist behavior is consistent in terms of Communist theory. Discussions with people who "represent the masses" can produce agreement about co-operation for peace and, to fit Communist theory, people who "represent the masses" must either already be sympathetic to Communism or also potentially sympathetic once the misunderstandings caused by anti-Communist propaganda have been cleared up. On the other hand, since judgments are determined by class standpoint, it is hopeless to expect that any agreement can be reached through discussions with people whose class standpoint is that of the bourgeoisie and someone who is well-informed on international affairs but still unsympathetic to Communism must be presumed to have a bourgeois class standpoint.

A much simpler motive which can also explain Communist behavior is that people do not like discussions in which their fundamental beliefs are likely to face criticisms to which they would probably find it hard to make an effective reply.

Thus it is unlikely that the Communists would spontaneously be willing to join in the sort of discussions which would be relevant to the problem of peaceful co-existence at either the official or the unofficial level. A willingness to do so would in itself be proof of readiness to make some modification in orthodox Communist doctrine.

My own experience has been that the normal Communist response to serious questions is evasion. The refusal in both China and Russia to co-operate in the project described in this book is only one instance.

In 1955 I wrote to the World Council of Peace asking them to explain why they refused to comment on East German rearmament while denunciations of West German rearmament played a large part in their publicity. This produced a very evasive and disingenuous reply, and when I wrote again indicating the points at which their explanation was obviously unsatisfactory I received no further answer.

When in China in 1954 I complained to the New China News Agency about their very misleading reports of Australian opinion. After a delay of two weeks a letter in reply was given me on the day I left China but the reply showed a complete misunderstanding of my criticism. (It argued that the particular facts reported were correct whereas my criticism was that these particular facts were an extremely biased sample.) When I wrote again putting my criticism more clearly my letters remained unanswered.

On the same visit to China I showed the manuscript of my book *China and the Cold War* to several people in the Chinese Communist Party and invited comments and criticism and I suggested that, if someone in the Chinese Communist organization would write a review, I would include it as a final section in the book. In fact no one was willing to discuss the manuscript either in conversation or in writing.

An earlier correspondence was started by a Communist sympathizer in China, Rewi Alley, but he also refused to continue the correspondence after I had stated the non-Communist case over the Korean war and other issues.

Other people's experiences point to the same conclusion. Some good illustrations have been provided by the cases in which people willing and able to state the non-Communist case have attended Communist sponsored conferences. There has very seldom been a reasoned statement of the non-Communist case followed by a reasoned Communist reply. On the contrary the normal procedure of the Communist organizers of such conferences has been to find ways of preventing discussion, by putting a non-Communist speaker as the last item on the agenda or by using various stategems to prevent non-Communist delegates from expressing their views at all.

Non-Communist Strategy

The argument so far has tried to establish three main points —Firstly, serious discussions between Communists and non-Communists would be extremely important. They could provide much clearer evidence than is at present available about how far Communism, in its present form and under its present leaders, is a system with which peaceful co-existence is possible or a system with which only a balance of power is possible. Such evidence is necessary for a reasoned decision about the basic principles of non-Communist policy. Also, if peaceful co-existence is possible, discussion of this kind is essential to enable both sides to plan their policy in such a way as to attain it.

Secondly, it is unlikely that the Communists, under their present leadership, would spontaneously join in such discussions. Up to now they have shown a strong reluctance to engage in serious discussion and have used contacts with non-Communists primarily to obtain an advantage in propaganda appeals to public opinion, often with some degree of success.

Thirdly, the Communist successes in appealing to public opinion have depended on the inept handling of the non-Communist case and they could not be prevented by a non-Communist policy of restricting contacts because such restriction would, in itself, put the Communists in a very favorable position for propaganda.

In this situation what is the best strategy for the non-Communist powers? It is not possible to compel the Communists to join in serious discussions if they are determined not to do so. On the other hand, it should be possible, in fact not very difficult, to create a situation in which the Communists would either have to join in serious discussion or else be largely discredited in the propaganda struggle and lose a great deal of their ability to appeal to the public opinion they wish to influence. One cannot predict the exact outcome of such a situation because this will depend on the Communist response; but one can predict that any possible Communist response will result in a situation more favorable than the present one. If the Communists respond by becoming willing to join in serious discussion then it will become possible to obtain clearer evidence about the Communist position. If this shows that peaceful co-existence is possible then further discussion and negotiation will lead to a lessening of world tension. (This would obviously be the most desirable outcome.) If, however, the extra evidence strengthens the case for believing that Communism is at present inherently aggressive then it will become easier to obtain general support for the necessary policy of building up a balance of power; the neutralist arguments against such a policy will be greatly weakened. If the Communists still refuse to join in serious discussions and the refusal is used to discredit their claims to want peace this will also weaken the neutralist position and weaken the ability of Communist propaganda to support subversion. In the long run, a situation in which the Communist claims to want peace had been discredited would favor the replacement of an inherently aggressive Communist leadership by a new leadership which was prepared to co-operate for peace.

One obvious move in such a strategy is to formulate the questions which can give the clearest tests of Communist readiness to co-operate for peace; to ask them; and to give the fullest possible publicity to a refusal to answer them.

The experiment described in this book was a very small scale test of this. I certainly do not claim any perfection or finality for the set of questions which I invited the Communists to answer. They are simply the work of one individual and, while I have been able to use a great deal of work by others, I do not know of anyone else who has been working on exactly the same kind of project. If more people were to work on the problem the resulting discussion and pooling of ideas would certainly make it possible for someone to produce a better selection of key questions to test the Communist position, to find out whether or not the present leaders of Communist regimes were actually willing to co-operate for peace.

It has been quite easy for the Communists both in China and Russia to ignore these questions coming from one private individual in a low ranking position in a new university. It would be very difficult to ignore them if they were raised at the official level by non-Communist governments, and some of them would quite well be raised in this way.

One of the important obstacles to successful negotiations is the low value which it is reasonable to place on any agreement made by a Communist regime in the light of their past performance in observing agreements. And what makes the value of any Communist obligation specially doubtful is the claim that Communist regimes have always strictly and faithfully honored their obligations in the past. In this situation the obvious reply to Soviet proposals for non-aggression pacts, such as the proposed pact between the Warsaw Pact group and the NATO group, would be to ask in what way these proposed pacts differed from the non-aggression treaties which the Soviet Government had signed in the past with Finland, Esthonia, Latvia, Lithuania and Poland. (It might be tactless for the British or American governments to include the treaty with Japan as the Soviet Government could probably show that they had instigated its breach but other governments, such as the Italian, could include it.) This could be an entirely serious question and not simply an attempt to score a point in propaganda. If the Soviet Government were willing to admit that the Soviet Union under Stalin's leadership had broken its treaty obligations in these cases it would repudiate an official line which Soviet statements and publications have consistently followed up to the present. If such an admission were made public in the Communist ruled world as well as in the non-Communist world it would suggest that the Soviet Government was seriously concerned to try to restore its reputation as a power likely to observe its agreements. There would then be reason to attach a fairly high value to Soviet promises in new agreements. If, on the other hand, the Soviet Government refused to answer the question and continued to claim that it had always strictly and scrupulously observed its treaty obligations, it would be clear that only bargains for simultaneous performance could usefully be made with the Soviet Government. And the evidence for this could be publicized.

Mr. Dulles and other non-Communist leaders have made speeches saying that the Communist record in breaking agreements makes it impossible to put much trust in the promises of Communist regimes, but these charges have usually been made in general terms and have not been made specifically in official replies to Soviet proposals. This type of statement is not very effective in appealing to public opinion. General denunciations of Communist bad faith may be stimulating to those who already agree with them but they are not convincing to those who do not agree. It is easy for neutralist opinion to feel that the denunciations from both sides cancel out. A request that a Communist regime should explain some particular aspects of its policy which seem to show that it cannot be trusted to keep agreements would have a much more effective appeal. It does not prejudge the issue. The same question might be asked by people with neutralist opinions; in fact, as I argue above, neutralists should ask this type of question themselves if they were really convinced of the opinions they defend and wished to obtain support for them. Because a satisfactory explanation from the Communist regime would strengthen the neutralist case, an evasive explanation or a refusal to reply would be clear evidence against the neutralist case.

Mr. Macmillan's remark that the proposed non-aggression pact between the NATO group and the Warsaw Pact group might do some good and would not do any harm suggested a failure to think out the basic issues involved. (And later statements suggest that he has realized this.) To make a pact whose actual value was probably completely different from its face value would simply add to uncertainty and confusion. If the pact were treated seriously and allowed to influence NATO policy it would be taking a gamble with non-Communist security; it would be a partial acceptance of the neutralist position without any evidence to show that this was justified. If, on the other hand, the pact was not allowed to make any difference to NATO defense preparations this would provide the Communists with an additional reason for suspecting the good faith of the non-Communist powers and would enable them to argue that the non-Communist powers did not treat agreements seriously. It would also put the non-Communist governments in a weaker position to resist neutralist criticism of their policies.

Even some of the more theoretical questions about the Communist position might be raised at the official level. Non-Communist statements on a possible summit conference have made the distinction between agreement on basic issues, which is regarded as not very hopeful, and agreement on minor points, which might be possible. They do not, however, show a realization of how far an attempt to discuss basic disagreements would have to bring in ideological issues. For example, it is argued that a top level meeting ought to discuss German re-unification and Eastern Europe. But to discuss these, except as subjects for possible bargains, would involve the sort of basic questions which are rasied in Sections (2) and (8) of my "Statement of the non-Communist case for suspicion of the Communist powers." Soviet arguments on the subject always start from the claim that the governments of East Germany and the "satellite states" are regimes representing the people they control. (And if the East German regime represents the people of East Germany in the same sort of sense as the West German regime represents the people of West Germany then the argument that unification should be decided by discussions between the two regimes is quite reasonable.) The non-Communist case depends on the claim that these regimes do not really represent the peoples they control but were imposed and are maintained by Soviet military intervention or the threat of it. (Both government and opposition statements in West Germany have justified the refusal to negotiate with the East German regime on the grounds that it has no right to claim that it represents the East German people.) In this situation any discussion of German unification or the "satellite states" would be completely at cross purposes unless it went back to the underlying basic questions: What standards and what sort of evidence can show whether or not a regime is justified in claiming to represent the people over whom it rules? and, What do these standards and the relevant evidence show about the regimes in East Germany and the "satellite states"?[1] And a discussion of these questions might quite well lead back to the still more basic question of whether there are any objective standards of judgment or only different standards of truth corresponding to different class standpoints.

It is probably true that the chances of reaching agreement on such fundamental questions at a summit conference are small. But it is also true that a Communist refusal to reach at least a partial agreement could be used very greatly to discredit Communist claims to want peace and to want the settlement of disputes by discussion and negotiation. The case for holding that no agreement is possible between non-Communists and the present Communist leaders would become much more convincing even to neutralist opinion if the Communist leaders stated explicitly that the claim of Communist regimes to represent the people could not be disproved by any empirical evidence; or if they themselves asserted that no agreement was possible between Communists and non-Communists because Communist truth was different from non-Communist truth. It would also discredit Communist claims of readiness to work for peace through discussion and negotiation if the Communist leaders simply refused to discuss the basic disagreements which could be shown to underlie the particular disputes which are a threat to peace. Thus, if the non-Communist representatives at any discussion thought out the basic issues involved and worked out the questions which provided the best tests of the Communist position, they would have a good chance of producing a

---

1. It seems likely that the agreement reached at the summit conference in July, 1955 accepting the standard of "free elections" for a decision on German unity was never more than a verbal agreement meaning different things to the different parties. (And even so it has been repudiated in later Soviet statements.) If the non-Communist representatives had thought out more clearly the basic issues involved they would have realized that, between Communists and non-Communists, "free elections" was an ambiguous term. To reach any genuine agreement they would have had to agree on an operational definition of what was meant by "free elections". If this had been discussed in July, 1955 it would probably have become clear that no agreement was possible and later developments would not have been confused by an apparent agreement.

situation in which either some genuine agreement was reached or else the failure to reach agreement could be used to discredit Communist claims.

The seriousness of a failure to reach agreement on basic issues is often obscured because people do not distinguish between bargaining agreements and agreements to co-operate. A bargain is simply an agreement that one party will do certain things in return for the other party doing certain other things. The parties need not agree on anything else and the making of a bargain does not necessarily produce any lessening of hostility and suspicion. It is rather confusing to say that there is hope of making some progress through limited agreements even though it is very unlikely that negotiations with the Communist powers will produce any agreement on basic issues. It is confusing because a series of bargains do not necessarily add up to progress towards a lessening of hostility or agreement to co-operate. Bargains on disputed issues show that both sides, for the time being, prefer to compromise rather than fight and they can do this while remaining mutually convinced that the other side is inherently aggressive and prefers not to fight only because of the balance of power. Bargaining may help to preserve a balance of power equilibrium by securing compromise on disputes which might otherwise lead to war, but it does nothing directly towards replacing a balance of power by peaceful co-existence. It can only help in this by giving time for other influences to operate which could lessen the basic disagreements between the systems and by producing a less immediately critical atmosphere more favorable to their operation.

The same arguments apply even more strongly to trading agreements. Trading will increase contacts between the two systems which could provide an opportunity for better understanding, but it will not produce better understanding unless the opportunity is used. And it is possible for trading to be used as a means for gaining advantage in a power struggle in ways which increase rather than diminish international tension. For example, though trade between Japan and the Chinese mainland could be to the economic advantage of both countries it seems clear that the Peking authorities have been mainly interested in using it as a means of applying political pressure. Or again, Communist regimes have used trading as a means to finance Communist activity in non-Communist countries.

A strategy aimed at securing a peace which is more than a balance of power equilibrium must, therefore, make clear that bargaining agreements can only provide the opportunity for reaching agreement on more fundamental issues and that progress towards peaceful co-existence is only possible if these opportunities are used.[1]

The most important type of possible bargaining agreement is probably disarmament because an effective agreement on disarmament could do so much to produce the sort of atmosphere in which it would become easier to settle more fundamental issues. The crucial difficulty in reaching agreement is the problem of securing guarantees for future performance and the Communist powers have a natural advantage in using disarmament as an issue for publicity because of the secrecy with which their governments operate. On many points a simple agreement without any inspection system to check observance would give the Communist powers a considerable degree of security for future performance because it is unlikely that the democratic countries could break their treaty obligations on any appreciable scale without the fact becoming public. (This would apply with special force to the United States where government operates with a specially high degree of publicity.) It would, for example, be

---

1. Some people have argued that it would be possible to reach a long term general settlement on the basis of pure bargaining. It has been suggested that the Communist and non-Communist powers should agree on a demarcation of their spheres of influence. Each system would obtain security in its sphere of influence by agreeing to avoid any sort of interference in the other sphere. There are a number of reasons for believing that such a scheme would be unlikely to produce any far reaching results even if an agreement could be reached about spheres of influence, which might be very difficult. It assumes that the populations concerned will play a passive role, which is unlikely. A boundary following the present demarcation of influence would not be accepted by the people on either side of it in Germany, Korea, China or Vietnam. Also it is doubtful how far the complete ending of outside interference would really give security to either system. Even if the Communist regimes genuinely withdrew all support from pro-Commu-

very difficult for a democratic country to maintain numbers of men in its armed forces above any limits prescribed by treaty without the facts becoming generally known. A totalitarian regime, on the other hand, could break its obligations under a disarmament treaty on a considerable scale without the fact becoming public.

Though the non-Communist powers have always insisted that a disarmament agreement would be no good unless it included effective provisions for inspection, it is only in a few fields that they have tried to give operational definitions of what they would mean by effective inspection. There are the various proposals for inspection from the air to guard against surprise attack and an effective inspection system for atomic weapons tests seems to be considered feasible. In other fields one gets the impression that people have no clear idea of how an effective inspection system could be devised and that this accounts for the curious unreality of so much of the negotiation on disarmament. The Communist powers seem to prefer agreements with the minimum of provisions for inspection. And, from the Communist point of view, these would be reasonably satisfactory. The non-Communist powers stress the need for inspection but seem hesitant to commit themselves fully to definite proposals, which is understandable if they have not been able to think of an inspection system which would really give them adequate security. In this situation the Communist powers can point to their readiness to accept simple and definite agreements and can interpret the hesitancy of the non-Communist powers as evidence of insincerity in wanting disarmament. To secure an effective agree-

---

nist organizations in the non-Communist world these would not necessarily disappear. On the other side, non-Communist propaganda and assistance have probably been only a minor factor in producing opposition to Communist rule. Any agreed demarcation might, therefore, be upset by revolution. And the mere existence of the other system and ideas coming from it would be a stimulus to revolution. Without a much greater degree of mutual confidence than at present exists neither side would really trust the other to keep the agreement so that any revolutionary movement would produce suspicions that the agreement was not being observed. And if either system is inherently aggressive the agreement would certainly not be observed for very long.

ment on disarmament or to remove this Communist advantage in publicity the non-Communist powers need to devise an inspection scheme which could be effective.

It is hard to see how the conventional type of inspection system could be effective against a totalitarian government which was trying to evade its obligations. The clearest case to show the ineffectiveness of a normal inspection system was the attempt to enforce the disarmament provisions of the Treaty of Versailles. The Inter-allied Control Commission was operating in a defeated country with considerable powers given it by the peace treaty. It was staffed by competent professionals and co-operation between the different national groups was good. The Weimar Republic was not a totalitarian state and only some groups in the country wanted to frustrate the activities of the commission. In spite of all this it was not possible to prevent a considerable amount of evasion. If the conventional type of inspection system had only limited success under these very favorable conditions it is extremely unlikely that any system of this kind could give reasonable security that a modern Communist regime was not evading its obligations.

To have even a reasonable chance of detecting evasions the inspection commission would need an extremely large staff with very wide powers and would have to exercise these powers in a way that would cause a good deal of unpleasantness even when no evasions were discovered. It would be very difficult to recruit a really large and competent staff from the genuinely neutral countries and very difficult to ensure that this staff continued to act with a sufficient degree of suspicion and readiness to be unpleasant to make their inspection effective.

There was, however, one aspect of the attempted control of German disarmament after 1919 which suggests the possibility of an unconventional type of scheme which might be effective. The successes of the Inter-allied Control Commission in detecting evasion of the treaty provisions depended to a considerable extent on the assistance received from German citizens of pacifist or left-wing political views,—workers would report stores of arms they had helped to hide, opponents of the Reichswehr would report its plans for evasion and so on. One reason for the ineffectiveness of control was that this type of assistance dried up when the German courts started to impose convictions for treason on those German citizens who had assisted the commission.

A power which could make an inspection commission really effective would be the power to offer rewards and protection (including political asylum in another country if requested) to people giving information leading to the discovery of evasions of a disarmament treaty. This would create a situation in which a government which wanted to evade its obligations would have to see that everyone connected with the treaty breaking project was of such a high security rating that they could be trusted not to reveal the project even when they could do so with impunity and perhaps with actual personal advantage to themselves. And the need for this security rating would not be confined to those directly concerned in the project. It would also be required for all those in a position to know that something was going on which might be an evasion of the treaty. This limitation would make it very hard to avoid detection of any treaty breaking project which involved considerable amounts of man power and other resources of installations or equipment which could be seen by the local population.[1]

The inspection commission would still need fairly wide powers but it would not need a very large staff. Most important, it could operate in a very different way when most of its investigations started on the basis of information supplied by people who had inside knowledge from which they could reasonably suspect the existence of such a project. The commission would know what evidence it was looking for to confirm or disprove its original information and could pursue its inquiries much more vigorously than it could if it were making only routine inspections or following up suspicions based on very slight evidence.

It is fairly certain that any substantial or prolonged breach of

---

1. A writer in the January, 1958 issue of the *Bulletin of the Atomic Scientists* argues that failure to reach a disarmament agreement earlier is irretrievable because no feasible inspection system could prevent the erection of launching sites for inter-continental ballistic missiles. Under this scheme the chances of detection would be quite high.

treaty obligations would be reported to the inspection commission. In all countries there are a great many people who do not agree with the slogan, "My country right or wrong," and who would consider that they had a stronger loyalty to the cause of peace than to a government which was evading its treaty obligations. In Communist ruled countries it is possible that a considerable proportion of the population would be only too glad of an opportunity both to discredit their government and also to become a refugee in a non-Communist country with enough money to start a new career. And this group might well include a number of people sufficiently high in government service to have a lot of information.

So far as I know this type of inspection scheme has not been suggested previously but it does seem to be a possible solution of the problem of getting a fairly high degree of certainty in checking the observance of a disarmament agreement by a totalitarian government.[1]

The Communist regimes have always shown their dislike of inspection schemes and they would almost certainly reject an inspection scheme that was likely to be really effective. But the proposal of a general disarmament agreement backed by such an effective inspection scheme would still be an important move in a strategy aimed at producing a situation in which the Communist powers either had genuinely to co-operate for peace or else be discredited in their claims to want peace. Non-Communist publicity would be able to say convincingly, "We have proposed a disarmament plan backed by an inspection scheme which could make practically certain that neither we nor the

---

1. Of course, a good many points would have to be worked out. It would, for example, be necessary to ensure that full publicity was given in all the countries involved to the provisions of the treaty so that people would know what actions by their governments would be breaches of the treaty and that the inspection commission had the power to give rewards and protection to its informants. A government which wished to evade its obligations would try to isolate the inspection commission from the public and it would be necessary to take special precautions and to give the commission the necessary powers to prevent this happening in a police state. But the working out of such points should not present insuperable difficulties.

Communist regimes could secretly break the agreement. The Communist regimes refuse to accept any agreement except under conditions which would leave them free to break it secretly if they wished to do so." If the Communist powers reacted by becoming willing to co-operate in a genuine attempt to work out a mutually satisfactory scheme they could be invited to suggest alternative inspection systems which could give the same sort of degree of security. On either alternative the resulting situation would be preferable to the present one in which disarmament negotiations are deadlocked on most issues and in which the hesitancy of the non-Communist powers, in producing definite plans which they would be prepared to stand by, works to the advantage of Communist propaganda.

A genuine desire for peaceful co-existence would imply an encouragement of contacts and discussion at the unofficial level. Part of the case for this has already been stated in Part I of this book, and in general the more that is known about the other system the better the chances of framing a policy likely to secure peaceful co-existence and of getting internal support for such a policy.

In fact, though Communist regimes have given some encouragement to contacts likely to promote international understanding in purely technical or cultural fields, in any contacts with a political aspect they seem to have been much more interested in propaganda than in the type of contact likely to help peaceful co-existence. It is not easy for the non-Communist powers to make an effective response to this situation because they cannot control unofficial contacts in the same way as a totalitarian regime. They cannot choose their "unofficial" representatives in the same way as a totalitarian system and they cannot simply cut off contacts because this, in itself, would provide a very strong point for Communist propaganda.

There is, however, a good deal that could be done. For instance, part of the Communist advantage in unofficial contacts is simply a matter of finance. Communist regimes are prepared to spend very large amounts in inviting visiting delegations, organizing "Peace Conferences" and so on. And when the initiative in contacts of this kind comes from the Communist side it is hard to prevent representation from non-Communist countries being biased in favor of Communist sympathizers or well-meaning people who are not sufficiently well-informed to raise the important questions in any discussion of international affairs or to make any useful judgment about internal conditions under a Communist regime. The situation could be changed a good deal if universities or learned societies in the non-Communist world were given financial assistance which would enable them to send people who were well-informed to Communist ruled countries or to Communist sponsored conferences,[1] or to organize conferences of their own to which people from Communist ruled countries would be invited.

Of course, Communist regimes might refuse entry to well-informed non-Communist visitors, but if the number of refusals became large enough to make it quite clear that such a policy was operating this would greatly diminish the propaganda value of those contacts which were allowed. And it would be within the powers of any non-Communist regime to exercise some control on contacts within its country, to see that visitors from Communist ruled countries did not confine their contacts to pro-Communist organizations. It would be possible to make an informal bargain that visas would only be granted to visitors from some Communist ruled country if invitations were ac-

---

1. A good illustration was provided by the conference at Helsinki organized by the World Peace Council in 1955. The organizers were very explicit in their publicity in claiming that they wished the conference to be representative and would welcome non-Communist delegates, so they would have found it hard to reject delegations from non-Communist countries containing people with some expert knowledge of international affairs. By encouraging the attendance of such experts the non-Communist powers could have obtained information about the Communist position which would have been very useful in preparing for the top level meeting in July 1955. The Communist delegates at the conference would not have been able to depart very far from the official Party Line while the non-Communist experts could have raised all sorts of questions without in any way committing their governments. (If they had not been allowed to raise questions this would also have been evidence about the Party Line and would have shown in advance that real agreement at the top level meeting was unlikely.)

cepted from non-Communist as well as from pro-Communist organizations.[1]

Again, suitable internal publicity in non-Communist countries could do something to ensure that even the unexpert visitor to Communist ruled countries had some background knowledge and would be likely to ask some important questions.

All these are only examples of the sort of policies which would be implied by the basic strategy suggested above. In each case the objective is to produce a situation in which the Communist regimes either have genuinely to co-operate in ways likely to promote peaceful co-existence or else discredit their claims to want peace.

It seems quite likely on present evidence that the question, Do the Communist powers really want peace?, is a question which cannot be answered by a simple yes or no. What many Communists really want is probably the ideal world of Communist theory in which there is no contradiction between wanting peace and wanting the indefinite expansion of Communist power. A great many Communists give the impression of complete subjective sincerity in claiming to want peace but, if one pursues the subject a little further, it becomes clear that they also have a strong emotionally charged inhibition against facing the possibility that peace can only be obtained by modifications in Communist policy which would imply a modification of the orthodox Marx-Leninist analysis of the world situation. One can say that most Communists do genuinely want peace in terms of a Marx-Leninist model of the world. Whether or not they want peace in the real world which differs considerably from the Marx-Leninist model is a hypothetical question. The answer depends on what Communists would decide if they faced a choice

---

1. For example, the Australian government (1958) recently refused a visa to a Chinese Communist to attend a congress of the Australian Communist Party as a fraternal delegate. It might have been better policy to have granted the visa on the understanding that the Chinese People's Institute of International Affairs would send a representative to some conference organized by the Australian Institute of International Affairs, or a China mainland university send a visiting professor invited by some Australian university.

which they have so far always tried to evade because, according
to their theories, the choice should not exist. (And emotionally
charged reluctance to face questions which would be disturbing
to strongly held beliefs is something which can be found in many
people besides Communists.)

The strategy suggested would increase the pressure on Communists to make the choice of whether or not they are willing
to co-operate for peace in the real world. If they do become
willing to co-operate this is obviously the most desirable outcome. If they still refuse, the strategy produces more and more
evidence to show that, so long as the Communist position remains unchanged, the rest of the world can only maintain peace
through a balance of power equilibrium.

Many people believe that it is not very important to make
more tests of the Communist position because they consider
that the existing evidence already shows that it is not possible
to expect co-operation for peace from the Communist regimes
and that the best that can be hoped for is a balance of power
with some bargaining to secure compromises on particular
issues which threaten to turn the cold war into a hot war. There
are two obvious arguments against this position. Even if it is a
correct analysis of the present situation it does not follow that it
will remain correct in the future. A policy which simply accepted that nothing better than a balance of power was possible
would be likely to miss any opportunities for reaching the much
more satisfactory state of peaceful co-existence which might be
provided by some change in the Communist position. Also, it is
clear that a great many people are not convinced that nothing
better than a balance of power is possible, many intelligent and
well-informed people are still sympathetic to neutralism. It is,
therefore, important to produce more evidence about the actual
Communist position and the only kind of evidence which can be
convincing is that from cases which allow the Communist regimes a further clear opportunity of choice. (In general terms,
the sort of evidence which can confirm an hypothesis is the sort of
evidence which could also disprove it.)

If is proves to be the case that the present Communist regimes
are not really prepared to co-operate to secure peaceful co-

existence but only want to influence public opinion by claims of wanting peace, then the proposed strategy could reverse the influence of the Communist sponsored peace campaigns. A steadily increasing number of test cases showing that the Communist regimes were not prepared to act in accordance with their claims to want peace and the settlement of disputes by discussion and negotiation, combined with effective publicity for this evidence, would erode the rational basis for neutralist views. Of course, human opinions seldom have an entirely rational basis and usually involve all sorts of emotional and non-rational factors. But rational judgment is the factor which can be influenced by evidence and argument, and opinions usually become more unstable as they lose a rational basis. It would be unreasonable to expect that even the most convincing demonstration that the Communist powers were not prepared to co-operate for peace would lead to a complete disappearance of neutralist views. What one could expect would be a steady weakening of the neutralist position and a steadily increasing realization that, so long as the Communist regimes refuse to join in co-operation for peace, there is no possible alternative to policies aimed at maintaining the balance of power.

It is also likely that, if this strategy fails in the short run to produce Communist co-operation for peace, it will still be the most effective method of helping to produce a change in the Communist position. The Communist peace campaign has not been simply for external consumption but has also played a large part in internal publicity. The Communist regimes would certainly try to isolate the people under their control from information showing that this peace campaign was being discredited but they would find it extremely difficult to maintain complete isolation for an indefinite period. In proportion as the peace campaign was discredited internally it would make the Communist systems more unstable and increase the chances of a change to a new leadership which could obtain support by demonstrating a readiness to co-operate for peace.

If one looks at the actual policies of the non-Communist powers it seems clear that they have paid far less attention to influencing public opinion than the Communist powers have done. This is not to say that they should copy the methods of Communist policy. Indeed, these methods have only been effective because the non-Communist powers have done so little to publicize the wide discrepancy between what the Communist regimes propose in general terms with a view to publicity and what they are prepared to do in practice when an attempt is made to reach any agreement based on these general proposals. What it does mean is that the non-Communist regimes should try to obtain the maximum publicity effect from proposals which they are prepared to implement and policies which they believe should command the support of an informed public opinion; and that publicity should be considered as one important factor in determining policy. It is important to devote more resources to publicity, but a publicity organization can only obtain limited results when it tries to secure support for a policy decided with little regard for publicity. What is needed is a process of policy decision in which the publicity factor is naturally considered, in which people will ask themselves, "What will be the effect of this policy on opinion which we hope to influence?" in the same sort of way as they naturally ask themselves, "What will be the effect of this policy on the military balance of power?" For example, great care is taken to see that official speeches or statements do not reveal classified information; why should not the same sort of care be taken to see that they do not contain remarks which can effectively be quoted in Communist publicity?

One can easily think of instances to illustrate the lack of concern for publicity. The most extreme case of failure to consider public opinion was probably Anglo-French policy over the Suez intervention. This is not the place to discuss the wider issues but there does seem to have been a complete failure to judge the reactions of public opinion even in those countries normally most sympathetic to Britain and France.

Policy over atomic weapons tests would seem to be another example. This is obviously an issue about which many people in all countries feel strongly, possibly with good reason. Scientific opinion seems to differ widely about how many tests would produce an appreciable biological danger but there is at least a possibility that continued testing even on the present scale would be a danger. Under these circumstances a proposal to stop all tests is extremely important in appeal to public opinion. A government concerned to influence public opinion would realize that it was an important policy decision to balance this gain against any possible losses in relative military preparedness. In fact, the rather confused reaction to the Soviet proposal to stop tests suggests that this policy decision had never been worked out. If the non-Communist powers are actually prepared to accept an agreement stopping tests why should the Soviet Union be allowed to obtain the advantage of proposing it? (Admittedly, the Soviet Government made its proposal at the time most advantageous to itself, when it had just finished a series of tests. But there may well have been earlier occasions when a proposal to end tests would have been relatively advantageous to the non-Communist powers.)

Yet another instance is provided by policy over Hungary. Communists defend Soviet intervention in Hungary with the argument that intervention was at the official request of the Hungarian Government. In fact, it is clear that the request for intervention did not come from the official government under Mr. Nagy, the Prime Minister, but from a rival regime set up by Mr. Kadar who was only one of the ministers in Mr. Nagy's cabinet. But the non-Communist powers have greatly weakened their case against the Communist argument by continuing to recognize the Kadar government as a legitimate successor to the Nagy government. They would have put themselves in a far stronger position if they had maintained that the legitimate Hungarian government which they had recognized and which had been admitted to the United Nations had been liquidated by Soviet military action so that Hungary was a territory under Soviet military occupation with no legitimate government but only a puppet organization set up by the Soviet authorities. It would have been possible to make a very strong case for holding that this was a correct view of the situation. And to have stated this as an official position would greatly have strengthened the case for demanding that United Nations observers should have the right to investigate the situation. An organization recognized as a government could plausibly claim the right to decide whether or not to admit U.N. observers to its territory. It would have been much harder to find a plausible excuse for excluding U.N. observers if one of the main issues requiring investigation had been whether there was a Hungarian government or merely local agents of the Soviet occupation forces claiming to be a government. Of course, all this would not have altered the ability of Soviet forces to retain control of Hungary so long as the non-Communist powers were not prepared to apply sanctions against the Soviet Union. What it could have done would have been to make it very much harder for Communist publicity to excuse Soviet action in Hungary.[1] As it is, by 1958, even in a debate in America the Soviet Ambassador can get away unchallenged with the statement that Soviet intervention was at the official request of the Hungarian Government.

The status of Berlin is another issue on which the Western powers do not seem to have made full use of their opportunities. The initiative has been left to Mr. Khrushchev who has argued that the position in Berlin is an anomalous remnant of the occupation regime of the immediate post-war period and has offered the solution of a Free City of West Berlin. Such arguments seem calculated to appeal to neutralist or potentially neutralist opinion and are sufficiently plausible to have a power of attraction. His tactics have managed both to keep the issue alive and, by postponing the dates on which he has threatened to take unilateral action, to provide a plausible claim that he is trying to reach a peaceful settlement. On the other side, Western official statements have usually appealed to treaty rights, which are related to the period of military occupation, and have stated a determination to preserve the freedom of the people of West Berlin, which is not obviously incompatible with proposals for a Free City. The Western powers have produced little in the way of positive proposals and have given the impression of merely fighting a delaying action.

---

1. This is not just being wise after the event. This paragraph is based on a letter of mine published in the *Sydney Morning Herald* in December, 1956.

The result has been to produce a situation in which a great deal of discussion in the West has been in terms of what concessions must ultimately be made to the Communists rather than in terms of what would be a genuinely satisfactory settlement or what concessions from the Communists should be required for a reasonable compromise.

The weak point in the Communist position is that they have been reluctant to state explicitly what are almost certainly their real grounds for disliking the present status of Berlin, that it is a serious gap in the Iron Curtain.

In recent years the population of the German Democratic Republic has been declining; the movement of refugees to the West has been greater than the natural increase of population. And Berlin is the route for the greater part of this movement because, with over 50,000 people travelling daily to work between the Eastern and Western sectors of the city, strict frontier control is not possible within Berlin. And there is also a leakage of ideas. People from the East can see in West Berlin the greater material prosperity of the non-Communist world and can read Western publications. Berlin is an advanced base for Western broadcasting and television and, in the other direction, for obtaining information about the Communist world. It is, therefore, quite reasonable to suspect that, while the immediate concessions demanded by the Communists may not be very serious, they are only demanded because they would weaken the ability of the Western powers to resist further Communist pressure aimed at preventing the movement of people and ideas between the Communist and non-Communist sections of the world through Berlin.

There are several points which the Western powers could make very effectively in their publicity. Firstly, the present status of Berlin is only anomalous because of the wider anomaly of the whole German situation, the control of East Germany by a regime which has no real claim to represent the people and which owes its power to Soviet military support. If the Soviet government honored its earlier undertakings to support German re-unification through free elections the anomalous situation of Berlin would automatically disappear. This of course brings in the wider issue of principle,—the non-Communist view that the claims of a government to have popular support are matters of fact which can only be decided by empirical evidence.

This general case has been made by Western commentators but not, so far as I know, in official Western statements.

Secondly, as an interim settlement pending German re-unification there might be some merit in plans for a Free City of Berlin under international guarantee, provided that the guarantees were effective and not subject to Communist veto. But here the obvious slogan for Western publicity would be, "If a Free City, then Berlin and not just West Berlin." This would mean the replacement of the four-power occupation regime, as a whole, by a new regime for the present situation. It would also be a genuine compromise. The Communists would gain some of their objectives because it would be easier to enforce frontier control between East Germany and the Free City than between the two sectors of the city. But they would have to make a real concession by giving up control over East Berlin. (Of course the Communists would have the theoretical possibility of winning elections in the new Free City, but this would be very unlikely.)

Though this would be a very effective reply to the Soviet proposals for a Free City of West Berlin it has not, so far as I know, been made at all from the Western side.

One can suggest a number of possible reasons for the failure of the non-Communist powers to make effective use of publicity. Especially in England one finds some indications in official statements of regret for the period when the public was prepared to leave the conduct of foreign policy in the hands of the professionals. Whatever advantages this system may have had it is not a possible alternative in the modern world. The public now realizes that international issues are of vital importance to them. If people who are trying to conduct a rational policy aimed at securing peace do not take the trouble to win public support for their policies the public demand for information and analysis of the international situation will simply be supplied from less reputable sources, such as Communist propaganda. Though it might perhaps be easier to settle international disputes in a world where no government engaged in psychological warfare, in the actual world a government which refuses to compete with the totalitarian regimes in influencing public opinion simply condemns itself to ineffectiveness.

American policy does not seem so inhibited by tradition but it does often seem that the people who decide policy think more in terms of how decisions or statements will influence Congress than in terms of how they will influence the people in other countries with which American foreign policy is concerned. Obviously American foreign policy has to obtain the support of Congress, but the sort of policy most attractive to Congress may differ from the sort of policy likely to attain American objectives. It may only be possible for an American administration to follow an effective foreign policy after an internal publicity campaign to win support for it from American public opinion.

Another factor is probably the influence of theories which imply that the sort of strategy suggested is bound to be futile. Though only a limited number of people concerned with the determination of non-Communist policy explicitly hold such theories they have a considerable influence because so many people try to avoid thinking out basic theoretical questions. It is not really possible to think about a highly complex subject such as international relations except in terms of some general concepts and theories. People who claim to be strictly empirical and uninterested in theory do not really avoid the use of theory but simply introduce their theory in the form of implicit assumptions. And a theory introduced in implicit assumptions often has more influence on people's thought than a theory which is used consciously with a knowledge of its limitations.

One can find a good many statements which imply an acceptance of the power politics analysis of the international system. It is assumed that the international system is one in which each nation always follows its national interest and that these national interests are naturally conflicting,—that the international system is a "zero sum game" in which one country can only gain at the expense of another. (If national interest is defined in terms of power over other countries or security based on superior power this natural conflict of interests follows logically.) In this theoretical system there is no room for anything but bargaining agreements and a balance of power is the only pos-

sible basis for peace. If national interests are naturally conflicting they cannot be harmonized by discussion and any hope
of replacing a balance of power by co-operation is "utopian".
The only possible form of co-operation is an alliance by which
some nations can increase their power against some other nation or alliance. The more extreme forms of this theory also
imply that people's beliefs are only what Marxists would call
"superstructure" and do not alter the real forces at work in
the international system. Professor Hans Morgenthau, for example, has argued that countries always really pursue their
national interests even when their leaders believe that they are
doing something quite different. And on this sort of view it
follows that nothing much can be accomplished by producing
a change in people's beliefs.

Power politics theories have been fashionable recently as a
reaction against earlier theories which tended to assume that the
international system was one in which national interests were
naturally harmonious. This assumption of natural harmony
implies that international conflicts can always be resolved if the
proper machinery exists for securing negotiation and mediation.
This general theory of the international system provides the
theoretical basis for neutralist views and it can be found very
clearly in many of Dr. Evatt's speeches.

In fact, it is just as unreasonable to assume that the international system is a system of naturally conflicting interests as it
is to assume that it is a system of naturally harmonious interests. It is unreasonable even to assume that it is a system which
can be explained in terms of interests. The Marxist analysis is
one example of a system which tries to explain everything in
terms of conflicting interests, in this case class interests and not
national interests. If the non-Communist powers wish to compete effectively with a policy based on Marxist theory they need
to work out more satisfactory theories and not to accept another
similar pseudo-scientific theory.[1]

---

1. I have criticized this type of theory at some length in Chapter VII
of my book *China and the Cold War,* so all I will try to do here is to
state one general objection to all the theories which try to explain the
very complex international system in terms of one single basic concept.
Though the ideal of scientific explanation is to produce a unified

Though the Marx-Leninist theory of the world situation is an inadequate and over-simplified one, a policy based on it is likely to be more effective than a policy based on an even more inadequate and over-simplified power politics theory or than a policy which tries to manage without any theoretical basis at all.

Though any simple general theory of international relations is bound to be unsatisfactory, international relations is still a field within which the basic principles of scientific method can be applied. It is possible to work out limited analyses which, within their fields, have the characteristics of the satisfactory scientific hypothesis, which yield conclusions which can be verified and which can be used with some degree of confidence as a basis for prediction and as a guide for the framing of policy. If the importance of adequate theory as a basis for effective action were fully realized in the non-Communist world it should be possible to work out policies considerably more effective than those based on the Marx-Leninist analysis.

The Long-Term Issues

Unless the present balance of power equilibrium breaks down in general war, the ability of different systems to attract support will be an important factor in determining the development of the international situation. If the situation develops towards peaceful co-existence it will become the main factor. If

---

theory it is certain that the study of international relations has not developed to the stage at which a satisfactory general theory could be produced. It is often useful to work out general theoretical models based on simplifying assumptions, provided one remembers how much the simplified model differs from the real world. The confusing theories are those which claim to be more than simplified models and which vary between narrow and wide definitions of their assumptions. If the assumptions are narrowly defined the theory is a definite hypothesis yielding deductions which can be empirically verified or refuted, and some of them can be refuted. If the assumptions are sufficiently widely defined the theory can be reconciled with all the empirical evidence but no longer yields any definite deductions. For example, one can say that power is the essential element in all international relationships if one gives a sufficiently wide definition of "power"; but a theory explaining international relations in terms of power then becomes unable

the cold war continues it may take second place to power but will still be important. The system which manages to offer the most satisfactory answers to the serious social problems of the modern world is likely to attract support from its competitors unless the the factor of power is strongly against it.

It is certainly an over-simplification to present the competition as between two systems, Communist-led socialism and Capitalism. The non-Communist world already contains a wide variety of systems which can only be lumped together if it is assumed that the only thing which matters about any society is whether or not there is some private ownership of the means of production. Orthodox Communists and extreme anti-Communists agree in believing that there can be only one form of socialism, but this is very doubtful. Jugoslavia has been trying something rather different and other Communist ruled countries have only been prevented from trying by Russian power. And many people want to try forms of socialism completely different from the Communist form.

To make any estimate of possible developments and to plan any long term strategy to influence developments one needs to consider what problems a satisfactory system has to answer. An attempt to do this is bound to be speculative, but a speculative estimate with some reasoned basis is better than none.

It is a commonplace that the modern world is one of rapid change and that science and technology are having profound effects on society, but fewer people try to put this into a long term perspective. In the long-run historical perspective, the changes which started in Europe a few centuries ago may mark a discontinuity in the trend of human history comparable to the

---

to distinguish the relationship between England and Australia from the relationship between the Soviet Union and Hungary.

These theories have a very confusing effect on those who believe in them. They feel satisfied that they have an adequate theoretical basis for their policy because they can always meet instances which might seem to refute their theories by using wide definitions of their assumptions. But if they want their theory to decide between practical alternatives they can only use the form based on the narrow definitions and, in this form, it is not a correct theory.

change produced several thousand years ago by the development of agriculture. The extra productivity of agriculture made civilization possible; and until recently all civilizations had a basis of peasant agriculture. The change from a hunting or nomad society to agriculture is not easy, as can still be seen in the case of such groups as the Australian aborigines. The agriculturist has to plan his activities far in advance and has to be ready to work hard for results which can only be obtained in the future. The changes in behavior required for the proper use of science and technology may be quite as great, and modern societies not only have to make the adjustment but also to find out what adjustment is needed. And they have to adjust to a comparatively rapid rate of change. An educated Chinese of less than a century ago might feel more at home in Han Dynasty China than in modern Shanghai. Even in Europe where the rate of change has been slower an educated European of the early 18th century might feel more at home in the Roman Empire than in modern Europe, both materially and even intellectually if his modern contacts were the scientists and technologists.[1]

The new situation offers very great possibilities, in particular a civilization in which all can share as opposed to the division of all previous civilized societies into a cultured ruling minority and an exploited majority. It also produces very serious problems. As compared with previous societies, a modern industrialized society requires for its efficient operation a much higher

---

1. One of the weak points in Toynbee's theory of history is that he does not seem to have any real understanding for science and so does not allow for the possibility that generalizations based on past civilizations may not hold for the future. He says a lot about technology but very little about science. (Quoting from memory, Galileo appears only once in the index of *A Study of History* and then only in a reference to the cosmology of Milton's *Paradise Lost*.) In fact the rapid development of modern technology has depended on basic science and this in turn has depended on a largely new way of thought which considers that the most reliable understanding of the world comes from a combination of working out theoretical models and the testing of their implications by experiment and observation and which recognizes that this kind of understanding is not final but may always need to be modified to allow for new evidence.

degree of co-ordination between the economic activities of all its members.[1] The problem is to work out a reasonably efficient system of co-ordination and also to ensure that the apparatus of co-ordination is not used to maintain the power of a new privileged exploiting group. The new society will almost certainly have to take conscious responsibility for things which most previous societies left to chance. (The population problem is an obvious example.) An industrialized society tends to break up former group organizations and to destroy former common cultural backgrounds and unless something is found to replace them many members of society will be dissatisfied and frustrated. All sorts of problems arise when very large numbers start to participate in political and cultural activities which were formerly confined to comparatively small ruling elites. (These are only a few of the most obvious problems.)

This kind of society will impose far greater strains on its members than societies which have a slower rate of change and are better adjusted to dealing with their problems. In the latter type of society a large proportion of the decisions which any individual has to make will be guided by established conventions or by the opinions of some group to which he or she belongs. In a rapidly changing society which has not made the adjustments needed to solve its problems an individual will have to make decisions with far less guidance and with far less confidence that acting according to accepted convention will produce the expected results. The new society may only be able to function efficiently if people develop new loyalties and new patterns of behavior, so people will face a conflict of loyalties and pressure to change accepted patterns of behavior.[2] Still

---

1. One illustration of this is the increased vulnerability of modern societies to a breakdown in co-ordination. In most pre-industrial societies trade and central authority could break down for considerable periods without having a very serious effect on a largely self-sufficient rural economy. (This could be seen in China during the war against Japan.) In a modern industrialized society with mechanized agriculture a breakdown of co-ordination would rapidly produce complete economic collapse.

2. Such problems of adjustment can be seen very clearly in those countries which are now trying to modernize themselves. To obtain an

greater strain is produced when it is obvious that some change is needed to solve social problems but when there is no agreement about what change is required. Even if people have managed to define the problems which their society faces they may still have to admit, if they are intellectually honest, that the most that can be said is that some lines of experiment look hopeful and might produce a solution. If social problems become really serious, people may be in the situation of wanting intensely to act but being quite uncertain about the right kind of action to take. And this is the type of situation which is used experimentally to produce neuroses. The economic crisis after 1929 was a good illustration. People wanted very strongly to attain what seemed a commonsense objective, to use unemployed resources to produce what society wanted. But the conventional policies prescribed by tradition completely failed to work and it took some time to develop an economic analysis capable of prescribing policies which could work. At present the sense of frustration is probably strongest among the educated minorities in under-developed countries who want intensely to develop their countries to catch up with the Western powers but do not see clearly how to do this.

In this sort of situation the acceptance of Communism, or some other totalitarian system, offers a subjective escape from the psychological strain. People can escape from a conflict of loyalties and the burden of personal responsibility for judging the right course of action by the single decision to transfer their loyalty to the Party or the Leader. At a slightly more rational

---

efficient administration they have to produce in their officials a new tradition of loyalty to the public service which will be stronger than the old traditions of loyalty to the family or other particular groups. To secure the efficient functioning of large scale industrial organizations requires patterns of behavior which are not important in small scale organization. When an organization becomes so large that most of its members have no personal contacts they can only co-ordinate their activities by developing a respect for conventional rules, accounting procedures, etc. which is not important in a small organization. (During the period when the Western powers were dominant in Asia their superiority depended quite as much on superior organizing ability as on superior weapons.)

level, Communism overcomes the uncertainty about the right
course of action by offering a general system of ideas which
claims to give all the answers and a system of organization and
tactics for getting the power to apply the answers.

And to some extent Communism actually does give answers.
Communism does offer a method by which an economically
backward country can industrialize itself. Communist mass organizations do something to offer people a sense of participation
in a common social life and to produce group loyalties which
will maintain social discipline in forms adjusted to a new society.
Marx-Leninism as an official orthodoxy offers some common
intellectual basis for society to fill the vacuum left by the collapse
of traditional systems. The Communist Party provides a new
ruling elite to replace those which had provided political and
cultural leadership in previous societies when they had been
functioning effectively. The centralized planned economy can
fairly easily prevent the development of mass unemployment;
and so on.

One can state a very strong case for holding that these answers
are not very satisfactory answers and are likely to become even
less satisfactory as Communist society develops. The establishment of Marx-Leninism as an official orthodoxy is not, as Communists claim it to be, the establishment of a scientific theory
for the guidance of society but is a rejection of the basic principle of scientific method that all theories are subject to possible
revision in the light of new evidence. And it does actually
inhibit adjustment and development. Industrialization under
Communism involves a very heavy price in human suffering
and one of the developments inhibited by Marx-Leninist orthodoxy is the sort of economic analysis which would enable a
planned economy to adjust itself to satisfy consumers' demands
efficiently when the standard of living has risen above subsis-
tence level.[1] There is a contradiction between securing mass
participation in social processes and maintaining the power of
the Communist Party; insofar as some organization in Com-

---

1. Cf. "The problem of 'success indicators' in Soviet economy." By A.
Nove, *Economica,* February, 1958.

munist ruled society is successful in satisfying the demands of its members for participation in social life it is likely to develop loyalties and ideas of its own and so become a threat to the Communist monopoly of power. Instead of exploitation disappearing and the state withering away as social conflicts lessen, which would mark an adjustment to the possibility of a civilization in which all can share, the actual trend of Communist ruled societies has been towards what Wittfogel calls "Oriental Despotism" or, to use another terminology, what Toynbee calls "arrested civilizations" in which social conflicts are so bitter that the ruling dominant minority can only maintain its power by resisting all social change.

But, however unsatisfactory the Communist answers to social problems may be, their power of attraction depends on whether or not more satisfactory answers are available. It is clear, for example, that Communism does have a considerable power of attraction for the intelligentsia in under-developed countries and this is quite understandable. Communism offers a proved technique for the seizure of power and it may be quite reasonable to believe that a process of social reform can only be started after a revolution has removed the control of the state from vested interests opposed to any reform. Communism offers a proved method of starting a process of rapid industrialization and making rapid social changes. A hierarchical monolithic party offers a method of securing a new public service with new loyalties. People may realize that the actual results of Communist-led revolutions have been much less attractive than they are pictured in Communist publicity and yet, if they feel sufficiently frustrated, be prepared to support Communism as a means of getting something done. And this feeling of frustration will arise if other systems do not offer any basis for an alternative program.

Non-Communist economics has now started to offer the theoretical basis for an alternative economic program, though interest in working out the theoretical problems of economic development in under-developed countries is fairly recent. In other fields the intellectual in an under-developed country will find that the non-Communist world has few suggestions to offer him. He will not find an alternative program for revolution. He will find a good deal about the values of liberty and democracy but very little about how these values can be realized in his society. Studies of the working of democratic institutions in countries with a long tradition of national solidarity and respect for law and with an educated population will have little relevance for a country in which none of these conditions exist. If he studies the history of the past century he will find that the institutions of Western representative government often fail to work when transplanted to countries with different background and traditions, even in the countries of Eastern and Southern Europe which share a great deal of the same cultural tradition. He will find that a number of non-Communists who are strong supporters of democracy in their own countries argue that democratic institutions are a luxury which an under-developed country cannot afford if it wants competent government or rapid economic and social progress.[1]

If non-Communist systems wish to compete with Communism in appeal to the intelligentsia of under-developed countries they will have to offer in other fields the sort of analysis they are beginning to offer in economics. It is quite unreasonable to conclude that the people of under-developed countries do not want liberty and democracy because they do not want the particular institutions through which Western countries have tried to obtain liberty and democracy. It is fairly certain that people in all countries would like to have the sort of security against arbitrary action by officials which is provided in Western countries by the rule of law. If they do not actively demand it this may only be because they have no experience that such security is possible. And it is fairly certain that the people in all countries would like to have the power to compel the government to change policies which are generally unpopular. Most countries which have failed to provide some measure of liberty and democracy in this sense have a long history of fairly frequent local revolts. And if people are prepared to risk their lives in a form of

1. This is not entirely a modern development. For example, one can find that foreigners who were professed believers in liberal democracy nevertheless supported Yuan Shih-K'ai and the warlord regimes in China.

protest against oppressive officials or unpopular policies which has a very small chance of success, it is fairly certain that there would be strong support for institutions which offered a much higher chance of successful protest with very much smaller risk. There are also a good many examples from recent history which show that a constitution modelled on those of the Western democracies does not necessarily provide this sort of liberty and democracy for most of the population. Again, as soon as people reach a certain level of education and political consciousness they are likely to want the right to discuss public affairs, to organize themselves to influence government policy and, if necessary, to replace the government by another one if the majority of the people dislike it. And they are likely to realize that if they want to discuss and influence public affairs they need some means of obtaining sufficient accurate information to form their own judgment on political and social questions.

What the non-Communist world needs to provide is a political theory and sociology of under-developed countries which is not simply descriptive but which can suggest the sort of measures through which these basic demands for liberty and democracy, and the equally basic demand for a competent administration, could be realized, starting from the existing social system. The result would certainly not be like what Communism offers, a single system of theory and strategy which claims to give all the answers in every case. There would probably be a number of different theories suggesting different programs and the theories would not claim to be more than reasonable hypotheses needing revision as more evidence appeared. But this would be quite enough for the purpose. People who wanted to work out a program of action for their country would be able to find the concepts and basic theories which they needed to think clearly about the subject and would not need to feel frustrated. Communism might still be attractive to people who did not like the responsibility of thinking for themselves and wanted a system which would tell them all the answers; but many people in all countries are sufficiently intelligent and mentally stable to see that many of the answers provided by Communism are not

really satisfactory and to realize that any system which claims
to give all the answers is promising more than it can perform.

I am not going to attempt a one man job on a vast subject by
trying even to outline the sort of theories which might be produced. I only suggest that the non-Communist countries have the
trained intelligence available to offer a great deal more than
they are offering now.

And it is not only in the under-developed countries that
competition exists between Communist and non-Communist
systems of ideas as the basis for programs trying to solve social
problems. One of the most important fields is within the Communist ruled countries themselves.

Since the death of Stalin many Communist regimes have ex-
perimented with some relaxation of their controls and the results
have provided evidence of a great deal of dissatisfaction with
Communist ideas as well as with living conditions under Communist rule. There have everywhere been demands for greater
freedom of thought and discussion and it seems clear that
Marx-Leninism as an official orthodoxy has not managed to win
general support even from the younger generation which has
never been taught anything else. Even in the Soviet Union there
are signs that many of the present generation of students are
thinking about questions to which the orthodox ideology does
not give satisfactory answers. However, dissatisfaction with a system does little to change it unless it is combined with support
for some alternative and a system of controls can inhibit the discussion and interchange of ideas which would make it possible
for people to work out an alternative for themselves.

Though there is strong evidence that there is a great deal of
dissatisfaction with the existing system in most Communist
ruled countries it also seems clear that the non-Communist world
does not, at present, provide a really attractive alternative. Even
when dissatisfaction with Communist rule has led to actual revolt the demands expressed have been for a different variety
of socialism and not for the reestablishment of a private enterprise system, except in peasant farming and family scale business.
Other evidence, such as studies of opinion among refugees, also
suggests that many people who strongly dislike Communist rule

still feel that really satisfactory answers to many social problems are not provided in the non-Communist world.[1]

In the situation of competitive co-existence, which will only be partly modified by a continuation of the cold war, one basic potential advantage of the non-Communist countries is their freedom to develop new ideas and try new experiments. Most of them are not tied down by anything like the Marx-Leninist official orthodoxy and their organization allows much greater scope for independent initiative and experiment. But this potential advantage counts for nothing unless it is used, unless the non-Communist countries do show initiative in working out ways of dealing with their problems which are obviously superior to anything the Communist system can offer.

At present many non-Communist regimes are much more stable than any Communist regime; the proportion of the population who might try to overthrow the regime by revolution if the state did not have organized force to prevent it is very much smaller. On the other hand, in many of them there is a great deal of not very clearly formulated dissatisfaction and there are some serious social problems which may become more serious in the future.

One obvious danger for the democratic powers is the tendency towards what might be called the "vested interest state". Normal democratic procedures are very effective for allowing pressure groups to work for their particular interests and the total of particular interests does not add up to the general interest. This can be seen most clearly in the economic field though it applies in others as well. Any particular group can often promote its economic interests most effectively by measures which increase its share of the national income even though they may involve some reduction in the total national income. Though everyone could benefit from a rise in total national income the benefit is so widely diffused that no particular group will feel inclined to press strongly for measures which would raise the total national income but might offend some vested interests. The efforts of

---

1. A very clear statement of this general view is given by a Polish refugee, Czeslaw Milosz, in a chapter entitled "Looking to the West," in his book, *The Captive Mind.* (Alfred A. Knopf, Inc., New York, 1953.)

rival pressure groups to get a larger share of the national income are likely very largely to cancel out and the result is a system working far below its possible efficiency to the disadvantage of almost everyone in it.

Such an economic situation is a degeneration of the free competitive market which, within fairly wide limits, is a far more efficient system for allocating resources in response to consumers' demand than anything yet devised by those in control of centrally planned economies. One can find the people in charge of planning in Communist ruled states making continual efforts with only limited success to cope with problems which would simply disappear if they allowed a competitive market system to operate. In fact, some observers of the Soviet Union have argued that the Soviet system has only worked as well as it has because a primitive and illegal market system has to some extent short circuited the confusion and delays of highly centralized planning.[1] However, when monopolies, cartels or price fixing agreements become sufficiently widespread the free competitive market has disappeared.[2]

The problems produced by vested interests are not confined to the field of economics. In many democratic countries they are very serious in political and cultural fields.

Such a system is extremely frustrating. Things which obviously need to be done will be held up by interminable negotiations to square the various vested interests involved and, since the various pressure groups are normally trying to gain at each others' expense, the first reaction of any group will be to suspect and oppose any proposals coming from other people rather than to co-operate.

1. Cf. Edward Crankshaw, *Khrushchev's Russia,* Penguin Books, Baltimore, 1959, pp. 72-75.

2. At the intellectually respectable level, the debate on free enterprise versus public ownership or control turns largely on the question of what should be done when a competitive market system does not work properly, because of this kind of degeneration, because of wide differences between individual and social costs or returns, or for various other reasons. The intellectually dishonest positions are those which refuse to admit the limitations and possible degeneration of a free market system or which refuse to admit the difficulties of getting an efficient and democratic planned economy.

The frustrations produced by this sort of system do often incline people to favor some totalitarian system in which the government can force through any measures it considers to be in the public interest regardless of the vested interests involved. Of course, a totalitarian system has one supreme vested interest, that of the ruling Party. But the ruling Party has at least to accept responsibility for the system as a whole which the particular pressure groups in a democratic system do not; and in some fields the Party's interests may not conflict with the public interest. Soviet progress in science is an important example of this. The Soviet Union is now benefiting from a long term program of investment in providing really good scientific and technical education. The leading non-Communist powers could have made the same investment with a proportionately smaller burden on their resources but no one was prepared to push for expenditure which would take a long time to produce its full results and which no particular pressure group was interested in supporting. Again, though some of the extremely wide income differences in Communist ruled countries represent exploitation by the ruling group, many non-Communist societies suffered from unwillingness to pay the salaries necessary to attract people of ability into work of importance to society.

This does not show that totalitarian systems are necessarily superior to democratic systems. The power of a totalitarian government to push through policies which are in the public interest can equally be used to push through measures which are extremely harmful to society, and often is so used. And when a democratic system is working for a common objective it is often much more efficient than an authoritarian system because the government is subject to criticism and pressure from public opinion.[1] What it does show is that totalitarian systems can provide some solution of problems which a number of democratic systems have not yet been able to handle satisfactorily.

There have been demands in most Communist ruled countries for freedom of discussion and freedom of publication and it seems fairly clear that the Party control of literature and art has

---

1. The two World Wars provided a good illustration of this. In both, Germany started with a more efficient organization than its democratic opponents and ended with a less efficient one.

been extremely unfavorable for the production of good original work. But it is doubtful whether the people in Communist ruled countries who demand more freedom would consider that the situation in the democratic countries provides a really attractive alternative. And many people in the democratic countries would agree that it is unsatisfactory in many ways. For example, the citizen of a democratic country has access to far more information than the citizen of any Communist ruled country, but he has to go to a fair amount of trouble to get it. Though an informed public opinion is very important for a democracy, extremely little information on public affairs is given by many newspapers which devote most of their space to sport, scandal, gossip and crime. A great deal of opinion in democratic countries is dissatisfied with the cultural standards which predominate under commercialized free enterprise and also with the working of various schemes of censorship and control. The dissatisfaction with the working of commercialized free enterprise has led a number of countries to put their broadcasting services under some form of state organized monopoly and there is a good deal of controversy about how these should be run. Altogether, though the situation in the democratic countries is clearly better than that in the Communist ruled countries (unless one attaches supreme importance to the avoidance of sex in literature and art), it is also clear that the greater degree of freedom leaves many problems unsolved.

One could easily continue with other instances to support the conclusion that, if the non-Communist countries wish to prove the more attractive in a situation of competitive co-existence, they cannot afford to be complacent about their existing institutions but need to study their defects and try to find ways of improving them.

There is no reason to suppose that improvement is impossible. There are, for example, very marked differences in the extent to which non-Communist regimes have been able to act in the public interest and overcome vested interests. And it should be possible to analyze the reasons for this and to suggest the sort of measures likely to reverse a trend towards the "vested interest state".

As in the case of international relations, it is fairly certain that attempts to work out general theories of society similar to the Marx-Leninist analysis would be confusing rather than helpful. The present state of the social sciences does not provide the basis for a general theory from which one could deduce the measures necessary to enable society to make satisfactory adjustments to the problems of a rapidly changing world. On the other hand, there is enough knowledge available to make it possible to work out limited analyses which would be really helpful in dealing with particular social problems. However, if non-Communist societies are to make use of their potential advantages in solving their problems, it is necessary to have a lot of people studying these problems at a fundamental level.

When the problems that some society faces are the result of gradual changes, it is probable that they can be dealt with fairly well if the people responsible for practical policy show common sense and goodwill. A process of trial and error will produce a fairly good adjustment to a gradually changing situation. However, when a society faces a rapidly changing situation and problems that are different both in scale and in quality from those which it has previously experienced, something more is needed. It is very unlikely that the new problems will be successfully handled unless they are studied scientifically and fundamentally, and this can seldom be done by the people responsible for practical policy. The commonsense practical approach will normally be inhibited by all sorts of implicit assumptions which may have been valid in the old situation but have ceased to be so in the new one; fundamental research will demand theoretical thinking and long term investigations for which the people responsible for practical policy do not usually have either the time or the qualifications.

Fundamental research may start from interest in particular practical problems but will try to evolve theories and concepts relevant to a whole class of problems and will try to follow out the full implications of some problem, which may often lead back to quite general theoretical and philosophical questions. There is nothing specially new about this. Many of the books which are now classics in social science or philosophy are to a considerable extent examples of fundamental research. Their authors started from an interest in the problems of their time and tried to work out concepts and theories in terms of which these problems could be handled.

Fundamental research depends on a belief that rational and scientific thinking can be applied to all problems with useful results, even when the limitations of human knowledge and the imperfections of the human mind make it impossible to obtain exact and certain answers, while the following out of the full implications of some problem implies a belief in the unity of knowledge. This belief in rational thinking is ultimately a matter of faith. Though some Roman Catholic theorists have argued that "the use of reason precedes faith" it is probably nearer the truth to say, "the use of reason implies faith." It is very doubtful whether it is possible to give any rational proof that the universe is an orderly system to which reason can be applied and attempts to do so can be shown to lead to paradoxes. It follows that fundamental research is not likely to flourish except in a culture which does have a faith which implies a belief in reason.[1] At a more practical level, fundamental research will be seriously hampered in a society where people are, for various reasons, afraid of fundamental thinking.

It seems fairly clear that Communist regimes are afraid of fundamental thinking and this can be explained by the hypothesis suggested above, that belief in Communism is a neurotic response to social problems. Faced with a situation in which it seems obvious that something needs to be done but in which it is very hard to decide on the right course of action, people escape from the strain by accepting an over-simplified analysis which claims to tell them what needs to be done. They can then devote themselves to working for the cause in which they believe, and it is obvious that working for a cause in which one believes is some-

---

1. A belief in reason is much wider than a belief in some particular system of reasoning. J. S. Haldane once defined materialism as a belief that the universe could be completely explained in terms of the existing working hypotheses of natural science. A belief that complete explanation was possible within any other known system would be equally restrictive.

thing which most people find extremely satisfying. So long as Communism appears to offer people the chance of devoting themselves to the building of a new and better society it has a real power of attraction. The difficulties arise when the new society turns out to be not so obviously better. One way out of these difficulties is to maintain the system of belief by refusing to admit any evidence incompatible with it, and this is a course which many Communists follow. They insist that any shortcomings or lack of popular support in Communist led societies are due to the influence of pre-Communist ideas or the activities of anti-Communist agents and not to any defects in the basic Communist analysis of social problems, and they avoid any discussion in which their theories would meet serious criticism. Another way out is to become cynical about Communist beliefs and to act simply for personal power or self-interest within the Communist system, and it seems that this has also happened to a considerable extent. The only other way out is to admit that Marx-Leninism has not given all the answers and that fundamental research is still needed to solve social problems. But this is "revisionism." If Marx-Leninism were really a scientific theory of society its continual revision to account for new evidence and to deal with new problems would be natural and accepted. The violent reaction against "revisionism" is explained by the hypothsis that belief in Marx-Leninism is a way of escape from problems. To accept revision would be to admit that the escape had not been successful and that the problems still remained in the real world.

The same sort of analysis can obviously be applied to the non-Communist world. One can find many cases in which people seem to have attained subjective satisfaction by devotion to over-simplified systems of belief to which fundamental research would be disturbing. But their influence as an obstacle to fundamental research is much smaller than in Communist ruled societies. There is, however, another form of neurotic response to social problems which is much more common in the non-Communist world and which can explain some important aspects of modern Western culture. The frustration produced by a desire to act and an uncertainty about how to act can also be removed by believing that the problems are insoluble, or at least that no rationally based course of action can do anything to solve them. Such a belief removes the feeling of frustration by removing any sense of responsibility for action to deal with social problems. This way of escape may not be quite so satisfying emotionally as devotion to a cause but it involves much less risk and sacrifice and it can give a feeling of superiority over those who are trying to solve problems.

The type of theory which completely satisfies the condition of removing any sense of responsibility for action to deal with social problems is one which implies that the development of society is completely determined by forces other than decisions based on rational judgment, and that when people believe that they can determine their actions by decisions based on rational choice they are simply deceiving themselves. A good many people do hold theories of this type in spite of the logical difficulty involved in any completely determinist theory. (If people's decisions are really always determined and cannot be based on rational choice, how can the people who believe in the determinist theory show that they have made a rational choice in deciding that the theory is true?)

What is far more common and far more important is a bias in attitude and emphasis. This whole analysis is in terms of unconscious or semi-conscious mental processes. People do not make conscious decisions to accept beliefs which provide subjective escape from a situation which they find too frustrating. It is very unlikely that anyone ever became a Communist by saying to himself, "I will accept Marx-Leninism even though I know it to be an over-simplified theory because it will provide me with a cause to which I can devote myself," or that anyone deliberately decided to believe in a determinist theory because it would free him from a sense of responsibility. What an emotional strain can do is to incline people to accept certain views and it can very easily influence attitude and emphasis which are usually only semi-conscious. It is one thing to accept beliefs which at some points are defective by the standards of rational judgment; it is much easier to consider a general subject with a certain bias in attitude and emphasis.

In modern Western culture there are signs of a bias in attitude against the sort of thinking involved in fundamental research related to the problems of society. And this bias can be explained by an unwillingness to face the responsibility of trying to deal with social problems. For example, two very different attitudes are possible towards the work which has shown that non-rational forces have a far greater influence on human behavior than the social scientists of fifty or a hundred years ago realized. If one is interested in social action based on rational judgment one can consider this work as something which makes it easier to distinguish rational judgment from rationalization and which provides an understanding of the possibilities and conditions for effective action.

The expectations of what can be achieved by action based on rational judgment may be much more limited than those of 19th century liberals, but they are much less likely to be disappointed. And one can find a number of people who approach the subject with this attitude. On the other hand, one can find many people whose writings suggest that they find a good deal of satisfaction in being able to show that human action is far less influenced by rational judgment than many people supposed and who take very little interest in those aspects of human behavior in which rational judgment can play a part.

To give an illustration of this last point directly relevant to this book:—a lecture I gave discussing what sort of foreign policy was most likely to promote certain objectives was criticized by someone of considerable academic reputation on the grounds that I had taken a wrong view of policy. Most modern work on policy, it was argued, studied policies as a result of social pressures and not as a means of attaining objectives. Now, of course, policy is influenced by social pressures and no policy can be carried out unless it can obtain the necessary support. However, as a matter of commonsense observation, governments and other organizations differ very greatly in the extent to which they follow policies likely to promote their objectives, that is, in the extent to which they act rationally in terms of their objectives. Any study of policy formation which considers policies only as a response to social pressures and refuses to consider them as a means to attain objectives has debarred itself from considering the interesting and important question, "What makes some organizations competent and others incompetent?" (Part of the answer is almost certainly that competent organizations which follow policies likely to attain their objectives are those in which some people do formulate objectives, work out the policies most likely to attain them, and try to secure the necessary support for these policies; while incompetent organizations are those in which policy is improvised in response to pressures which often represent partial or unconsidered judgments, that is, organizations in which people do not think about policies as a means of attaining objectives.)

If people want to avoid a sense of responsibility for the problems of society it is natural that they should emphasize the irrational elements in social behavior and tend to avoid study of the problems relevant for effective social action.

Another attitude which can be explained in the same way is extreme emphasis on exactness and certainty in knowledge. Obviously exactness and certainty are desirable but in many fields there is a choice between exact and certain knowledge which gives no answer to interesting and important questions and rather less exact and certain knowledge which does give some answer.

One can trace a long way back in Western culture a distinction between people who have been interested in trying to form general theories or to answer interesting questions, even though the results could only be speculative and uncertain, and people who have been interested in establishing exact and certain results, even though this involved restriction to limited fields and narrow questions. Ideally the two types of work are complementary. Speculation becomes hopelessly vague unless it has a basis of well established detailed knowledge, exact research becomes largely futile unless its choice of topics is guided by more general theory. In practice, unfortunately, the two interests are often competitive.

Wittgenstein's saying, "Whatever can be said at all can be said clearly,"[1] could be a slogan representing a widespread attitude.

---

1. In the introduction to *Tractatus Logico-philosophicus.*

It is assumed that all worthwhile knowledge must be exact and certain. All the interesting and important problems to which it is not possible to give an exact and certain answer are relegated to a field in which no proper standards can be applied, in which one opinion is as good as another and in which decisions can only be made on the basis of expediency or emotional preference.[1]

This attitude has had an increasing influence in Western intellectual life. In many fields it has become fashionable to produce monographs on very restricted topics, compilations from established sources, purely abstract theoretical models, or purely descriptive studies and to avoid any general interpretations or any attempts to draw conclusions relevant to actual problems. The underlying assumption seems to be that work which is of general interest or which is relevant to actual problems involves some loss of academic integrity.

Such an intellectual atmosphere is extremely unfavorable to the sort of fundamental research which could suggest answers to social problems. Work relevant to actual problems cannot expect to produce certain and definite conclusions. It could only hope to produce analyses with the characteristics of a scientific hypothesis, and a scientific hypothesis cannot in principle give certain knowledge but is always subject to revision in the light of new evidence.

Practical decisions nearly always have to be taken on the basis of limited information which can only yield uncertain knowledge. But there is still a wide difference between rational action which is guided by such knowledge as can be obtained, and irrational action which is not so guided. The view that all worthwhile knowledge must be exact and certain has an important influence in discouraging rational action, in so far as such a view is accepted. One of the most effective statements on this was

---

1. One quite influential variety of this attitude is the view that, as a matter of principle, social scientists should confine themselves to fields in which they can produce quantitative results which can be expressed in mathematical forms. This automatically excludes from the field of possible scientific study a large proportion of the interesting and important questions in social science.

made by R. G. Collingwood in describing the influence of the "realist" school of philosophers at Oxford.[1]

"Their pupils, with habits and characters yet unformed, stood on the threshold of life; many of them of public life. Half a century ago, young people in that position had been told that by thinking about what they were doing, or were about to do, they would become likely on the whole to do it better. . . . The 'realist', on the contrary, said to his pupils, 'If it interests you to study this, do so; but don't think it will be any use to you. . . .' . . . The inference which any pupil could draw for himself was that for guidance in the problems of life, since one must not seek it from thinkers or from thinking, from ideals or from principles, one must look to people who were not thinkers (but fools), to processes that were not thinking (but passion), to aims that were not ideals (but caprices), and to rules that were not principles (but rules of expediency)."

This gloomy picture is only one aspect of Western culture, though a fairly important aspect. If it ever became dominant the prospects for the non-Communist societies would be poor. They might still succeed even though they did very little to solve their problems if the Communist regimes made sufficiently serious mistakes. Otherwise, a non-Communist leadership, improvising policy in response to the pressures of the moment and lacking the courage and initiative which come from ideas, would probably lose against a fanatical Communist leadership. And many of the Western intellectuals whose attitudes make them sceptical about the possibility of rational action to deal with social problems are, in fact, completely defeatist about the possibility of competing with Communists, even when they have no liking for Communism.

One can find quite prominent intellectuals in the non-Communist world who claim to be supporters of democracy but whose underlying theoretical position is quite incompatible with democracy. The assumption behind democratic institutions is that a process of discussion and study of the evidence will tend to produce a consensus of opinion about what is the right thing to

1. *An Autobiography.* By R. G. Collingwood, Oxford University Press, 1939.

do. And there is a good deal of evidence to suggest that a society co-ordinated by such a consensus is more efficient than a totalitarian system, that freedom and discussion can produce more initiative and more rapid correction of mistakes. But discussion and study of the evidence will only tend to produce a consensus of opinion if human opinions are influenced by reason. This basic assumption is denied, not only by the Marxists who hold that beliefs are determined by class status, but also by those who hold that scientific reasoning can only be applied in limited fields of human interest (e.g. only to the quantitatively measurable), by the more extreme behaviorists, and by those who hold that beliefs are completely determined by cultural tradition. On such theories about the determination of human beliefs there is no reason to suppose that democratic processes will ever produce a consensus of opinion and it follows quite logically that the co-ordination needed for the effective functioning of any society can only be produced by submission to authority.[1]

To some extent it is possible for people not to accept the logical implications of their basic beliefs. Many people are quite sincere in maintaining that they believe in democratic institutions while holding theoretical views which imply that society must be either authoritarian or anarchic. But people in this confused position are not capable of thinking clearly about the principles of democracy or offering useful guidance for possible means of developing towards democracy from a primitive or a totalitarian society. They also quite often provide interesting instances on a small

1. This paragraph is, of course, a simplification of a very large problem. Scientific reasoning does not, in principle, give final and certain knowledge and, dealing with complicated questions on the basis of limited evidence, is unlikely often to produce complete consensus. But all that is needed for the working of a democratic system is that there should be general agreement that there is a reasonable case for a limited number of alternative policies and that it is better to choose between them on the basis of some convention such as majority vote or delegation of power to an individual rather than to continue indecision beyond a certain time.

Also, the various forms of relativist theory are reactions against over-simplified absolutist theories. Cultural traditions or class status certainly play some part in determining people's opinions. It is not possible to defend the crude rationalist view that rationally demonstrated conclusions must inevitably be accepted. It is possible to defend

scale of the way in which relativist theories of truth lead logically to the types of behavior one finds in totalitarian society. If someone believes that truth, in the field of social science, is a matter of opinion not testable by rational objective standards he has no logical obstacle against drawing the conclusion that he is making a true statement when he says something calculated to produce results which he considers expedient. Equally, if truth is only a matter of opinion, authority can only be maintained against criticism by penalizing the critic,—to admit that criticism was justified would be to accept the authority of the critic's opinion.

If this relativist view of truth became dominant in Western culture the ultimate victory of some totalitarian system would be almost certain. It may, however, already have passed the peak of its influence and, in American academic life, one can find a growing awareness of its implications.[1] One can also see a growing interest in fundamental research of the type which would be likely to help non-Communist societies in solving their problems and would make them better able to compete with totalitarian systems.

It is extremely difficult to predict developments because one is dealing with a situation with a good deal of instability, (in differing degrees many people are dissatisfied in both Communist ruled and non-Communist societies), and also with processes in which there may be a great deal of positive feedback, (the successful handling of some problems will stimulate the successful

---

a view that reason plays some part in determining human beliefs and actions, and that it can play a larger part in so far as men come to understand the influence producing irrationalism. And it is this latter view that some theories deny.

Just before making these final corrections I was reviewing two books on the influence of cultural tradition on modern China which provided an interesting illustration of the difference in basic assumptions discussed above. One argued, "Valid conclusions of science . . . are empirically demonstrable, hence ultimately irresistible." The other argued, "The intrinsic truth or falsehood of a doctrine . . . is purely a matter of academic dissertation. What matters to the historian and to the man of action is its effectiveness."

1. E.g. the article by Professor Hans Morgenthau in the *New York Times Magazine* of 22nd. November, 1959.

handling of others and attractive ideas may spread very

If the non-Communist societies are able to make prope.
their opportunities their prospects in competitive co-ex.
should be very good. If they are able to use their greater fre
of thinking and experiment to develop ideas which can hel,
handle the general social problems of the modern world, the non-
Communist societies will not only become stronger in themselves
but also be able to exercise a strong power of attraction both in
the under-developed countries and in the Communist ruled
countries. And the influence of ideas might be quite rapid in both
types of country. The case of the under-developed countries has
already been discussed. In the case of the Communist ruled
countries the potential demand is for ideas which would enable
people to formulate the questions they are starting to think about
but which cannot be adequately expressed or handled in terms of
the concepts of Marx-Leninism. In both cases the type of non-
Communist scholarship which avoids interpretation or refuses
to attempt answers to interesting and important questions is
likely to seem unattractive and may even seem to confirm the
Communist criticisms of non-Communist society, but ideas which
were relevant to social problems might spread very rapidly. Some
recent accounts of the intellectual atmosphere in the Soviet
Union suggest the possibility of a situation in which the right
type of idea might have a catalytic effect and produce a rapid
change to something considerably different from Marx-Leninist
orthodoxy.

For people who would like certainty and security the instability of the situation is probably very worrying. For people
who want interest and opportunity the unstable situation offers
both because it is one in which comparatively limited initial
actions could produce far reaching results.

Is peaceful co-existence possible?

The main theme of this book has been that this is a question
which cannot be answered definitely without more evidence and
that people on both sides who want peaceful co-existence should
co-operate to clear up the uncertainties about whether or not

peaceful co-existence is possible at present and, if it is not, to consider what changes would be needed to make it possible. Any answer given on the basis of present evidence can only be tentative.

It seems that Communists could give a satisfactory alternative explanation of the evidence which suggests that the Soviet Union under Stalin's leadership was an aggressive power, at least from 1939 on after the replacement of Litvinov by Molotov. One cannot be sure about the relative importance of the different motives for aggressiveness; how far it came from a desire for security against a non-Communist world which was assumed to be irreconcilably hostile, how far it came from a fanatical desire to realize the Marx-Leninist prediction that Communism must dominate the world, or how far it came from the need of the Communist ruling group for international tension as a means to retain its internal power.

One can make some estimate of the change away from the Communism of the Stalinist period needed to make peaceful co-existence possible. There would have to be enough revision of Marx-Leninist orthodoxy to make it possible for Communists to believe that capitalist regimes genuinely wanted peace, provided that these regimes gave reasonable evidence of their peaceful intentions. (This would remove the motive for aggressiveness based on the desire for security.) There would have to be enough revision of Marx-Leninist orthodoxy to make Communists willing to admit the Communist-led movements did not necessarily have mass support. (This would remove the motive for aggressiveness to help the spread of Communism.) There would have to be a willingness to join in discussions trying to reach genuine agreement with people who, in the Communist view, had different class standpoints, which would also involve some modifications of Marx-Leninist orthodoxy. And there would have to be sufficient internal stability to make it unnecessary for the regime to rely on international tension to maintain its internal power. The regime remaining after these changes might still call itself Communist but it would be a revisionist version of Communism, at least as revisionist as Jugoslavia under Tito or Poland under Gomulka.

The immediate prospects for peaceful co-existence seem less good now than they did in 1956 because of the reversal of the trends away from Stalinism. China in particular has become violently anti-revisionist since the middle of 1957 and it is hard to see how Mao Tse-tung could make another experiment in liberalization. Many of the people who expressed criticisms during the more liberal period began by saying that formerly they had been afraid to speak and only did so because Chairman Mao had promised that people could speak freely without fear of reprisals. Now that the "anti-rightest" campaign has taken reprisals against those who trusted in Mao's promise and expressed criticisms, it will be a long time before anyone will believe in similar promises. (1957 may prove to be the decisive year in which Mao Tse-tung finally destroyed the possibility of basing his power on popular support.) As implied by this violent anti-revisionism, Chinese policy towards the non-Communist world has become more intransigent and more hostile.

In the Soviet Union the anti-revisionist movement does not seem to have gone nearly so far or to have taken a form so difficult to reverse. Soviet foreign policy under Khrushchev is certainly much less intransigent and hostile than under Stalin though Khrushchev's pronouncements still leave room for serious doubts as to whether he really wants peaceful co-existence or whether he has merely come to realize that a general war fought with atomic weapons would be too dangerous and costly a way of trying to extend Communist power.

In the long run, the prospects are a good deal more hopeful. It has become clear since 1956 that orthodox Communist indoctrination has not produced a stable system of belief and has not managed to eradicate a tendency to rational thinking. Not only in Eastern Europe but also in China and the Soviet Union the youth and students (who in the Soviet Union had never known anything but a Communist regime) showed strong dissatisfaction with the ideas with which they had been indoctrinated. One of the more hopeful features of Soviet society is that, according to many reports, the younger generation now just beginning to rise to positions of responsibility has an independence of thought and interest in the truth which is largely lacking in the generation which survived in public life under Stalin.* This suggests that, unless a new set of purges eliminates all the independently minded people in the new generation, the chances of the Soviet system changing in a way which would make peaceful co-existence possible are likely to increase in the future.

This statement of the problem has assumed that any changes needed to make peaceful co-existence possible are much more likely to be on the Communist side than on the non-Communist side. I think that this assumption could be justified.

It would be much more satisfactory if Communist representatives were prepared to make a clear and consistent statement of their reasons for suspecting that the non-Communist powers were aggressive. In fact, as has been argued in an earlier section, Communist statements on this subject have been neither clear nor consistent. Insofar as Communist suspicions are based on theoretical deductions from Marx-Leninist theory showing that capitalist regimes must be aggressive the non-Communist powers could only remove them by becoming Communist. Insofar as Communist statements cite empirical evidence of non-Communist policy and statements, this evidence can nearly all be explained as a reaction to a fear of Communist aggression. If one were dealing with a sort of science fiction situation in which the Communists were an unknown race with whom it was impossible to communicate it might be worthwhile speculating about what possible changes in non-Communist policy might be taken as convincing evidence of peaceful intentions. In fact, the Communists could easily provide an answer to this sort of question, if they wanted to. Given that they refuse to make a clear statement of their position and that they refuse to consider the possibility that what they consider evidence of aggressiveness could be explained as a reaction to a fear of Communist aggression, the most likely hypothesis is that the main basis for Communist suspicions of the non-Communist powers is subjective. And until this hypothesis has been tested the value of further speculation is doubtful. Non-Communist policy can be criticized at many points for lack of skill in dealing with people whose theories

---

* Cf. Crankshaw, *Op. cit.,* pp. 127-131.

incline them to delusions of persecution, but it is doubtful whether any major changes in the non-Communist position would be needed to make peaceful co-existence possible. This is not to say that non-Communist societies are entirely peace loving. One can point to some influences which are aggressive and also to some evidence of a fear that non-Communist societies might lose under conditions of competitive co-existence. But there are strong reasons for believing that these influences are not likely to be strong enough to have a decisive influence on policy.

However, non-Communist policy could do more positively to promote peaceful co-existence. The most effective basic strategy would be one which continued to offer the Communist powers as clear a choice as possible. It would be made clear that the non-Communist powers would prefer peaceful co-existence if the Communist powers were willing to enter into the sort of negotiations and discussions through which it might be attained and showed themselves willing to modify those aspects of their policies which were incompatible with it. This would involve as clear a formulation as possible of the conditions of peaceful co-existence and a policy, especially in negotiation and publicity, which did not try to evade or slur over disagreements but tried to force a clear-cut decision on cases which provided test cases of Communist intentions and good faith. Leaders on the Communist side who genuinely wanted peaceful co-existence would then know what they had to do to secure co-operation from the non-Communist powers and, in planning their strategy against their internal opponents, they would know how far they would have to go before their policy would produce responses from the non-Communist powers which they could use in internal publicity to win popular support.

It would be equally important to make clear that the non-Communist powers were prepared to maintain a balance of power or deterrence if peaceful co-existence could not be obtained and that effective publicity would be used to discredit Communist claims to want peace which were not accompanied by readiness to act in ways likely to promote peace. An effective balance of power or deterrence, however unpleasant and costly it may be, is the only possible reaction (except surrender) to Communist aggressiveness based on a determination to spread Communism or to a situation in which Communist ruling groups might be inclined to use aggression as a means of maintaining their internal power. And a readiness to discredit Communist claims to want peace which were not accompanied by a readiness to act for peace would be the most effective way of forcing Communist opinion to face questions about their position which have to be answered if peaceful co-existence is to be attained but which they have been inclined to evade.

This sort of general strategy would yield the clearest evidence of whether or not peaceful co-existence has become possible at any time, and would also do the most to promote its possibility.

The answer to the question, is peaceful co-existence possible, can, therefore, only be, we do not at present have enough evidence to give a definite answer. More detailed study of the information now available might somewhat reduce the degree of uncertainty, but any substantial progress in answering the question is likely to come from getting new evidence. And the main conclusion of this book is that it would be possible to obtain a great deal more evidence by following appropriate procedures.

As in any scientific inquiry, the sort of evidence which can confirm a hypothesis is the sort of evidence which could also disprove it. Policies designed to test the possibility of peaceful co-existence might end by showing that peaceful co-existence is not possible with the Communist powers, at least while they are under their present leadership. If this proved to be the case, the best that could be hoped for would be to maintain a balance of power or balance of deterrence until such time as changes had taken place within the Communist powers which would make peaceful co-existence possible.

This may seem a very pessimistic conclusion but it is, perhaps, not quite so pessimistic as it seems. Firstly, it has yet to be clearly proved that peaceful co-existence is impossible with the existing Communist regimes. Secondly, even if it is now impossible, changes in the Communist regimes might make it possible. And, thirdly, correct policies on the part of the non-Communist powers could greatly increase the likelihood of changes within the Communist system which would make peaceful co-existence possible.

In conclusion it may be worth commenting on two recent books which have discussed the question of peaceful co-existence, Bertrand Russell's *Common Sense and Nuclear Warfare*[1] and C. Wright Mills' *The Causes of World War Three*.[2] Both are very good illustrations of one of the main theses of Part III of this book, that it is foolish for the non-Communist powers to base their policies on the assumption that nothing better than a balance of power is possible because, even if this assumption happens to be true, so long as it has not been proved beyond reasonable doubt, policies based on it cannot obtain the degree of support needed by a democratic system. Both Lord Russell and Professor Mills are quite rightly dissatisfied with non-Communist policies which have no apparent aim beyond maintaining the balance of power. But both seem seriously to underestimate the possibility that this may be the only attainable short term objective. Both rather uncritically assume that non-Communist policies aimed at peaceful co-existence with present Communist regimes would be almost certain to succeed.

Professor Mills is the more naïve of the two. He devotes less than a tenth of his book to considering the policies which the United States ought to follow and the remainder to considering how the United States government might be induced to follow the policies which he favors. But, in describing his proposals for a radical change in United States policy, he simply assumes that no obstacle to peaceful co-existence will arise from the Communist side. It has been argued above that the non-Communist powers ought to do all they can to secure genuine negotiations. But when Professor Mills proposes this he does not even consider the problems discussed in the section of this book on "Negotiation",—the possibility that Communist regimes may not be prepared to negotiate in any meaningful sense so that nothing beyond limited bargains for simultaneous performance may be possible. Professor Mills wishes, quite rightly, for a great increase in discussion and intellectual contacts between the Communist

1. London, George Allen & Unwin, 1959.
2. London, Secker & Warburg, 1959.

and non-Communist sectors of the world; but he does not consider the possibility that the Communist regimes might restrict
such contacts because the resulting inflow of "dangerous
thoughts" would threaten their stability. At one point he says,
"The pertinent question now is: Do the Russian elite recognize
that World War III would *not* be to Russia's advantage and that
an equitable treaty structure is the only hope for avoiding war?
The answer is yes every bit as much for the Russian elite as it
is for the American elite." (page 105.) But he does not seriously
try to give evidence to support this answer; and in the case of the
Chinese elite one can point to statements claiming that World
War III would be disastrous for the non-Communist world and
not for the Communist. Another begged question is whether
Communists and non-Communists could agree on the operational
meaning of "an equitable treaty structure". In short, while a
good many of Professor Mills' proposals might, in some form,
have a place in a rational United States policy, his basic approach
to international affairs is the uncritical neutralist position.

Bertrand Russell's approach is not nearly so uncritical, though
he may underestimate the irrationality of Communist leadership. He is willing to face the possibility that peaceful co-
existence may not be possible, and it is his argument from this
point onwards which is most open to criticism. He argues,
"There are those in both camps who think that the extermination
of the human race would be a smaller evil than the victory of
the 'enemy'. I regard this view, whether held by A or by B, as
insane." (pages 86-7.) The fallacy in the argument is that a
victory of the "enemy" does not rule out the possibility of a
subsequent extermination of the human race; it may even make
it more likely. There is no good reason for believing that an
inherently aggressive system would remain united after it had
conquered the entire world by using the threat of unlimited
atomic warfare. Lord Russell argues that tyrannies do not last
for ever (page 75) but he fails to follow up his historical analogy.
In most empires established by military power there have been
civil wars over the succession or large scale rebellions, so that
the victory of an aggressive system has not meant the end of war.
If some inherently aggressive system conquers the world, because

its leaders are prepared to risk the extermination of mankind rather than forego their conquest, are not these leaders, or their successors, likely to be equally reckless in the pursuit of their internal disputes? And when external enemies have been eliminated internal quarrels are more likely. The real alternatives may be: a risk of the extermination of mankind now through resistance to the "enemy", or a greater risk of the extermination of mankind some years later after surrender to the "enemy".

The correct conclusion from Lord Russell's argument is, surely, that the development of atomic weapons has made historical analogies inapplicable; and that the long term survival of mankind depends on working out institutions which will prevent an inherently aggressive group from obtaining control of any country able to wage atomic war. This may not be an immediately obtainable objective, but it must be the aim of any rational long term policy.

Postscript, August 1960

Developments since the main part of this book was written seem to confirm two of its main arguments, that it is futile to work for a lessening of tension between the Communist and non-Communist systems without coming to grips with the underlying issues causing suspicion between the two systems, and that a major weakness of non-Communist policy has been unwillingness to compete in psychological warfare.

As far as one can judge from the published accounts of the proceedings leading up to the abortive summit conference, the basic assumption of the non-Communist leaders was that Mr. Khrushchev was sufficiently rational to realise that an atomic war would be disastrous for the Soviet Union. There is a good deal of evidence to support this assumption even from Mr. Khrushchev's public statements and he may well have been even more explicit in private conversations. What they seem to have underestimated was the rigidity of Mr. Khrushchev's commitment to aspects of the orthodox Communist ideology which were certain to make it extremely difficult to reach any genuine agreement with him; and this wrong estimate could have been avoided if they had studied the evidence available to them.

In 1957 both the Poles and the Yugoslavs had hoped that the reaction against Stalinism would lead Mr. Khrushchev to tolerate "revisionist" views, and had been disappointed. Some Polish theorists had hoped for some modification of the dictatorship of the proletariat (represented by the Communist Party) towards greater popular control and some respect for moral standards other than that of what was considered expedient for "the inevitable progress of history." The Jugoslav leaders had hoped for some modification of the model of the world sharply divided into the two hostile camps of socialism and imperialism in favor of a model which allowed different and not necessarily hostile forms of development towards socialism. (Both of these modifications of Communist orthodoxy would obviously facilitate peaceful co-existence between the Communist and non-Communist parts of the world.)

Mr. Khrushchev's actual position is described in a recent study[1], "The Jugoslavs, much like the Poles, . . . placed false hopes on the person of Khrushchev. Yet there has never been one iota of evidence that Khrushchev was predisposed toward anything but a firm commitment to a rigidly dichotomic approach. [A view of the world sharply divided into two hostile camps.] Every one of his speeches, his press interviews, has reflected a commitment typical of a self-taught peasant who has perceived certain immutable laws and will not be shaken from his insight. He has been able to couple this, however, with an elasticity in tactics and a willingness to experiment which apparently made it possible for him to convince Tito that his desire to shake off the inexpedient remnants of Stalinism also involved a departure from his dichotomic vision. But it was only on this tactical level that Khrushchev was willing to adopt occasionally more flexible positions than his more rigid colleagues in the camp."

The same author also points out that Mr. Khrushchev seems firmly committed to a belief that the victory of Communism is an inevitable historic process which it is wrong to oppose. "Khrushchev was most probably deeply sincere when he said to Adlai Stevenson: 'you must understand, Mr. Stevenson, that we live in an epoch when one system is giving way to another. When you established your republican system in the eighteenth century the English did not like it. Now, too, a process is taking place in which the peoples want to live under a new system of society; and it is necessary that one agree and reconcile himself with this fact. The process should take place without interference.' "[2]

[1] *The Soviet Bloc; Unity and Conflict.* By Zbigniew K. Brzezinski, Harvard University Press, 1960, p. 313.
[2] *Op. Cit.,* p. 394.

It is easy to fit a sincere desire to avoid atomic war into this ideological framework. While the capitalist imperialists will always be hostile and will try to oppose the spread of Communism, they are subject to increasing pressure from the masses against opposing the spread of Communist power by means which might produce an atomic war and they may be rational enough to realise that an atomic war would only hasten their doom. The problem in these terms is one of timing and tactics. What degree of risk is it worth taking to accelerate the "inevitable progress of history"? If Communists are not in too much of a hurry to control the entire world there may never be an occasion on which the imperialists have both the will and the power to risk an atomic war, while premature attempts to secure the final defeat of imperialism might drive the imperialists to desperate and mutually suicidal measures of resistance. So long as he believes that this is the kind of choice he faces it is easy to understand that Mr. Khrushchev should be in favor of going rather slower without risking an atomic war and should disagree with the more fanatical Communists prepared to take bigger risks.

For non-Communists the interesting questions are rather different. How would Mr. Khrushchev choose if the alternative to atomic war turned out to be the indefinite postponement of the expansion of Communist power or even a set back through failure to suppress revolts against Communist rule? More generally, when Mr. Khrushchev talks of "competitive co-existence" is he willing to compete under conditions which would allow people not only to choose Communism but also to reject Communist rule after trying it, or is he only willing to compete on terms which would allow Communists to win but never to lose?

One important objective of non-Communist policy in the preliminaries to the summit meeting should have been to find out the answers to these questions, to find out whether or not Mr. Khrushchev's desire to avoid atomic war carried an implicit qualification, "so long as the avoidance of atomic war does not produce a permanent set back to the spread of Communism." There was a real problem of tactics. The questions important for non-Communists would almost certainly be emotionally disturbing to Mr. Khrushchev. He would be more likely to answer them if they were

asked by someone who had established a friendly personal relationship with him. There was, therefore, a difficult problem of
judgment in deciding the point in a series of discussions at which
it was essential to get down to business by pressing the important
questions even if Mr. Khrushchev resented them. Mr. Khrushchev's obvious tactics were to secure the indefinite postponement
of questions which he did not want to answer by indicating that
he would treat them as evidence of hostility and perhaps as the
occasion for breaking off relations. These were the tactics which
he followed at his public appearances in America and they were
successful except on a few occasions such as his meeting with
American trade union leaders. It seems likely that they were
equally successful at Camp David and at his meetings with other
Western leaders.

In his letter to Mr. Macmillan, Mr. Khrushchev repeated the
old Soviet claim that, "The Soviet government has never sought
to expand the sphere of its influence by grabbing foreign territory
and bringing other peoples into submission."[1] It has been pointed
out earlier in this book that this Soviet claim implies that other
countries cannot possibly have any valid reasons for suspicion of
the Soviet Union or for taking precautions against possible Soviet
aggression and that so long as, on this vital point, the Soviet
authorities insist on maintaining a position quite clearly contrary
to the evidence there can be no basis for serious discussion or
negotiations on the most important international issues. The
letter also follows the old Soviet line of denouncing West German
rearmament while avoiding all mention of the prior East German
rearmament.

If Mr. Khrushchev had the slightest expectation of influencing
Mr. Macmillan by his letter he could only weaken his case by
including statements which Mr. Macmillan had previously attacked as completely contrary to the evidence and as serious obstacles to any useful negotiations. This suggests that Mr. Macmillan had not pressed the important underlying issues in February 1959 when, in Mr. Khrushchev's words, "we exchanged views
rather freely and frankly on the questions which we deemed it
necessary to discuss."

[1] *New York Times.* 6th. August, 1960.

Another passage in the letter complains of speeches by Secretary of State Herter and Vice President Nixon and says, "The spirit of these speeches was hostile to the Soviet Union. How can one prepare a summit meeting and at the same time pronounce hostile speeches against one of the parties to the conference?" These speeches could not have been unexpected by Mr. Khrushchev if the discussions at Camp David had made clear the very profound differences between the American and Soviet positions on fundamental issues.

An alternative explanation in both cases would be that Mr. Khrushchev is a man whose mind is completely closed to ideas which will not fit into his ideology so that points made by Mr. Macmillan or President Eisenhower had made no impression.

On this analysis it seems unlikely that the summit meeting at Paris could have accomplished anything more than the previous summit meeting at Geneva even if it had not been broken off because, as in 1955, the Western leaders were not prepared to press the questions which could have yielded the most important evidence about Soviet intentions and shown whether or not any agreement could be hoped for going beyond temporary bargains on immediate issues.

Commentators seem to differ widely in their speculations about the exact motives which led Mr. Khrushchev to break off the Paris meeting. He did, however, manage to do it in a way which was a considerable victory for the Soviet Union in psychological warfare, even though its effects were lessened by his performance at the subsequent press conference.

Mr. Khrushchev succeeded in getting considerable sections of opinion, even in America, to accept the view that there was something especially serious in espionage by high flying aircraft (the particular form of espionage against which Soviet counter-measures had been least effective); and managed to project widely a picture of the United States as a power whose reckless behavior made it a dangerous ally. These successes depended on his being allowed to present the U-2 incident out of its context in the continuing Cold War and could almost certainly have been prevented if United States policy had been conducted with more attention to its effect on public opinion.

Within the United States a great deal of the more serious
criticism of American action was directed against the decision to
admit responsibility for the U-2 incident instead of following the
traditional convention of officially denying responsibility for all
espionage and clandestine activities. The critics do not seem to
have faced the consequences which would have resulted from following the traditional convention.

The Soviet government had an American aircraft shot down
over 1,000 miles inside Soviet territory with equipment especially
designed for high level photography. A denial that it had been
engaged in aerial reconnaissance over Soviet territory would have
been an obvious falsehood which would have discredited future
American official statements. One big potential advantage which
democratic powers have over totalitarian powers is that many
people recognize their rather higher standards of veracity and it
would have been foolish to weaken this advantage. (If the U.S.
government had attempted denial in the U-2 case, public opinion
would have been much less ready to accept the truth of American
statements that the B-47 later shot down by Soviet aircraft had
never been over Soviet territory.)

A claim that those at the head of the U.S. government did not
know of the U-2 flights would not have been obviously false but
would have been highly discreditable by exaggerating the lack of
co-ordination in Washington. It would have provided a very
plausible argument that the U.S. system of government was a
danger to world peace because the President had no control over
agencies which could act quite independently to involve their
country in serious international complications.

A more valid criticism would be that the U.S. government had
not reconsidered the whole problem of espionage and clandestine
activities long before the U-2 incident because the traditional convention of disclaiming responsibility works to the advantage of
those governments which are least scrupulous. One of the things
which might well have been said to Mr. Khrushchev at Camp
David was that, so long as the Soviet Union maintained a large
apparatus of espionage in the United States and until agreements
had been negotiated and implemented, which would remove the

grounds for fear of possible Soviet aggression, the U.S. government was compelled by reasons of national security to do what it could to obtain information about Soviet military preparations.

The use of spies and clandestine agents long precedes any modern concepts of national sovereignty or normal diplomatic relations and has been continued by almost all powers seriously involved in international politics because it has appeared necessary for national security. A government which did not at least use espionage to obtain information about a potentially hostile country would greatly weaken its position. (The arguments for and against a unilateral decision to abandon espionage involve the same principles as the arguments for and against a unilateral decision to disarm in certain types of weapon.)

On the other hand, all such activities are incompatible with strict respect for the sovereignty of other countries. The domestic jurisdiction of any state includes the right to control entry to its territory and to decide what activities are lawful within its territory. It follows that any government which sends agents who evade such control into the territory of another government or uses agents who act illegally is thereby violating the sovereignty of the country. There would probably be fairly general agreement on principles relating the seriousness of the violation to the activities of the agents, that the use of violence as in sabotage or assassination is more serious than espionage which simply obtains information and that armed raids or assistance to a rebellion are still more serious. There is no obvious general principle which would relate the seriousness of the violation to the technical means which agents use to evade the control of the government against which they are operating.

Almost all governments have, therefore, been in the false position of claiming to respect the sovereignty of other states while actually violating it. The contradiction has been evaded by the traditional convention of disclaiming official responsibility for any agents who happen to be found out. This convention has favored totalitarian states which find it easier to maintain secrecy about clandestine operations and have less of a reputation for veracity to lose through obviously false denials of official responsibility. Quite apart from the U-2 case there were, therefore, arguments for abandoning the traditional convention and admitting what most people already knew, that, for reasons of national security, the U.S. government considered it necessary to conduct espionage against the Soviet Union. Attempts might have been made to negotiate mutual agreements restricting clandestine activities going beyond simple espionage. A statement of this position would have been more effective if it had been stated as a general principle before the U-2 incident.

The main part of this book has argued for a non-Communist strategy which would aim at presenting the Communist leaders with as clear a choice as possible between joining in genuine negotiations to reduce international tension or facing a contest in psychological warfare in which the bad faith of their claims to want peace would be exposed. This strategy would have implied an immediate counter-attack against Mr. Khrushchev's attempt to present the U-2 incident outside its context in the Cold War which could have been made by President Eisenhower in something like the following terms:

"Mr. Khrushchev is demanding an apology for flights over Soviet territory by high altitude photo-reconnaissance aircraft. I do not consider that he has any right to demand such an apology unless he, on his part, is willing to apologize for much more serious violations of sovereignty by agents of the Soviet government.

"The flights over Soviet territory by U-2 aircraft had no effect at all on the Soviet Union except a loss of military secrecy. On the other hand, the Soviet authorities have maintained a large apparatus of espionage agents in other countries who have not only caused losses of military secrecy to the United States and its allies but have also corrupted their citizens. (If Mr. Khrushchev wishes to challenge this statement I could cite numerous instances to substantiate it.) In some countries Soviet agents have not confined themselves to espionage but have also engaged in criminal activities such as assassination and kidnapping. (Here again I could cite instances.) Moreover, Soviet violations of the sovereignty of other countries have not been confined to the activities of clandestine agents. In November, 1956 regular units of the Soviet army intervened in the internal affairs of Hungary after the Hungarian government had requested the withdrawal of

Soviet forces, an action for which the Soviet Union was condemned
by the United Nations. In 1953 Soviet armed forces suppressed an
attempt by the people of the Eastern Zone of Germany to liberate
themselves from a regime imposed by Soviet armed force. In the
period before the death of Stalin the Soviet record was even worse.
In 1939 the Soviet government became the ally of Hitler and the
Nazi German government and made an attack on Poland in violation of a mutual security treaty. Soviet forces attacked Finland,
again in violation of a mutual security treaty. In 1940, the Soviet
Union annexed the Baltic States, again in violation of treaties.
Later, Soviet forces intervened in the internal affairs of Roumania, Poland, Bulgaria and Hungary in violation of agreements
reached at Yalta and Potsdam with the United States and other
allies. Soviet agencies gave important assistance to forces in rebellion against the Greek government. (This is not a complete
list of Soviet actions violating the sovereignty of other countries.
I have only picked out some of the more serious cases.)

"Mr. Khrushchev might plead the defense of superior orders for
his complicity in Soviet policy before the death of Stalin, though
I would remind him that such a defense was not accepted by the
international tribunals at Nuremberg and Tokyo. It is, however,
reasonable to ask Mr. Khrushchev to accept responsibility for
Soviet policy since the death of Stalin. Therefore, if Mr. Khrushchev is willing to apologize for the espionage and more serious
criminal activities of Soviet agents in the United States and other
countries, and if he is willing to apologize for the actions of the
Soviet army in Hungary and the Eastern Zone of Germany, I will
then apologize to him for the flights of U.S. photo-reconnaissance
aircraft over Soviet territory.

"Alternatively, if Mr. Krushchev is willing to withdraw his demands, I am still prepared to continue with this conference in
the hope that we may be able to work out plans for a more
peaceful world in the future. Our ultimate long term goal should
be a situation in which both military secrecy and espionage would
become unnecessary and obsolete.

"If, however, Mr. Khrushchev continues to demand that other
countries should show the most scrupulous respect for Soviet
sovereignty while the Soviet government considers itself free to

engage in serious violations of the sovereignty of other nations, I could only conclude that his professions of desire for peace are not sincere. Such behavior by Mr. Khrushchev would strengthen the arguments for holding that Soviet professions of desire for peace are only camouflage for aggressive designs and that the peace loving nations of the world must, for the sake of world peace as well as their own national security, do all they can to obtain information about Soviet military preparations."

A reply on these lines would have put the whole affair clearly into the general context of the Cold War and shown that Mr. Khrushchev was demanding standards of international conduct from the United States which his own government had never been willing to observe. It would also have shown that, despite the past, the U.S. government was still willing to join in attempts to reduce international tension by negotiation.

In the later U.N. proceedings the U.S. representatives did make counter-charges against the Soviet Union but with far less than the possible effectiveness. The counter-charges were confined to Soviet espionage, thus missing the most effective point that Soviet interference in other countries had often gone far beyond simple espionage; and the charges of Soviet espionage in the United States were made in a very ineffective form—a mere list of names of Soviet agents with no supporting details. The U.S. representatives also accepted the Soviet position in considering only the issue between the U.S.A. and the U.S.S.R. and not bringing in the wider issue of Soviet actions against many other countries of the non-Communist world.

Thus the possibility of peaceful co-existence remains a question about which there is a good deal of indirect evidence but to which one cannot give a really confident answer because the questions which could provide the clearest evidence have never been pressed in ways which might force an answer. And the reluctance of the leading non-Communist governments to think in terms of a struggle for men's minds as well as in terms of a purely military struggle has produced further set backs in a field where their potential advantages could produce successes.

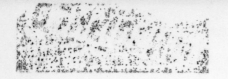